Gothic Literature

Edinburgh Critical Guides to Literature
Series Editors: Martin Halliwell, University of Leicester and
Andy Mousley, De Montfort University

Published Titles:
Gothic Literature, Andrew Smith
Canadian Literature, Faye Hammill
Women's Poetry, Jo Gill
Contemporary American Drama, Annette J. Saddik
Shakespeare, Gabriel Egan

Forthcoming Titles in the Series:
Asian American Literature, Bella Adams
Children's Literature, M. O. Grenby
Eighteenth-Century Literature, Hamish Mathison
Contemporary British Fiction, Nick Bentley
Contemporary American Fiction, David Brauner
Victorian Literature, David Amigoni
Crime Fiction, Stacy Gillis
Renaissance Literature, Siobhan Keenan
Modern American Literature, Catherine Morley
Scottish Literature, Gerard Carruthers
Romantic Literature, Richard Marggraf Turley
Modernist Literature, Rachel Potter
Medieval Literature, Pamela King
Women's Fiction, Sarah Sceats

Gothic Literature

Andrew Smith

Edinburgh University Press

For my father, Arthur Stanley Smith

© Andrew Smith, 2007

Edinburgh University Press Ltd
22 George Square, Edinburgh

Reprinted 2008

Typeset in Ehrhardt
by Servis Filmsetting Ltd, Manchester, and
printed and bound in Great Britain by
Antony Rowe Ltd, Chippenham, Wilts

A CIP record for this book is available from the British Library

ISBN 978 0 7486 2369 3 (hardback)
ISBN 978 0 7486 2370 9 (paperback)

Contents

Series Preface

The study of English literature in the early twenty-first century is host to an exhilarating range of critical approaches, theories, and historical perspectives. 'English' ranges from traditional modes of study such as Shakespeare and Romanticism to popular interest in national and area literatures such as those of the United States, Ireland, and the Caribbean. The subject also spans a diverse array of genres from tragedy to cyberpunk, incorporates such hybrid fields of study as Asian American literature, Black British literature, creative writing, and literary adaptations, and remains eclectic in its methodology.

Such diversity is cause for both celebration and consternation. English is varied enough to promise enrichment and enjoyment for all kinds of readers, and to challenge preconceptions about what the study of literature might involve. But how are readers to navigate their way through such literary and cultural diversity? And how are students to make sense of the various literary categories and periodisations, such as modernism and the Renaissance, or the proliferating theories of literature, from feminism and Marxism to queer theory and eco-criticism? The Edinburgh Critical Guides to Literature series reflects the challenges and pluralities of English today, but at the same time it offers readers clear and accessible routes through the texts, contexts, genres, historical periods, and debates within the subject.

Martin Halliwell and Andy Mousley

Acknowledgements

I would like to thank Andy Mousley and Martin Halliwell for inviting me to write this book and for their helpful editorial advice. I would also like to thank my colleagues in English at the University of Glamorgan who enabled me to take a sabbatical from teaching during the spring term of 2006, in which much of the book was written. Thanks to Diana Wallace for arranging this, and to Martin Willis and Hilary George who took over my teaching. Also, thanks to my colleagues on the Senior Management Team for enabling me to arrange meetings in a way that optimised research time. I would also like to thank a number of people who commented on drafts of various parts of this book, especially Professor Benjamin Fisher, Professor Charles Crow, Professor William Hughes, my colleague Professor Richard J. Hand, and Ian Scoones.

My thinking on the Gothic has been shaped over the years by my teaching of it. So special thanks are due to the undergraduates I have taught and to the students taking the MA in Gothic Studies at Glamorgan. In particular I would like to thank Tracy Edmunds for allowing me to reproduce her essay.

Finally, and as always, I would like to thank my wife, Joanne Benson, for her love, support, and tolerance throughout the writing of this book.

Chronology

Date	Historical and Cultural events	Gothic texts
1742		Edward Young, *Night Thoughts* (1742–5)
1743		Robert Blair, *The Grave*
1745		James Hervey, *Meditations among the Tombs* (1745–7)
1746	Dom Augustine Calmet, *Treatise on Vampires and Revenants: The Phantom World*	
1747		Thomas Warton, *On the Pleasures of Melancholy*
1751		Thomas Gray, *Elegy written in a Country Churchyard*
1756	Seven Years' War between Britain and France (1756–63)	
1757	Edmund Burke, *A Philosophical Enquiry into the Origin of Our Ideas of the Sublime and the Beautiful*	

Date	Historical and Cultural events	Gothic texts
1759	Edward Young, *Conjectures on Original Composition*	
1762	Richard Hurd, *Letters on Chivalry and Romance*	
1764		Horace Walpole, *The Castle of Otranto*
1767	William Duff, *An Essay on Original Genius and its Various Modes of Exertion in Philosophy and the Fine Arts, Particularly in Poetry*	
1768		Horace Walpole, *The Mysterious Mother* (drama)
1773	John Aikin and Anna Laetitia Aikin (later Barbauld), 'On the Pleasure derived from Objects of Terror, with Sir Bertrand, A Fragment'	
1775	American War of Independence (1775–83)	
1777		Clara Reeve, *The Champion of Virtue; A Gothic Story* (re-issued in 1778 as *The Old English Baron*)
1782	Hector St. John Crèvecouer, *Letters From an American Farmer*; James Beattie, 'On Fable and Romance'	
1783		Sophia Lee, *The Recess* (1783–5)
1786		William Beckford, *Vathek* (published in English)

Date	Historical and Cultural events	Gothic texts
1787	John Pinkerton, *A Dissertation on the Origin and Progress of the Scythians or Goth*	
1789	The French Revolution (1789–94)	Ann Radcliffe, The *Castles of Athlin and Dunbayne*
1790	Edmund Burke, *Reflections on the Revolution in France*; Immanuel Kant, *The Critique of Judgement*, Ann Radcliffe, *A Sicilian Romance*	
1791	Thomas Paine, *The Rights of Man*	Ann Radcliffe, *The Romance of the Forest*; The Marquis de Sade, *Justine; or, Good Conduct Well Chastised*
1792	Mary Wollstonecraft, *A Vindication of the Rights of Woman*	
1793	William Godwin, *Enquiry Concerning Political Justice*	
1794		William Godwin, *Things as They Are; or, The Adventures of Caleb Williams*; Ann Radcliffe, *The Mysteries of Udolpho*
1795	Friedrich Schiller, *Naïve and Sentimental Poetry*	
1796		Matthew Lewis, *The Monk*
1797	Mary Wollstonecraft, *The Wrongs of Woman*	Ann Radcliffe, *The Italian*; Matthew Lewis, *The Castle Spectre* (drama); Samuel Taylor Coleridge, *Christabel* (1798–1801)

Date	Historical and Cultural events	Gothic texts
1798		Charles Brockden Brown, *Weiland; or The Transformation*; Wordsworth and Coleridge, *Lyrical Ballads*, including Coleridge's 'The Rime of the Ancient Mariner'
1799	Napoleon Bonaparte made Consul in France	Charles Brockden Brown, *Edgar Huntley; or the Memoirs of a Sleepwalker*
1801		Wordsworth and Coleridge, second edition of *Lyrical Ballads* with Wordsworth's Preface
1803	The Napoleonic Wars (1803–15)	
1805	Hugh Murray, *Morality of Fiction*	Walter Scott, *The Lay of the Last Minstrel*
1806		Charlotte Dacre, *Zofloya, or The Moor*
1807	Slave trading ended in Britain	Charles Robert Maturin, *The Fatal Revenge*
1810		Percy Shelley, *Zastrozzi*
1811		Percy Shelley, *St. Irvine, or, the Rosicrucian*
1813		Lord Byron, *The Giaour*
1816		E.T.A. Hoffmann, 'The Sand Man'
1817		Lord Byron, *Manfred*

Date	Historical and Cultural events	Gothic texts
1818		Jane Austen, *Northanger Abbey*; Thomas Love Peacock, *Nightmare Abbey*; Mary Wollstonecraft Shelley, *Frankenstein*
1819		John Polidori, *The Vampyre*; John Keats, 'La Belle Dame Sans Merci' and 'The Eve of St Agnes'; Percy Bysshe Shelley, *The Cenci*; Lord Byron 'Fragment of a Story'
1820		Charles Robert Maturin, *Melmoth the Wanderer*; John Keats, *Lamia*; J. R. Planché, *The Vampyre* (drama)
1824		James Hogg, *The Private Memoirs and Confessions of a Justified Sinner*
1826		Anne Radcliffe, 'On the Supernatural in Poetry' and *Gaston de Blondeville*
1830	Walter Scott, *Letters on Demonology and Witchcraft*	
1831		Mary Wollstonecraft Shelley, revised edition of *Frankenstein*
1832	Passing of the first Reform Act (Britain)	

Date	Historical and Cultural events	Gothic texts
1837	Thomas Carlyle, 'The Age of Romance'	
1838		Charles Dickens, *Oliver Twist*; Edgar Allan Poe, 'Ligeia', *Narrative of A. Gordon Pym*
1839		Edgar Allan Poe, 'The Fall of the House of Usher'
1842		Edgar Allan Poe, 'The Pit and the Pendulum'
1843		Edgar Allan Poe, 'The Black Cat'; Charles Dickens, *A Christmas Carol*
1844		G.W.M. Reynolds, *The Mysteries of London* (1844–8)
1847		Charlotte Brontë, *Jane Eyre*; Emily Brontë, *Wuthering Heights*; James Malcolm Rymer, *Varney the Vampire*; or, *The Feast of Blood*
1848	Karl Marx, *The Communist Manifesto*	
1849		William Harrison Ainsworth, *The Lancashire Witches*
1851	The Great Exhibition, London	Nathaniel Hawthorne, *The House of the Seven Gables*
1853		Charles Dickens, *Bleak House*

Date	Historical and Cultural events	Gothic texts
1854	The Crimean War (1854–6)	
1856		Wilkie Collins, *After Dark*
1857	Indian 'Mutiny'	
1859	Charles Darwin, *The Origin of Species*	Edward George Bulwer–Lytton, 'The Haunted and the Haunters'
1860		Wilkie Collins, *The Woman in White*
1861	American Civil War (1861–5)	
1862		Mary Elizabeth Braddon, *Lady Audley's Secret*; Christina Rossetti, *Goblin Market*
1864		Sheridan le Fanu, *Uncle Silas*
1865	Sabine Baring-Gould, *The Book of Were-Wolves*	
1866		Charles Dickens, 'The Signal-Man'
1867	Passing of the second Reform Act (Britain)	
1868		Wilkie Collins, *The Moonstone*
1869	Matthew Arnold, *Culture and Anarchy*; John Stuart Mill, *The Subjection of Women*	
1870		Charles Dickens, *The Mystery of Edwin Drood*

Date	Historical and Cultural events	Gothic texts
1871	Charles Darwin, *The Descent of Man*	
1872		Sheridan Le Fanu, *In a Glass Darkly* including *Carmilla*
1873		Amelia B. Edwards, *Monsieur Maurice*
1875	Founding of the Theosophical Society	J.H. Riddell, *The Uninhabited House*
1876	Cesare Lombroso, *Criminal Man*	
1882	Founding of the Society for Psychical Research	
1884	Passing of the third Reform Act (Britain)	
1886		Robert Louis Stevenson, *The Strange Case of Dr Jekyll and Mr Hyde*; Vernon Lee, *A Phantom Lover*
1887		Henry Rider Haggard, *She*
1888		Rudyard Kipling, *The Phantom Rickshaw and Other Tales*
1891		Oscar Wilde, *The Picture of Dorian Gray*
1892	Max Nordau, *Degeneration*	Charlotte Perkins Gillman, 'The Yellow Wallpaper'

Date	Historical and Cultural events	Gothic texts
1893		Ambrose Bierce, *Can Such Things Be?*; John William Waterhouse, 'La Belle Dame Sans Merci' (painting)
1894		Arthur Machen, *The Great God Pan* and *The Inmost Light*
1895	Sigmund Freud and Joseph Breuer, *Studies in Hysteria*	George Macdonald, *Lilith*
1896		H. G. Wells, *The Island of Dr Moreau*
1897		Bram Stoker, *Dracula*; Richard Marsh, *The Beetle*
1898		Henry James, *The Turn of the Screw*
1899	Boer War (1899–1902)	Charles W. Chesnutt, *The Conjure Woman*
1900	Sigmund Freud, *The Interpretation of Dreams*	
1901	Sigmund Freud, *The Psychopathology of Everyday Life*; death of Queen Victoria	
1902		Arthur Conan Doyle, *The Hound of the Baskervilles*
1903		Bram Stoker, *The Jewel of Seven Stars* (revised, 1912); Arthur Benson, *The Hill of Trouble*

Date	Historical and Cultural events	Gothic texts
1904		M. R. James, *Ghost Stories of an Antiquary*; Arthur Benson, *Isles of Sunset*
1905	Albert Einstein proposes Theory of Relativity	
1911		Gaston Leroux, *The Phantom of the Opera*; Bram Stoker, *The Lair of the White Worm*
1912		Edmund Gill Swain, *The Stoneground Ghost Tales*; E. F. Benson, *The Room in the Tower, and Other Stories*
1914	First World War (1914–18)	
1917	Dorothy Scarborough, *The Supernatural in Modern English Fiction*	
1918	Suffrage for British women	
1919	Sigmund Freud, 'The Uncanny'; suffrage for American women	Robert Wiene, dir. *The Cabinet of Dr Caligari*
1920	Sigmund Freud, 'Beyond the Pleasure Principle'	Paul Wegener, dir., *The Golem*
1921	Edith Birkhead, *The Tale of Terror*	
1922	Tomb of King Tut discovered by Howard Carter	F. W. Murnau, dir, *Nosferatu: Eine Symphonie des Grauens*
1923		May Sinclair, *Uncanny Stories*
1925		Rupert Julian, dir. *The Phantom of the Opera*

Date	Historical and Cultural events	Gothic texts
1927	Eino Railo, *The Haunted Castle*	H. P. Lovecraft, *The Case of Charles Dexter Ward: A Novel of Terror*; Fritz Lang, dir. *Metropolis*
1928	Montague Summers, *The Vampire*	E.F. Benson, *Spook Stories*
1929	Ernest Jones, *On the Nightmare*; stock market crash on Wall Street, New York	
1931		M. R. James, *Collected Ghost Stories*; Tod Browning, dir. *Dracula*; Rouben Mamoulian, dir. *Dr Jekyll and Mr Hyde*; James Whale, dir. *Frankenstein*, *The Witch's Tale* (radio) (1931–8); Ernest Jones, *On the Nightmare*
1932	J.M.S Tompkins, *The Popular Novel in England 1770–1800*	Carl Theodor Dreyer, dir. *Vampyr*; Tod Browning, dir. *Freaks*; Karl Freund, dir. *The Mummy*
1933	Aleister Crowley, *The Book of the Law*; Mario Praz, *The Romantic Agony*; Marie Bonaparte, *The Life and Works of Edgar Allan Poe: a Psycho-Analytic Interpretation* (published in French)	
1934		Dennis Wheatley, *The Devil Rides Out*; E. F. Benson, *More Spook Stories*, *Lights Out* (radio) (1934–47)

Date	Historical and Cultural events	Gothic texts
1937		Edith Wharton, *Ghosts*; Charles Addams, *The Addams Family* (cartoon book)
1938	Monague Summers, *The Gothic Quest: A History of the Gothic Novel*	Daphne du Maurier, *Rebecca*
1939	Second World War (1939–45)	
1940		Alfred Hitchcock, dir. *Rebecca*, *The Hermit's Cave* (radio) (1940–43)
1941		*Inner Sanctum Mysteries* (radio) (1941–52)
1942		Jacques Tourneur, dir. *Cat People*, *Suspense* (radio) (1942–62)
1943		Jacques Tourneur, dir. *I Walked with a Zombie*, *The Mysterious Traveler* (radio) (1943–52), *The Black Castle* (radio) (1943–4), *Appointment with Fear* (radio) (1943–55)
1944		Lewis Allen, dir. *The Uninvited*, *Stay Tuned for Terror* (radio) (1944–5)
1945		Elizabeth Bowen, *The Demon Lover, and Other Stories*
1946		Mervyn Peake, *Titus Groan*
1947		*Quiet Please* (radio) (1947–8)

Date	Historical and Cultural events	Gothic texts
1949		A. N. L. Munby, *The Alabaster Hand*
1950	Korean War (1950–3)	Mervyn Peake, *Gormenghast*
1951		John Wyndham, *The Day of the Triffids*
1954		Isak Dinesen, *Seven Gothic Tales*; Richard Matheson, *I Am Legend*
1957	Devendra P. Varma, *The Gothic Flame*; Soviet satellite Sputnik 1 launched	Terence Fisher, dir. *Dracula*; John Wyndham, *The Midwich Cuckoos*; Terence Fisher, dir. *The Curse of Frankenstein*
1958		Terence Fisher, dir. *The Revenge of Frankenstein*
1959		Robert Bloch, *Psycho*; Shirley Jackson, *The Haunting of Hill House*; Mervyn Peake, *Titus Alone*
1960		Roger Corman, dir. *The House of Usher*; Alfred Hitchcock, dir. *Psycho*
1961	Yuri Gagarin, first man in space	Roger Corman, dir. *The Pit and the Pendulum*
1962		Ray Bradbury, *Something Wicked this Way Comes*
1963	Betty Friedan, *The Feminine Mystique*	Robert Wise, dir. *The Haunting*
1964		Robert Aldrich, dir. *Hush, Hush, Sweet Charlotte*

Date	Historical and Cultural events	Gothic texts
1965	Vietnam War (1965–73)	Roman Polanski, dir. *Repulsion*
1966		Jean Rhys, *Wide Sargasso Sea*
1968		George A. Romero, dir. *The Night of the Living Dead*; Roman Polanski, dir. *Rosemary's Baby*
1969	The first moon landing	
1970	Germaine Greer, *The Female Eunuch*	Roy Ward Baker, dir. *The Vampire Lovers*
1972	Watergate scandal begins	
1973		William Freidkin, dir. *The Exorcist*
1974	Juliet Mitchell, *Feminism and Psychoanalysis*	Stephen King, *Carrie*; Tobe Hooper, dir. *The Texas Chainsaw Massacre*
1975		James Herbert, *The Fog*
1976		Anne Rice, *Interview with the Vampire*; Brian de Palma, dir. *Carrie*
1977		Dario Argento, *Suspiria*; Stephen King, *The Shining*; Jim Sharman, dir, *The Rocky Horror Picture Show*
1978	Edward Said, *Orientalism*	John Carpenter, dir. *Halloween*

Date	Historical and Cultural events	Gothic texts
1979		Angela Carter, *The Bloody Chamber*; Werner Herzog, dir. *Nosferatu: Phantom der Nacht*; Ridley Scott, dir. *Alien*
1980	David Punter, *The Literature of Terror*	Suzy McKee Charnas, *The Vampire Tapestry*; Stanley Kubrick, dir. *The Shining*
1981		Whitley Streiber, *The Hunger*; John Landis, dir. *An American Werewolf in London*
1982	Julia Kristeva, *The Powers of Horror*	
1983		Tony Scott, dir. *The Hunger*
1984		Iain Banks, *The Wasp Factory*; William Gibson, *Neuromancer*; Jody Scott, *I, Vampire*; S. P. Somtow, *Vampire Junction*; Wes Craven, dir. *A Nightmare on Elm Street*; Neil Jordan, dir. *The Company of Wolves*
1985	Donna Haraway, *The Cyborg Manifesto*	Anne Rice, *The Vampire Lestat*
1986		David Lynch, dir. *Blue Velvet*
1987		Toni Morrison, *Beloved*; Alan Moore and Dave Gibbons, *Watchmen*; Joel Schumacher, dir. *The Lost Boys*; Kathryn Bigelow, dir. *Near Dark*

Date	Historical and Cultural events	Gothic texts
1988		Clive Barker, *The Books of Blood*; Neil Gaiman, *The Sandman No.1*; Thomas Harris, *The Silence of the Lambs*
1989		Nancy Collins, *Sunglasses After Dark*
1990	The Gulf War (1990–1)	Tim Burton, dir. *Edward Scissorhands*; David Lynch, dir. *Twin Peaks* (TV series begins)
1991		Brett Easton Ellis, *American Psycho*; Patrick McGrath, *Spider*; Jonathan Demme, dir. *The Silence of the Lambs*
1992		Poppy Z Brite, *Lost Souls*; Francis Ford Coppola, dir. *Bram Stoker's Dracula*; Bernard Rose, dir. *Candyman*
1993	The World Wide Web launched	Barry Sonnenfield, dir. *Addams Family Values*
1994		Alex Proyas, dir. *The Crow*
1995		Joyce Carol Oates, *Zombie*; David Fincher, dir. *Seven*; Kenneth Branagh, dir. *Frankenstein*
1996		Robert Rodriguez, dir. *From Dusk till Dawn*; Andrew Fleming, dir. *The Craft*

Date	Historical and Cultural events	Gothic texts
1997		*Buffy, the Vampire Slayer* (TV series begins); Jean-Pierre Jeunet, dir. *Alien Resurrection*; Michael Cohn, dir. *Snow White: a Tale of Terror*
1998		Alex Proyas, dir. *Dark City*; Hideo Nakata, dir. *The Ring*
1999		Sarah Waters, *Affinity*; Tim Burton, dir. *Sleepy Hollow*; Thomas Harris, *Hannibal*; Daniel Myrick and Eduardo Sánchez, dirs. *The Blair Witch Project*
2000		Mary Harron, dir. *American Psycho*
2001	Terrorist attacks on the World Trade Center, New York and the Pentagon, Washington, DC	Iain Sinclair, *Landor's Tower*; Alejandro Amenábar, dir. *The Others*; The Hughes Brothers, dir. *From Hell*
2002		Marc Evans, dir. *My Little Eye*; Danny Boyle, dir. *28 Days Later*
2003	The Iraq War begins	A. S. Byatt, *Little Black Book of Stories*; Barbara Vine (Ruth Rendell), *The Blood Doctor*; Dan Brown, *The Da Vinci Code*

Date	Historical and Cultural events	Gothic texts
2004		Joel Schumacher, dir. *The Phantom of the Opera*; Stephen Sommers, dir. *Van Helsing*
2005		Hideo Nakata, dir. *The Ring 2*
2006		Thomas Harris, *Hannibal Rising*

Introduction

This book is mainly aimed at readers who are either new to studying the Gothic or who have some basic understanding of the form and want to know more. How to critically read the Gothic is the principal issue addressed in this volume, which examines a range of Gothic texts and non-textual Gothic forms from the eighteenth century to the present day. The approach here is avowedly cultural and historical in emphasis as this helps us to observe the connections between texts and authors, and to appreciate how a Gothic tradition developed.[1]

In a book of this kind there will inevitably be omissions, and the texts sampled here are representative rather than definitive. The Guide to Further Reading at the end of the book in the Student Resources section lists information on secondary material concerning specific periods, forms (such as film, for example), theoretical approaches, and author-based studies. The Glossary provides a synoptic explanation of some of the key terms, and a sample essay is discussed in a section on advice on essay writing. The book's structure is broadly chronological and each chapter concludes with a specific reading of a Gothic text from the period discussed in that chapter. However, before looking in detail at such texts it is important to consider the historical contexts from which they emerged and the kinds of critical approaches which are available to us.

GOTHIC HISTORIES

The word 'Gothic' means different things in different contexts. The Goths were a Germanic tribe who settled in much of Europe from the third to the fifth centuries AD. In architecture the term refers to a revival (more accurately a cultural reconstruction) of a medieval aesthetic that was in vogue in Britain from the early eighteenth to the late nineteenth century. Such reconstructions of a somewhat fantasised version of the past (combined with a sense of 'barbaric' Germanic tribes) provide a context for the emergence of Gothic as a literary mode.

This cultivation of a Gothic style was given new impetus in the mid-eighteenth century with the emergence of Enlightenment beliefs that extolled the virtues of rationality. Such ideas were challenged in Britain by the Romantics at the end of the eighteenth century, who argued that the complexity of human experience could not be explained by an inhuman rationalism. For them the inner worlds of the emotions and the imagination far outweighed the claims of, for example, natural philosophy. The Gothic is at one level closely related to these Romantic considerations, and poets such as Coleridge, Keats, Shelley, and Byron at various times used the Gothic to explore, at different levels of explicitness, the role that the apparently irrational could play in critiquing quasi-rationalistic accounts of experience. This view was given intellectual support by philosophies which explored the limits of thought and feeling. Edmund Burke's *A Philosophical Enquiry into the Origins of Our Ideas of the Sublime and Beautiful* (1757), which will be discussed in depth later in this chapter, suggested that the sublime (a key Romantic concept) was associated with feelings of Terror (rather than with a benign pantheism which characterised some other models of sublimity). Transgressive, frightening feelings (in Burke, relating to largely imagined imminent violent death) are the most powerful that people are subject to and therefore the most sublime. Immanuel Kant's more rigorously philosophical account of the sublime in *The Critique of Judgement* (1790) observed a distinction between phenomena (a world of objects) and noumena (a world of ideas), in an exploration of the relationship between the mind and the external world. For Kant the sublime indicated the limits of subjective experience, and this emphasis on introspection privileges thought and understanding above certain Enlightenment ideas about the presence of an independent or 'objective' reality that can be rationally comprehended. However, although the Gothic often shares in such anti-Enlightenment ideas (because it focuses on thoughts and feelings), it is important to acknowledge that the early Gothic appears to be highly formulaic, reliant on particular settings, such as castles, monasteries, and ruins, and with characters, such as aristocrats, monks, and nuns who, superficially, appear to be interchangeable from novel to novel. Nevertheless, these stories are not as stereotyped as they may seem, and it is necessary to look beyond such narrative props in order to consider the anti-Enlightenment impulses and related themes and issues which are central to the form.

A second key aspect in any analysis of a Gothic text concerns its representation of 'evil'. The demonisation of particular types of behaviour makes visible the covert political views of a text. This is perhaps not surprising, given that the 1790s were a period in which the fears of, or enthusiasm for, revolutionary ideas, exemplified by their practical implementation by the French Revolution, profoundly influenced the British Gothic. The relationship between the Terror in France (the term used to apply to the mass executions, which included many of the first generation of revolutionary leaders) and literary versions of Terror can, for example, reveal the moral outlooks and political sympathies of specific writers. Nevertheless, it is necessary to approach such apparent clarity with circumspection. David Punter in his seminal study of the Gothic *The Literature of Terror* (1980, revised 1996) rightly notes that one of the key terms in the Gothic is that of ambivalence, because the Gothic so often appears to delight in transgression.[2] This is a key issue which this book explores in depth.

The Gothic is also a form which is generated in different genres as well as national and social contexts. The American Gothic tradition, for example, reveals particular concerns about race which are closely tied to issues of slavery and how it shaped a black identity politics which emerged in the post-Civil War period. America, unlike Britain, had a revolution (1775–6, although fighting with Britain continued until 1781) and was thus free of the images of threatened political turmoil that colour a strand of late eighteenth-century

British Gothic writing. In Germany the emergence of the *Schauerroman*, or 'shudder novel', in the late eighteenth century has its roots in a German Romantic tradition which included Schiller and Goethe. The shudder novel was a form which influenced the Gothic from other nations, and this illustrates how nationally specific manifestations of the Gothic played a role in shaping the aesthetic considerations of the Gothic in other countries. The Gothic also encompasses different forms, including drama, poetry, the novel, the novella, and the short story, and in the twentieth century it was taken up by radio, film, and television. In the late twentieth century to the present day it has also shaped certain subcultural experiences built around the Goth scene, which encompasses music and stylised dress codes, as well as influencing video games and the images on specialist Internet websites. The Gothic, in other words, mutates across historical, national, and generic boundaries as it reworks images drawn from different ages and places. The roots of the British Gothic can be found in the mid-eighteenth-century 'Graveyard Poetry' of Collins, Young, Blair, and Gray, a quite different point of origin from that of the German *Schauerroman*. In addition Gothic theatre's heyday in Britain coincides with the popularity of the Gothic novel, approximately 1780s to the 1820s, whereas in France Gothic drama was staged at the infamous Grand Guignol theatre in Paris from 1897 until its closure in 1962.

Different nations therefore generate different types of Gothic that develop and feed into other Gothic forms which proliferate in one place but seemingly die out in another. Space precludes the opportunity to explore this in depth, but the relationship between the British and American traditions will be focused on in this study; information concerning other national and cultural developments is given in the Guide to Further Reading.

Despite the national, formal, and generic mutations of the Gothic, it is possible to identify certain persistent features which constitute a distinctive aesthetic. Representations of ruins, castles, monasteries, and forms of monstrosity, and images of insanity, transgression, the supernatural, and excess, all typically characterise the form. In order to appreciate how we might read these Gothic motifs, it is helpful to acknowledge how criticism on the form has developed.

READING THE GOTHIC

The first major academic study of the Gothic was Dorothy Scarborough's *The Supernatural in Modern English Fiction* (1917), which was followed by Edith Birkhead's *The Tale of Terror* (1921) and Eino Railo's *The Haunted Castle* (1927). These early critical readings attempted to locate the Gothic within certain literary cultures, or to explain them in terms of an author's oeuvre. Important studies in the 1930s include J. M. S. Tompkins's *The Popular Novel in England, 1770–1800* (1932), which explored in detail Gothic themes and how they contributed to a suspense tradition. Mario Praz in *The Romantic Agony* (1933) examined the Gothic in relation to Romanticism, and Montague Summers's *The Gothic Quest: A History of the Gothic Novel* (1938) provided a broad, if somewhat eccentric, history of the form.[3] They also, in their various ways, attempted to culturally locate the Gothic as a literary mode. In 1928 Summers had also written *The Vampire*, which is an early study of vampires in literature and folklore. A later important study was Devendra P. Varma's *The Gothic Flame* (1957).[4] However, the modern era of theoretically informed criticism was inaugurated by David Punter's *The Literature of Terror*, published in 1980, which provided the first rigorous analysis of the Gothic tradition and suggested ways in which Gothic texts could be read through a combination of Marxist and psychoanalytical perspectives. The following year Rosemary Jackson's *Fantasy: the Literature of Subversion* (1981) was published, in which she examined the Gothic through Freud's concept of the uncanny (a concept which will be discussed at the end of this chapter). Since then there have been many groundbreaking contributions from scholars working in Britain, mainland Europe, the United States, Canada, and Australia, indeed often in those very countries where the Gothic took root. Such studies have helped to shape approaches to the Gothic, and in order to acknowledge this I will briefly outline a range of possible critical approaches (see Guide to Further Reading): the psychoanalytical, historicist, feminist, and colonial and postcolonial perspectives. Psychoanalytical approaches indebted to Sigmund Freud tend to read Gothic narratives as if they could be interpreted as dreams. Freud in *The Interpretation of Dreams* (1900) examined how a dream worked through two levels of content: the latent and the manifest. The manifest content of a dream refers to the story of the dream. Dreams, like some Gothic narratives, possess a peculiar surrealism and a rich symbolism. Such tales appear to be 'fantastical', and require the work of the analyst, or literary critic, to decode them so that they give up their latent content which is what the dream (or story) is really about. For Freud, this was only possible if we knew something of the dreamer and his or her life experiences. The author is treated like the patient, so that the tale corroborates the presence of anxieties that are specific to their life, as well as confirming the presence of more generalisable neuroses such as those generated by the Oedipus complex. Marie Bonaparte's study of Edgar Allan Poe (1933), discussed in Chapter 2, is a classic of this kind of analysis. However, it is also possible to psychoanalyse the text by examining how the symbolism articulates anxieties that are inherent to a culture, as well as to consider the kinds of effects that reading such narratives might have on a readership.

Freud's essay 'The Uncanny' is an important critical text and will be explored in depth in a concluding section to this chapter. In the essay Freud attempts to account for feelings of unease, and relates them to anxieties about the return of the dead in which the dead are reanimated and the living become corpse-like. In his interpretation of E.T.A. Hoffmann's Gothic tale 'The Sand Man' (1816) he constructs a model of the double which is relevant to a reading of many Gothic texts. For Freud, the double suggests that the self is haunted by repressed feelings which threaten to disrupt commonplace notions of everyday reality. Julia Kristeva's *Powers of Horror: An Essay on Abjection* (1982) moved away from the Freudian idea of doubling to argue that a culture needs to represent as abject any experiences which compromise the 'norm'.[5] Such a view has obvious applications to the Gothic conception of 'evil' and suggests that it is a necessary concept that ensures the well-being of the 'norm'. Psychoanalytical readings can also be used in conjunction with more historicist approaches to the Gothic as it enables us to decode the form's symbolism and discuss the critically retrieved narratives (or latent content) in historical terms. However, it is important to note that whilst early readings of the Gothic from the 1980s frequently relied on predominately psychoanalytical approaches, such a perspective has, in recent years, been criticised by more robustly historicist critics.

Reading the Gothic historically enables us to see how writers respond to earlier Gothic texts; it also enables us to relate such texts to the historical contexts within which they were produced. Such an approach does not, as mentioned, necessarily preclude using a psychoanalytical perspective to help decode certain scenes or characters, which can then be related to the wider historical picture. Such an approach is implicit in much of the analysis of the texts discussed throughout this book. A historically sensitive approach helps to illustrate the points of cultural contact between Gothic narratives and the events (the French Revolution, for example) to which they respond. However, the danger in this is that such texts can merely be seen as doing history by other means and it is important that due acknowledgement is made of the literary histories which they also drew upon and which played a role in shaping a Gothic aesthetic. One can say, for example, that Ann Radcliffe's novels make covert reference to conservative British fears concerning the spread of seditious ideas during a time of revolution, but it is also important to see how she reworks ideas and concepts which are familiar from Romanticism, as well as reworking scenes and characters which possess a clear Shakespearian imprint. In addition, how we understand history is not an objective process as it is inevitably influenced by selectivity and because the past is always mediated for us through accounts (even contemporary 'eye witness' accounts) of historical events. History also means different things to different critics – how a Marxist, a cultural materialist, a new historicist, or a feminist interprets history is dependent upon the significance accorded to specific events. For some critics a historical approach provides a rebuttal to the apparent ahistorical tendencies of a strict psychoanalytical reading. Robert Mighall, for example, has argued that psychoanalytical criticism can find itself co-opted to support stereotypes about repression. To argue that *Dracula* (1897) uses vampirism as a coded reference to sex implies, in this argument, little more than a cliché about the Victorians and sexual repression.[6] Michel Foucault has argued that we can map histories of sexuality which are not complicit with such a repressive hypothesis, a hypothesis which merely indicates just how far Freudian ideas have become critically internalised within our analytical procedures and cultural practices.[7] However, this is really another way of saying that reading Gothic texts should not become an oversimplified process of ahistorical symbol spotting. The advantage of a historicist approach is that it enables us to examine Gothic transgressions within the context of the prevailing norms which generated notions of the transgressive in the first place. In Kristeva's terms, what a society chooses to abject or jettison tells us a lot about how that society sees itself, and this process can also be read archaeologically to make sense of the historically and culturally specific manifestations of 'terror' that are central to the Gothic.

One of the most important contributions made to scholarship on the Gothic has been made by feminist critics. Ellen Moers in 1976 coined the term 'Female Gothic' in order to distinguish between male- and female-authored texts from the early part of the Gothic tradition.[8] This has generated a considerable amount of scholarship which either develops or challenges many of the issues raised by Moers (especially relating to whether the Female Gothic simply refers to writing by women or whether it constitutes a literary form which has also influenced certain male-authored Gothic texts).[9] This type of criticism helps to decode Gothic symbolism in order to reveal the covert presence of patriarchal plots, and to examine the relationship between aesthetics and gender. It is also important to note that a particular strand of the Gothic, like that of Shirley Jackson, Angela Carter, and Toni Morrison (all of whom are discussed in Chapter 4), is quite self-conscious in its use of Gothic imagery. In the case of Carter, her rewriting of folk tales in *The Bloody Chamber* (1979) represents an explicit attempt to make visible the concealed gender narratives inherent to the tales collected (and often rewritten) in the late seventeenth century. This type of self-conscious critical rewriting also makes visible one of the most significant issues about the Gothic: that it should not be read as a form which passively replicates contemporary cultural debates about politics, philosophy, or gender, but rather reworks, develops, and challenges them. The engagement may often be ambivalent, but the Gothic is a mode which searches for new ways of representing complex ideas or debates, and it is therefore not coincidental that the form has so often appealed to women writers. Such an approach to gender has also stimulated discussion about the presence of a 'Male Gothic' tradition which arguably has its roots in Matthew Lewis's violent and semi-pornographic novel *The Monk* (1796), which is examined in Chapter 1 in relation to Ann Radcliffe's *The Italian* (1797). Feminist approaches to the Gothic often utilise elements from feminist inflected critical theory, such as that of Julia Kristeva and Hélène Cixous. However, it is a mode of criticism which cannot be easily pigeon-holed by association with other critical theories. Feminist readings examine historical evidence, but that does not mean that they simply accept the claims made by Marxists or cultural materialists about historical and cultural evidence. Indeed, for historical and political reasons feminist critics are often, quite rightly, cautious about the claims made by Marx and Freud as their deliberations frequently overlook the contribution that women make to the economy (Marx) or can help to confirm troubling gender stereotypes (Freud). This study will highlight the presence of gendered narratives in order to illustrate how this approach provides a perspective on the Gothic which illuminates how these issues are generated in historically contextualised terms.

That certain types of critical theory can be used in a way that is mutually supportive is indicated by how critics have examined the Gothic in terms of race, colonialism, and postcolonialism. Stephen D. Arata, for example, has (in an article discussed in depth in Chapter 3) examined how vampirism in *Dracula* can be read not only in gendered terms but as a symbolic representation of colonisers parasitically feeding off the colonised.[10] In addition a novel such as Toni Morrison's *Beloved* (1987) is a gender-aware reconstruction of a range of anxieties (psychological, historical, and economic) which reflect on the history of slavery in North America. To that end it invites an analysis that is grounded in feminist, psychoanalytical, and historical enquiry. This historicist approach would not just reflect on the nineteenth-century setting of the novel but would explicitly address how and why such issues about history are important in understanding black identity politics in the late twentieth century. Also relevant here are writers such as Edgar Allan Poe, Charles W. Chesnutt, George Washington Cable, and Kate Chopin, for they illustrate how issues about race and slavery were developed within an American Gothic idiom in the mid- to late nineteenth century, which covertly influenced many of the issues in *Beloved*. Discussions of colonialism and postcolonialism acknowledge that these terms are open to contestation. India, for example, a former British colonially administrated country, could rightly be considered as a postcolonial nation. However, given that much of its industrial economy is dependent upon North America and Europe for its sustainability, it could be argued that it is subject to a new kind of economic colonialism. Other complications are technical ones relating to, for example, Commonwealth countries such as Canada, Australia, and New Zealand, which are economically independent of Britain but which have dominion status. How nationality (itself a highly contested term) is represented in the Gothic helps to explain why there are periodic anxieties about the meaning of national identity, especially but not uniquely at the *fin de siècle* in Britain.

The Gothic can represent a confluence of many issues reflecting on gender, race, history, class, nation, and the self, and a number of critical strategies are available for understanding how these issues relate to one another. This book places Gothic texts within their historical contexts and indicates how they address some, or occasionally all, of these issues. However, there are, historically speaking, two major intellectual contributions made to an understanding of the Gothic – Burke's *A Philosophical Enquiry* (1757) and Freud's 'The Uncanny' (1919) – which need to be outlined as they will underpin much of the discussion of the Gothic in this study and represent two theoretical accounts of anxiety which have played an important role in shaping Gothic criticism on Romantic and post-Romantic Gothic.

BURKE

Edmund Burke's *Philosophical Enquiry* takes its place in a history of treatises on the sublime. The sublime had acquired conceptual significance in Britain during the seventeenth century after the publication of Boileau's 1674 French translation of *Peri Hypsous* ('On the Sublime'), written around the first century AD and attributed to

Longinus, which examines how rhetoric can be used as a form of persuasion. The abuse of rhetoric found in propagandist political speeches might move the soul but also trick the mind, and so indicates the potentially deceptive nature of sublimity which would dog later accounts of it (especially debates about its natural or cultural provenance).[11] Burke's influential account of the sublime distinguished between sublimity and beauty. The sublime was associated with grand feelings stimulated by obscurity and highly dramatic encounters with the world in which a sense of awe was paradoxically inspired by a feeling of incomprehension. Beauty was of a different order, and was linked to notions of decorum and feelings for society. This distinction is also gendered, with the sublime implicitly associated with a strong masculine presence, and beauty with a decorous feminine presence. Central to Burke's treatise is the claim that death, or more precisely the fear of death, provides the clearest example of sublimity. He states that:

> Whatever is fitted in any sort to excite the ideas of pain, and danger, that is to say, whatever is in any sort terrible, or is conversant about terrible objects, or operates in a manner analogous to terror, is a source of the *sublime*; that is, it is productive of the strongest emotion which the mind is capable of feeling.[12]

This view provided the Gothic of the late eighteenth century with an influential representation of states of terror. Burke's treatise is notable for its attempt at cataloguing the possible causes of sublimity. He discusses a series of concepts which articulate these feelings of anxiety, including Obscurity, Power, Privation, Vastness, and Infinity. All imply experiences in which the subject is diminished, and behind it all lies, for Burke, the presence of an omnipotent creator who, given these implied links to fear, anxiety, and a terror of death, seems to be an Old Testament God of punishment and damnation. Burke claims that within our conceptions of 'the Deity' (p. 62) we invest God with such an awesome power that 'we shrink into the minuteness of our own nature, and are, in a manner, annihilated before him' (p. 63).

Burke's account of the sublime is important because his is the first major treatise to claim that the sublime is associated with absence. Instead of the sublime leading us to a contemplation of our place in a world of natural majesty (the natural sublime), which implies the presence of a benign divine creator, he claims that the sublime is a negative experience because it reinforces feelings of transience (our passing) and insignificance (our smallness).

For Burke these feelings appear as intimations of danger, and this suggests that fears and anxieties are subtly generated via subjective associations and expectations. His formulation of God, for example, explicitly depends upon a particular conception of the divine. As we shall see, Ann Radcliffe frequently exploits the potential solipsism which is implicit in Burke's idea of the sublime, and in her hands this is used to suggest that terror can easily be falsely manufactured. In *The Italian* (1797), for example, Vivaldi, the ostensible hero, is given an object lesson in how his overstimulated imagination makes him prone to conceiving imaginary terrors which make him susceptible to manipulation by the villain Schedoni. Radcliffe also provides a corrective to Burke by replacing his terrifying God with a more paternalistic divine presence who, through providential design, helps the virtuous. Gothic writers do not, therefore, simply copy from Burke, but they do respond to his formulation of Terror, seeing in it a language for representing fear, and a debate about the role that the imagination plays in generating emotionally heightened states.

Burke's version of the sublime therefore makes a contribution to an understanding of accounts of subjectivity. What it means to feel is his principal concern, and the hesitations and oddly schematic structure of his *Philosophical Enquiry* are the consequence of accounting for emotions within the discursive limitations of a philosophical examination. At its heart is the idea that the subject is not defined by noble or lofty feelings, but by anxious feelings relating to self-preservation. This version of the subject seems at one level to be manifestly Gothic, whilst its suggestion that the self is defined by moments of trauma anticipates Freud's conception of the subject as shaped by childhood anxieties. Or as the Freudian analyst Adam Phillips puts it in his introduction to the *Philosophical Enquiry*, Burke discovers 'the impossibility of rational classification' and that 'nearly two hundred years later Freud would describe something comparable between Thanatos, the Death Instinct, and

Eros' (p. xxiii). Freud gives specific voice to these Burkean anxieties about death in his essay 'The Uncanny', which is regarded as a critically important attempt at understanding the psychological complexities which characterise the post-Romantic Gothic.

FREUD

The problem with classification that Phillips noted in Burke is echoed in Freud's attempt to define the uncanny. For Freud the uncanny, or *unheimlich*, exists in opposition to the *heimlich*, or 'homely'. The *unheimlich* 'is undoubtedly related to what is frightening – to what arouses dread and horror', whereas *heimlich* refers to domesticity and security.[13] However, these terms are prone to slipping into each other, so that '*heimlich* is a word the meaning of which develops in the direction of ambivalence, until it finally coincides with its opposite, *unheimlich*. *Unheimlich* is in some way or other a subspecies of *heimlich*' (p. 347, italics in original). Freud's hesitancy ('is in some way or other') is indicative of his inability to produce a rigorous, putatively scientific, analysis of feelings of uncanniness. The reason why the two terms slip into each other is due to the Oedipus complex which Freud explores in his reading of Hoffmann's 'The Sand Man'. In his interpretation of the German tale he identifies the references to eyes and threats to sight as representing Oedipal anxieties about castration (in which 'eyes' take on a symbolic form). His reading of the tale reworks an idea which earlier in the essay he regarded as central to the uncanny when he claimed that 'the uncanny is that class of the frightening which leads back to what is known of old and long familiar' (p. 340). The home, or the *heimlich*, is for Freud the place where Oedipal desires and anxieties are generated, so that the home is not, because of the sexualised family tensions which inhere in the Oedipus complex, such a safe place after all. Indeed the home considered in this way is the place which generates repression and becomes uncanny because it involves incestuous sexual feelings that evoke fear, dread, and horror.

Freud's view of uncanniness is allied to Burke's notion of terror because it represents an attempt to account for fear. Burke suggested that such fears were a response to dangers in the external world, but his account of subjectivity implies that these anxieties inform us about the inner emotional world of the subject rather than about the specific objective conditions which give rise to fear. The problem in Burke is how to find a language which can represent the emotions, and for this reason he asserts the importance of external stimuli even though his principal focus is on why the subject feels in the way that they do. For Freud, such feelings of uncanniness may represent repressed Oedipal anxieties which are revealed in disturbing ways. As with Burke, the issue is how to find a language or a set of images which captures this feeling of fear. Freud, however, suggests a further modification of his theory of Oedipal subject formation by linking the uncanny to images of the double.

For Freud, the subject, when a child, goes through a stage of primary narcissism which they grow out of once they develop a conscience that enables them to regulate their moral conduct. However, the very presence of this conscience suggests a capacity for self-criticism which paradoxically reflects, because it is a self-regarding process, 'the old surmounted narcissism of earliest times' (p. 357). This adult self-reflection is thus a continuation of childish primary narcissism but with an added morbid twist. In primary narcissism the child experiences the double 'as a preservation against extinction' (p. 356). The child, in other words, has no conception of death. In the adult experience of doubling, implied by the presence of a conscience which enforces moral censorship, the relationship to the double is changed – 'From having been an assurance of immortality, it becomes the uncanny harbinger of death' (p. 357) – as we become aware of the morally constricting and finite adult world. The uncanny is thus closely associated with images of death, and Freud states that 'Many people experience the feeling in the highest degree in relation to death and dead bodies, to the return of the dead, and to spirits and ghosts' (p. 364). Such images also represent an image of repetition, 'the return of the dead', which is a fundamental characteristic of the uncanny. The urge to repeat, or to relive a past experience, suggests a desire to confront as yet unresolved, because repressed, Oedipal dramas. This can manifest itself as an adult anxiety about death (concerns about the future), or as a neurotic anxiety about the past.

Avril Horner has noted that 'Freud's essay and terminology have been adopted by critics of the Gothic who thereby read texts as codified forms of instinctual drives and mechanisms of repression'.[14] Freud's essay has proved to be very productive for psychoanalytically orientated critics, but the uncanny can also be used to historicise such anxieties. This is exemplified in Chapter 3 in a reading of Dickens's *A Christmas Carol* (1843) in which the uncanny helps to draw out an underlying dynamic concerning economics (and so aids in placing the tale in the context of the economic depression of the 1840s). Freud's essay is important because it enables us to explore motifs of doubling in the Gothic which we can find in texts as diverse as *Frankenstein*, *Dr Jekyll and Mr Hyde* and *Dracula*. It also enables us to see how the Gothic creates an uncanny mood in which characters become doubled with places (which, as we shall see, is a key element in the ghost story). Freud intriguingly also suggests in 'The Uncanny' that uncanny tales should be read not solely for their hidden psychological meaning but also for how their literary qualities generate new forms of uncanniness. He notes of such literature that 'it is a much more fertile province than the uncanny in real life, for it contains the whole of the latter and something more besides, something that cannot be found in real life' (p. 372). The very unreality of the Gothic text becomes, paradoxically, the special place for the uncanny.

In Chapter 2 Marie Bonaparte's classic Freudian reading of Edgar Allan Poe's 'The Murders in the Rue Morgue' will be discussed and contrasted with some historicist approaches which explore Poe's representation of race. However, it is important to re-emphasise that the uncanny, whilst a psychoanalytical concept, can also be used to bring to light historically contextualised anxieties.

The chapters follow a chronological approach to the Gothic and discuss a range of different literary and non-text-based forms (including radio and film). As mentioned at the beginning of this chapter, this book should be seen as stimulating discussion about the Gothic; it is not intended to be the last word on the topic. The principal ambition of this study is to show how the Gothic can be read for its contexts, and to do that we have to begin with the eighteenth century.

NOTES

1. It is also important to appreciate that the academic study of the Gothic, as with any mode, is conditioned by the formation of literary canons. What constitutes a course of study on the Gothic is not a static affair because it is conditioned by changes in critical theory and by other issues such as the availability of new editions of long out-of-print texts. In other words, we need to be aware that a Gothic canon (and this book inevitably builds it own version of that) should not be seen as carved in stone but rather subject to critical scrutiny and revision. The reasons for these changes are an implicit theme in this study.

2. David Punter, *The Literature of Terror*, 2 vols (London: Longman, [1980] 1996): see pp. 1–19.

3. See Punter, *Literature of Terror*, vol. 1, pp. 14–15.

4. Dorothy Scarborough, *The Supernatural in Modern English Fiction* (New York: Putnam, 1917); Edith Birkhead, *The Tale of Terror: A Study of the Gothic Romance* (London: Constable, 1921); Eino Railo, *The Haunted Castle: A Study of the Elements of English Romanticism* (London: Routledge, 1927); J. M. S. Tompkins, *The Popular Novel in England, 1770–1800* (Lincoln, NB: University of Nebraska, [1932] 1961); Mario Praz, *The Romantic Agony* (Oxford: Oxford University Press, 1933); Montague Summers, *The Gothic Quest: A History of the Gothic Novel* (London: Fortune, 1938); Montague Summers, *The Vampire* (London: Senate, [1928] 1995); Devendra P. Varma, *The Gothic Flame: Being a History of the Gothic Novel in England: Its Origins, Efflorescences, Disintegration, and Residuary Influences* (London: A. Barker, 1957).

5. See Julia Kristeva, *The Powers of Horror: An Essay on Abjection* (New York: Columbia University Press, 1982).

6. Robert Mighall, 'Sex, History and the Vampire', in *Bram Stoker: History, Psychoanalysis, and the Gothic*, ed. W. Hughes and A. Smith (Basingstoke: Macmillan, 1998), pp. 62–77.

7. Michel Foucault, *The History of Sexuality: An Introduction*, vol. 1, trans. Robert Hurley (Harmondsworth: Penguin, [1976] 1984).

8. See Ellen Moers, *Literary Women* (London: Women's Press, [1976] 1978).

9. See also special issue of *Gothic Studies*, 6: 1 (May 2004) on 'The Female Gothic', ed. Andrew Smith and Diana Wallace, and special issue of *Women's Writing: The Elizabethan to Victorian Period*, 1: 2 (1994) on 'Female Gothic writing', ed. Robert Miles. See also Alison Milbank, *Daughters of the House: Modes of Gothic in Victorian Fiction* (Basingstoke: Macmillan, 1992); E. J. Clery, *Women's Gothic: From Clara Reeve to Mary Shelley*, Writers and Their Work series (Tavistock: Northcote, 2000), and Suzanne Becker, *Gothic Forms of Feminine Fiction* (Manchester: Manchester University Press, 1999).

10. Stephen D. Arata, 'The Occidental Tourist: *Dracula* and the Anxiety of Reverse Colonization', *Victorian Studies*, 33 (1990), 621–45. Reprinted in *Dracula: A Casebook*, ed. Glennis Byron (Basingstoke: Macmillan, 1999), pp. 119–44, p. 129.

11. Cassius Longinus, *On Sublimity*, trans. D. A. Russell (Oxford: Clarendon, 1965).

12. Edmund Burke, *A Philosophical Enquiry into the Origin of Our Ideas of the Sublime and Beautiful*, ed. Adam Phillips (Oxford: Oxford University Press, [1757] 1998), p. 36 (italics in the original). All subsequent references given in the text are to this edition.

13. Sigmund Freud, 'The Uncanny', in *Art and Literature: Jensen's Gradiva, Leonardo Da Vinci and Other Works*, trans. James Strachey, ed. Albert Dickson, Penguin Freud Library, 14 (Harmondsworth: Penguin, 1985), pp. 339–76, p. 339. All subsequent references given in the text are to this edition.

14. Avril Horner, 'Unheimlich (The uncanny)', in *The Handbook to Gothic Literature*, ed. Marie Mulvey-Roberts (Basingstoke: Macmillan, 1998), pp. 287–8, p. 288.

CHAPTER I

The Gothic Heyday, 1760–1820

DEFINING THE GOTHIC: *OTRANTO*

Horace Walpole's *The Castle of Otranto* negotiates a series of anti-Enlightenment themes in its construction of a debate concerning the relationship between the medieval and the modern. The medieval, associated with castles and malign aristocrats, becomes recast as symbolically representing some highly politicised issues of the 1760s. Anti-Enlightenment ruins and irrationality can ultimately be decoded to reveal some historically specific political, social, and economic anxieties.

It is important to note that critical discussion of *Otranto* has focused as much on the novel's two prefaces as it has on the novel itself. The first edition of the novel was published on 24 December 1764, and purported to be a translation by one William Marshal of a sixteenth-century edition of an Italian manuscript by the fictitious Onuphrio Muralto, which had originally been written at some point between 1095 and 1243. Walpole, seemingly emboldened by the novel's commercial success (and, in the main, reasonable reviews), brought out another edition in 1765 in which he admitted authorship in what has become a critically significant second preface.

Whilst the preface to the first edition attempts to pass the novel off as a genuine medieval romance, the preface to the second edition tried to define a new mode of writing initiated by the novel. Crucially, this is to be found in Walpole's claim that the novel 'was an attempt to blend the two kinds of romance, the ancient and the modern. In the former all was imagination and improbability: in the latter, nature is always intended to be, and sometimes has been, copied with success'.[1] This means that the first preface helped to situate the novel as an ancient romance, dealing in fantastical improbability, whereas the second preface emphasised that the novel can be read 'realistically'. Walpole therefore claims that in the second edition the novel is really about how 'moral agents' would act 'according to the rules of probability' (p. 9), so that the central ambition was 'to make them [his characters] think, speak and act, as it might be supposed mere men and women would do in extraordinary positions' (p. 10). As critics such as Clery, Miles, and Norton have noted, Walpole is essentially claiming that his fantastical figures should be read as ciphers for 'real' psychological situations and political circumstances.[2] Indeed during the period there was a considerable reassessment of how the medieval romance should be interpreted, which suggested that if such texts were read historically then their political visions would be understood. The key precursors to such a rereading of the medieval romance are Thomas Warton's *Observations on the Faerie Queene of Spenser* (1754) and Richard Hurd's *Letters on Chivalry and Romance* (1762), in which he argued that medieval romances should be understood as coded references to the political upheavals of the period. As Clery has noted, Hurd writes that the 'oppressive feudal Lords' of the time became represented through fantastical forms in which 'every Lord was to be met with, like a Giant, in his stronghold, or castle'.[3] Therefore, symbolically these giants represent the scale of feudal authority.

Walpole's second preface is thus important because it outlines the roots of the Gothic and attempts to define some of its key features and ambitions. Walpole expresses this in modest terms (although ones which suggest that he knows that he has begun something important) when he states:

> if the new route he has struck out shall have paved a road for men of brighter talents, he shall own with pleasure and modesty, that he was sensible the plan was capable of receiving greater embellishments than his imagination or conduct of the passions could bestow upon it. (p. 10)

Walpole is thus supremely self-conscious of this new literary form which he has helped to fashion (indeed the second edition indicates that the first was a knowing hoax), and acknowledges that the book is not as fantastical as it might appear. In fact the first preface asks us to read the novel as a medieval romance, but the second suggests that we should interrogate this notion of medievalism (via Hurd's idea that such romances encrypt political realities) more closely in order to discover what the novel is 'really' about. To do this there are a variety of covert strands which we need to disentangle, including references to religion, class authority, models of the family, and images of demonic patriarchs. However, one issue which links the prefaces to the novel itself is that of legitimacy – as Walpole claims ownership of the text, so that text explores ownership of territory, land, political power, and the self.

The novel examines the idea of aristocratic inheritance by addressing how Manfred, Prince of Otranto, attempts to secure his family's claim on the principality by having his fifteen-year-old son, Conrad, marry Isabella (a descendant of another noble family). Manfred has arranged this marriage because he requires a male heir to whom the principality can eventually be passed. Conrad is his only son and is described as being in poor health, which means that there is some urgency for another male heir to be produced from the marriage between Conrad and Isabella. Manfred is also conscious of the fact that his claim on the principality is an illegitimate one. His grandfather Ricardo had poisoned Alfonso the Good, the last legitimate Prince, and falsified his will, making him and his descendants the new princes. Conrad dies before the wedding takes place when he is crushed beneath a giant helmet 'an hundred times more large than any casque ever made for human being' (p. 19). This strange supernatural intervention is in part explained by the disappearance of the helmet on a statue of Alfonso in the nearby church of St Nicholas. Manfred, conscious of the pressing need for a male heir, and believing that his wife, Hippolita, would not be able to bear him another son (although they have a daughter, Matilda), attempts to physically force himself upon Isabella. His pursuit of her in the castle is interrupted by a second supernatural intervention when a portrait of Ricardo sighs and the image of Manfred's grandfather 'quit its panel' to 'descend on the floor with a grave and melancholy air' (p. 26).

Manfred, understandably distracted, loses sight of Isabella, who is able to escape to the church of St Nicholas with the help of a local peasant, Theodore, whom Manfred had earlier attempted to forcibly detain for alleged involvement in the death of Conrad.

Manfred's attempts to secure Isabella are thwarted by the arrival of a group of knights led by Isabella's father, Frederic, who is searching for his daughter and who also makes a claim on the principality. Frederic is subsequently wounded in a sword fight with Theodore (with whom both Isabella and Matilda have become enamoured), who is revealed to be the long-lost son of Jerome, a friar who presides over the church of St Nicholas. Manfred, ever vigilant for possibilities of securing his lineage, suggests to Frederic that he marry Matilda, whilst Manfred marries Isabella, thereby uniting the two families. However, it transpires that Jerome has married a direct descendant of Alfonso, meaning that Theodore is the legitimate heir to Otranto. Jerome tells Manfred 'Thou art no lawful prince . . . thou art no prince' (p. 97). Manfred triumphantly tells Jerome of his plans for the wedding of Frederic and Matilda, at which moment 'three drops of blood fell from the nose of Alfonso's statue' (p. 97). Earlier a giant knight, resembling Alfonso, had been seen by the servants in the castle.

Manfred's plans are unsuccessful; he accidentally stabs Matilda, believing her to be Isabella secretly meeting with Theodore. When Matilda dies so does Manfred's claim on Otranto, at which point the castle is reduced to rubble by a gigantic Alfonso, who declares 'Behold in Theodore, the true heir of Alfonso!' (p. 112). Manfred confesses everything and he and Hippolita separately enter monastic orders. Theodore marries Isabella and legitimacy is restored.

This highly convoluted plot is delivered at some speed, but the theme of legitimacy is foregrounded throughout. The periodic appearance of a gigantic supernatural Alfonso heralds the restoration of the principality to its legitimate bloodline, whilst the sighing animated portrait of Ricardo suggests the guilty conscience of those who have usurped such legitimacy. Walpole's second preface, in which he claims that the tale is a blend of both ancient and modern romances, indicates that the story should be read 'realistically' as a kind of allegory. The supernatural elements in the story are linked to the past and suggest the presence of an illegitimate aristocratic claim on forms of political power. Critics such as Miles and Clery have noted that Walpole's Whig political background (he was a member of parliament for twenty-eight years) informs his allegorical representation of the aristocracy.[4] The Whigs saw themselves as the inheritors of a political power base extending back to the Saxons, and they were largely anti-monarchical and anti-establishment in attitude (if not always in reality: Walpole was also a member of the aristocracy).[5] The issue of aristocratic legitimacy had a particular potency during the period because of an ongoing political debate about the rights of ownership which centred on whether an aristocrat had the right to dispose of property and land, when technically it could be argued that these were held in trust by them for future generations. Also, the wishes of the dead, such as those codified in a will for example, could determine what an aristocrat could do with 'their' property. The issue had a particular significance because of the emergence of a new trading middle-class that was dependent upon the flexibility of the developing laissez-faire economy. The aristocracy in comparison suddenly look shackled to the past.

Walpole's novel is ambivalent about these matters. At one level it is clearly concerned with the legitimate restoration of an aristocratic line and the destruction of an illegitimate one (indicated in Alfonso's triumphant destruction of Manfred's castle). However, the narrative is more complex than this. Theodore becomes the new prince, and although he possesses a nobility of spirit (noble thoughts seemingly being the product of a noble birth), he is deeply unhappy. There is an interpolated love story involving Theodore and Matilda (and Isabella's jealousy over this), and his subsequent marriage to Isabella does not alleviate Theodore's gloom. The concluding sentence of the novel suggests that Isabella only partially helps him to reconcile himself to feelings of loss, so that 'he was persuaded he could know no happiness but in the society of one with whom he could forever indulge the melancholy that had taken possession of his soul' (p. 115). Not exactly a happy ending, despite the apparent restoration of the legitimate family line. It is at the level of identity that these debates about authority are expressed.

Theodore is initially portrayed as a peasant but is revealed to be the son of the friar Jerome, who had been the Count of Falconara before taking holy orders. From peasant to prince, from count to friar, identities change, or will out, as the social relations between characters in the novel become transformed. Also, as in the concerns about aristocratic inheritance, the dead do not stay dead: Alfonso is given an epic physical form; a despondent Ricardo walks out of his portrait. Identity is mobile, both literally and figuratively, and these movements generate misunderstandings, such as Theodore wounding Frederic and Manfred killing Matilda. The social (and, in the case of Alfonso and Ricardo, metaphysical) world is in a state of flux and the attempt to stabilise relations through a concluding socially corrective marriage merely generates, at least for Theodore, a new kind of emptiness.

This moment of triumph, which is in some respects a moment of defeat (given that up until this point Theodore's interests have been personal rather than demonstrably political), captures one of the key terms of the Gothic: ambivalence. The novel is both pro- and anti-aristocratic in its central political narrative relating to lineage. Restoring the old aristocratic class privileges is, however, ultimately not enough. To appreciate this the novel should be seen within the context of the economic upheavals which characterised Britain in the eighteenth century, ones in which aristocratic power was progressively replaced by the new economies largely generated through international trade which were controlled by, and helped to consolidate, the new middle classes. Therefore *The Castle of Otranto* can be read as an allegory of political decline, in which the restoration of a form of legitimacy does not in itself re-empower the aristocracy. A certain form of in fighting might have been eradicated, but a future presided over by a melancholy Theodore looks at best an uncertain one.

Whilst the novel illustrates some historically specific concerns relating to the aristocracy, it also introduces some formal elements which later Gothic writers would have to contend with, including images of religion, the family, and particular representations of gender. Superficially it may seem that these elements constitute common narrative props. However, it is important to consider how later narratives use these elements in different ways, illustrating the critically self-reflective nature of the Gothic tradition.

In the first preface the novel purports to be written by Onuphrio Muralto, a Catholic priest from the church of St Nicholas. During the period an extensive anti-Catholicism was generated within predominantly Protestant Britain, and this becomes reworked within the Gothic of the time through the repeated suggestion that Catholic countries were associated with 'superstition, arbitrary power and passionate extremes'.[6] Such countries therefore lacked Protestant self-restraint and were prone to generating fantastical 'Gothic' terrors. However, this view is problematised by the second preface, partly because the 'hoax' has been discovered, but in the main because Walpole suggests that we need to read the novel allegorically. Such a reading supports the view that the novel suggests that the aristocracy are tied to the past, a medieval past in which superstitious religious beliefs function as a metaphor for self-generated aristocratic decline. The novel represents a fantastical world and although there is a sense of political rectitude, there is no real impression that it possesses a recognisable theological dimension. Convents and monasteries appear to be places one goes to in order to escape a kind of worldliness, rather than to cultivate spirituality. Therefore, how to read this 'Catholicism' poses particular problems for the critic because its allegorical function is unclear. At one level it suggests aristocratic attachments to outmoded beliefs, but its presence in the novel also seems to be part of the 'hoax' from the first preface. Nevertheless, it is important to bear in mind that religion in the novel looks like a structural rather than a theological presence, and, as we shall see, later writers address Catholicism in a more direct way.

The novel is also about families, an issue that is central to Manfred's plotting. However, his political manoeuvrings mark him out as the Gothic villain in the novel. At one level his seemingly 'evil' designs destroy the family that he claimed was so important to him. Conventional family relations do not exist for Manfred because they have become politicised, as he tells Isabella on Conrad's death: 'Think no more of him [. . .] he was a sickly puny child, and heaven has perhaps taken him away that I might not trust the honours of my house on so frail a foundation' (p. 24). He subsequently attempts to replace Hippolita with Isabella and kills his daughter. Thus, the destruction of Manfred's family is a consequence of his support for the rather more politically abstract notion of aristocratic lineage. This disjunction between political vision and family intimacy becomes a key factor in the later writings of Ann Radcliffe, and indeed notions of what constitutes 'normal' family life will pervade the Gothic tradition, and are, as we shall see, central to later Gothic narratives such as *The Haunting of Hill House* (1959) and *Beloved* (1987).

The novel also addresses (perhaps largely unconsciously) the role of gender in constructions of power. In *Otranto* aristocratic women are represented as morally virtuous but lacking social and economic power. The aristocracy is clearly a man's world and this is apparent not just in Manfred's threatened rape of Isabella and aggressive attempts to manipulate the political situation, but also in the gigantic form of the righteous Alfonso, who, quite literally, towers over everyone else. Alfonso's size suggests the scale of masculine authority, an endorsement of which is also given in Manfred's scathing comments on Conrad's 'puniness'. However, such authority is prone to abuse and even the wronged Alfonso is associated with a capacity for destruction. Responses to such authority figures illustrate how this power operates. Hippolita, for example, whilst struck by the abuses of Manfred, nevertheless sees her role as a compliant one. Whilst this confers a martyr-like dignity upon her, it also highlights the destructive capacities of male authority figures, an issue which will run through the Gothic (it includes such obvious later manifestations as Count Dracula and Hannibal Lecter).

The importance of *Otranto* cannot be underestimated. The second preface is key to understanding both how the Gothic emerged and how it needs to be read. Walpole's representations of the aristocracy, the family, and above all gender played an important part in the very different work of Ann Radcliffe and Matthew Lewis, who also address and foreground the anti-Catholicism implied in Walpole's novel.

RADCLIFFE AND LEWIS

The implicit anti-Catholicism which coloured *Otranto* is given more explicit treatment in Radcliffe's *The Italian* (1797) and Matthew Lewis's *The Monk* (1796) set respectively in Catholic Italy and Spain. However, they are quite different novels in emphasis and tone, and this is reflected in how they approach the issue of religion. *The Italian* is fundamentally a love story in which the two lovers, Ellena and Vivaldi, are separated by the interference of Vivaldi's mother, the Marchesa, who has employed the apparently malevolent monk Schedoni to keep the lovers apart. The Marchesa is concerned that Ellena is not of noble birth and is therefore unfit for Vivaldi. Schedoni has Ellena abducted and imprisoned in various convents. The solution appears to be Ellena's murder, but Schedoni is unable to assassinate her and changes his view of her because a locket that she wears leads him to falsely believe that he might be her father. Vivaldi, meanwhile, despite temporarily being able to rescue Ellena, has been imprisoned by the Inquisition. Ellena discovers her long-lost mother, Olivia, in a convent and discovers that she is of noble birth. Schedoni dies in the Inquisition, Vivaldi is released, and the novel concludes with the wedding between Vivaldi and Ellena.

In *The Italian* the key to understanding the novel's anti-Catholicism is through its representation of sublimity because it both endorses a moderating Protestantism (one which enables self-control) *and* operates within Burke's notion of Terror, which was outlined in the Introduction. For Burke the sublime can be generated by obscurity and lack of clarity; it is about gesture and implication rather than direct representation. Burke may posit a fear of death as *the* source of the sublime, but this is necessarily abstract (because how can we know what we have not experienced?), so that it is an *idea* of death which is important. If Terror is about gesture and implication, its opposite, Horror, is about showing. Radcliffe commented on these issues in her posthumously published essay 'On the Supernatural in Poetry' (1826), where she noted that, 'Terror and horror are so far opposite that the first expands the soul, and awakens the faculties to a high degree of life; the other contracts, freezes, and nearly annihilates them'.[7] In *The Italian* the debate about emotion is constructed between three characters, the monk Schedoni, who is too intellectual, the ostensible hero, Vivaldi, who is too imaginative, and the heroine, Ellena, who is a model of self-control and moderation.

Ellena's self-control appears to be an antidote to the excesses of Gothic horror that the novel heads towards but importantly never develops, and therefore it seems as though Radcliffe is writing against Gothic excess. The novel repeatedly puts Ellena in situations where she could justifiably consider her life at risk (implying Burke's idea of Terror), but where she refuses to give in to negative feelings. When she is abducted by agents working for Schedoni (in order to stop her romantic attachment with Vivaldi) she is taken through a dramatic mountainous terrain. Although her position is dangerous (having seemingly been abducted by banditti) she nevertheless looks out at the dramatic scenery and finds a sublime landscape in which, for her, 'It is scarcely possible to yield to the pressure of misfortune while we walk, as with the Deity, amidst his most stupendous works!'[8] This becomes the antidote to danger, and it is this godly presence which means that 'during the rest of the journey she preserved a strenuous equality of mind' (p. 63). That this is a Protestant God, one that instils fortitude and self-control, rather than superstition and fear, is emphasised during Ellena's incarceration in a convent. She gains access to a room from which she gazes out on nature:

> Here, gazing upon the stupendous imagery around her, looking, as it were, beyond the awful veil which obscures the features of the Deity, and conceals Him from the eyes of his creatures, dwelling as with a present God in the midst of his sublime works; with a mind thus elevated, how insignificant would appear to her the transactions, and the sufferings of the world! (pp. 90–1)

The clear message is that God is to be found outside of the convent.

Ultimately the novel suggests that there is a providential design at work which protects and rewards the innocent, such as Ellena. Lewis's *The Monk*, however, is of a very different order. First it should be noted that there is a tacit dialogue taking place between Lewis and Radcliffe. Radcliffe's earlier Gothic writings are to some degree lampooned in *The Monk*, which provides a highly visual, semi-pornographic and violent version of her Gothic world. Radcliffe responds with *The Italian*, as an attempt to recuperate the Gothic and to incorporate some of the new elements which Lewis had introduced into the form.

The Monk corresponds to Radcliffe's idea that horror relies upon explicit representations of danger. The highly complex plot has many interpolated shorter Gothic narratives, concerning the story of the Bleeding Nun and the Wandering Jew, amongst others, as well as a longer narrative relating to the doomed love of Raymond and Agnes (and the child which they have out of wedlock). However, essentially the story revolves around the monk Ambrosio and Antonia (a kind of Radcliffean surrogate heroine). Ambrosio is a grand orator who is much admired, but he is seduced by a demon in the guise of a woman, Matilda, who had infiltrated his monastery by pretending to be a fellow monk, Rosario. Matilda has modelled herself on a picture of the Madonna which had stimulated some erotic feelings in Ambrosio. He tires of Matilda and she helps him seduce Antonia. In order to effect this he murders Elvira, Antonia's mother, and abducts, rapes, and finally murders Antonia. He is imprisoned by the Inquisition but calls upon Satan to save him from the prison (it transpires he would have been found not guilty by the Inquisitors); the fiend then drops him from a great height and consigns him to a painful and lingering death.

The importance of visuality is emphasised from the start when the crowd ostensibly congregates to admire the oratory of Ambrosio. However, Lewis indicates that the congregation are not there for reasons of piety: 'The Women came to show themselves, the Men to see the Women'.[9] This emphasis on seeing is very different from the discretion employed by Radcliffe (and her heroines). Whilst Radcliffe's plots unfold in often highly complex ways, Lewis, in keeping with the theme of explicitness, gives the plot away in the first chapter when Lorenzo falls asleep and has a highly symbolic dream that relates to Antonia and Ambrosio. In the dream Ambrosio, in the guise of a 'Monster', assaults Antonia 'with his odious caresses', kills her and is sent to hell whilst she, angel-like, with 'a wing of brilliant splendour spread' from each of her arms, ascends to heaven (p. 28).

In Radcliffe, there is always the possibility of transcendence, whilst in *The Monk* there is no possibility of redemption because the world is presided over by the Devil. In Radcliffe, the world is presided over by God, and any apparently 'evil' acts are later revealed to be the consequence of a misguided view of the world.

The clearest way to appreciate these different approaches is to compare Ambrosio with Schedoni. Ambrosio's character and likely dilemmas are stated by Lorenzo to Antonia. In the opening scenes, he says of Ambrosio:

Ambrosio's character is perfectly without reproach; and a Man who has passed the whole of his life within the walls of a Convent, cannot have found the opportunity to be guilty, even were He possessed of the inclination. But now, when obliged by the duties of his situation, He must enter occasionally into the world, and be thrown into the way of temptation, it is now that it behoves him to show the brilliance of his virtue. The trial is dangerous; He is just at that period of life when the passions are most vigorous, unbridled, and despotic; His established reputation will mark him out to Seduction as an illustrious Victim; Novelty will give additional charms to the allurements of pleasure; and even the Talents with which Nature has endowed him will contribute to his ruin, by facilitating the means of obtaining his object. Very few would return victorious from a contest so severe. (p. 21)

The political dramas of *Otranto* are replaced by sexual intriguing as Ambrosio is seduced by a demon in the guise of Matilda and is led to rape and murder Antonia (who it transpires is his long-lost sister) and his mother, Elvira. Such a moral decline inevitably means that the Devil has won his soul. However, the novel is ambivalent about ascribing blame to Ambrosio. As Lorenzo's speech makes clear, it is not Ambrosio's fault that he is subject to temptation, and this appears to be in keeping with the emphatic masculine ambience of the novel in which the semi-pornographic incidents in Ambrosio's downward journey are lingered over. The novel also claims that Ambrosio's failings are the consequence of his associations with the church. We learn that: 'He had a Warrior's heart, and He might have shone with splendour at the head of an Army' (p. 236). As a youth he was forced to enter the church, where 'the Monks were busied in rooting out his virtues, and narrowing his sentiments' (p. 237) so that ultimately he becomes the 'Monster' of Lorenzo's dream who cannot reconcile his sexual feelings with the world of the monastery. As a result his desires, because long repressed (or sublimated, as in his sexualised attachment to the picture of the Madonna), become expressed in a distorted way.

The Monk appears to be a peculiar offshoot of Romanticism because it emphasises that passions cannot be controlled, even if they lead to damnation, whereas *The Italian* celebrates the virtues of self-restraint. In *The Italian* 'evil' represents an estrangement from God: however, redemption is always an option and the villain, Schedoni, is ultimately not as capable of 'evil' as he thinks. Whilst Schedoni, like friar Jerome in *Otranto*, turns out to have an aristocratic past, it is one associated with fratricide and rape that suggests, like Ambrosio, that he is unable to resist his passions. As a monk, he becomes a rather different figure, a scheming Machiavellian in pursuit of possible political influence, but through a misplaced faith in logic and rationality. Schedoni supplants his passions with his intellect but this generates a false view of the world because he lacks the sensibility that is required in order to intimate God's presence. We discover that Schedoni:

> seldom perceived truth when it lay on the surface; he could follow it through all the labyrinths of disquisition, but overlooked it when it was undisguised before him. In fact he cared not for truth, nor sought it by bold and broad argument, but loved to exert the wily cunning of his nature in hunting it through artificial perplexities. (p. 34)

However, later Schedoni is unable to carry out the assassination of Ellena in a moment of comic bungling in which he needs to fortify himself with wine, becomes confused about whether he has the dagger or not, forgets what role the servant is to play, and neglects to take a lamp so that he cannot see what he is doing. This comic deflation suggests that Schedoni is capable of redemption, and this is in keeping with how other characters and institutions that appear corrupt are redeemed. Vivaldi's scheming mother, the Marchesa, is more humane than she initially appears to be, the convents which also function as prisons are not all dangerous, and Ellena will discover her mother in one of them, even the Inquisition (which Lewis had used to dramatic effect in *The Monk*) becomes a place associated with honesty and the truth.[10] However, these are not simply matters of different aesthetic outlook: they are also closely related to specific political visions, which are apparent in three linked considerations – gender and literary form, class, and the political context of the 1790s.

Any discussion of Radcliffe has to acknowledge her contribution to the Female Gothic. This term was first used by Ellen Moers in *Literary Women* (1976) and referred to writing by women within the Gothic tradition.[11] For Moers the Female Gothic represented fears about women's entrapment within domestic spaces and anxieties about birth. The term has been subject to further critical discussion which has explored its development of a subtle, or understated, mode of feminism in which its heroines strive for some version of a better, more emancipated, life.[12] The Female Gothic's focus on the opportunities for social advancement suggests an optimism about possibilities for change, although one that is frequently conditional upon discovering a long-lost mother that facilitates a mother and daughter relationship which can withstand patriarchal authority.

It is important to note that much of the Gothic novel writing in the late eighteenth century is by women. Other notable contributions to this tradition are Clara Reeve's *The Old English Baron* (1777) and Sophia Lee's *The Recess* (1785). Mary Robinson and Sarah Wilkinson also made significant contributions to the 'Blue Books', which were often synoptic accounts of full-length novels. In Radcliffe it is difficult to disentangle ideas about gender from class-bound considerations, such as the role of sensibility. Sensibility implied the presence of moral virtue and an empathy with others and was not uniquely associated with women's writing: indeed Henry Mackenzie's *The Man of Feeling* (1771) made an important contribution to a tradition of writing about sentiment. During the period there was much discussion about sensibility. Mary Wollstonecraft regarded sensibility as a middle-class affectation designed to inhibit women's conception of a future which did not involve marriage.[13] In the 1790s the debate on sensibility in part concerned how one should temper one's emotions so that they do not become too dangerously self-indulgent, which is one of the main themes of Radcliffe's *The Mysteries of Udolpho*

(1794). For Radcliffe excessive sentiment is always controlled by virtuous self-restraint.

Ellena's sensibility enables her to discern the presence of the divine, which gives her the fortitude to control her feelings. Those who lack sensibility, such as Schedoni, or are unable to temper it, such as Vivaldi, are estranged from this divine presence and consequently are lost in either the world of abstract ideas or over-stimulated Gothic imaginings. Sensibility leads to the divine, which enables self-restraint within a providential design that protects and ultimately rewards Ellena with social and economic advancement.

Ostensibly the wedding between Ellena and Vivaldi with which the novel concludes is a celebration of aristocratic authority, as it is revealed that Ellena is of noble birth. However, the picture is more complicated than this because Ellena's journey of upward social mobility seems more in keeping with middle-class ambitions than with aristocratic authority. Radcliffe is writing at a time when the French aristocracy were deposed during the French Revolution and when there was considerable concern about the spread of revolutionary ideas to Britain. Ellena's journey sees her find her mother and make a socially advantageous marriage. Along the way she demonstrates some good, middle-class, Protestant virtues. Ellena represents a new bourgeois Protestant outlook, and, as Miles has noted, Radcliffe achieves this by politicising sensibility so that it becomes the antidote to the 'social bigotry' which characterised the aristocracy.[14] Radcliffe therefore situates the middle classes within a history that does not belong to them by suggesting that they emerged out of the aristocracy, rather than appeared as a result of the kinds of ruptures that characterised the French Revolution. Radcliffe, seemingly aware of this historical anomaly if the novel is read literally, invites the reader to consider it not as a narrative about 1758 (when it is set) staged in Italy, but about the problems confronted by present-day Britain. A comment in the final chapter refers to the gardens where the wedding of Ellena and Vivaldi takes place, where it is noted that: 'The style of the gardens, where lawns and groves, and woods varied the undulating surface, was that of England, and of the present day, rather than of Italy' (p. 412). Finally, as Miles argues, it is about here and now, rather than there and then, and this, in ideological terms, suggests the new middle-class presence emerging from the older class hierarchies in what is a new myth about belonging.[15]

In keeping with the Female Gothic *The Italian* is optimistic about the new possibilities of advancement for women, possibilities that were, paradoxically, in part generated by the radical ideas stimulated by the French Revolution (and by the earlier American Revolution). Lewis's *The Monk* is much more pessimistic about the idea of social change, as indicated by a world presided over by demonic forces. For Lewis sensibility is a false emotion because it fails to defend you against the realties of a dangerous world. As Punter notes, Antonia's sensibility 'betokens an unworldly faith in other people's goodness and sensitivity, and Lewis has her abducted, poisoned, raped and murdered as a savage indication of the inadequacy of this faith'.[16] The novel also indicates an anxiety about mob rule which for a contemporary readership would clearly have referred to concerns about French revolutionary mobs, an issue addressed in the crowd's assault on the Mother Superior responsible for the incarceration of Agnes, in which she is trampled upon until she 'became no more than a mass of flesh, unsightly, shapeless, and disgusting' (p. 356).

Lewis's world is one of chaos and anarchy, whereas for Radcliffe order is restored. Lewis represents society as imploding because of its hypocrisies, whereas for Radcliffe the truth will out in the end. It is important to note that these differences are not just due to matters of moral vision, but are the consequence of the highly politicised ambience of the time which was shaped by radical debates about the existing social order. However, Britain did not experience a revolution, but America did, and it is important to consider how such changes affected an American Gothic tradition which like the British tradition has its roots in the eighteenth century.

AMERICAN GOTHIC

So far the Gothic has been explored in a British context which has enabled us to see how national issues relating to class, wealth, and political power came to bear upon the form. However, the eighteenth century also saw the emergence of an American Gothic tradition which was subject to quite different pressures. The chief exponent of eighteenth-century American Gothic, and one of the first professional writers in America, was Charles Brockden Brown, who wrote a series of novels that profoundly influenced the direction of the American Gothic, the most famous of which is *Wieland* (1798).

The novel is written from the point of view of Clara Wieland, who recounts how her father came to America from Europe in order to spread his religious views. His somewhat severe Puritan beliefs prompted him to pray several times a day at a small temple which he had specially built in his garden. One night whilst praying he dies in a moment of spontaneous combustion (indicative of the pressures of his oddly solipsistic life). The novel then dwells on the activities of the adult Clara; her brother, Theodore; his wife, Catherine; and her brother, Pleyel. This quartet pursue a leisured life that revolves around religious and philosophical debate. Their intellectual idyll is interrupted by the arrival of Carwin, who is a mischievous ventriloquist (or biloquist, as he is referred to in the novel), who by projecting imitated voices from members of the group challenges many of their religious and philosophical beliefs. The final drama of the novel concerns Theodore's murder of Catherine and their children because he believes that God has told him to do it (the novel is loosely based on an actual murder case from 1781 when a New York farmer killed his wife and four children). Carwin confesses to Clara that he was responsible for many of the misunderstandings between members of the group because of his voice projection, but protests that he did not pretend to be the voice of God in order to test Theodore's faith by commanding him to murder his family.

Teresa A. Goddu has noted that in order to understand this seemingly eccentric narrative it should be seen within the context of post-revolutionary America. Goddu argues that:

> Father Wieland's death by spontaneous combustion signifies the loss of authority and raises central questions: How can the new nation succeed if its citizens are powder kegs of passion rather than rational beings? How can the nation reinstitute authority in a body that can self-destruct?[17]

Spontaneous combustion here refers to the potentially explosive qualities of the body politic. In a society supposedly governed by republican virtues of self-control (an idea which Goddu notes is central to Benjamin Franklin's widely read *Autobiography*, 1791) *Wieland* suggests the inherent instability of the new order.[18]

The novel examines the merits of a variety of religious and philosophical positions which have their roots in Enlightenment beliefs that extolled the merits of rationality and supported religious tolerance. Clara, for example, sees the world in a way which suggests her ability to exercise an almost Radcliffean control over the dangers of the Gothic imagination:

> I am not fearful of shadows. The tales of apparitions and enchantments did not possess that power over my belief which could even render them interesting. I saw nothing in them but ignorance and folly, and was a stranger even to that terror which is pleasing.[19]

However, the arrival of Carwin, who uses his ventriloquist skills to suggest that Clara has only just escaped being murdered in her bedroom, changes that. Now: 'My fears had pictured to themselves no precise object. It would be difficult to depict, in words, the ingredients and hues of that Phantom which haunted me' (p. 178). This disembodied voice compromises not only Clara's sense of personal safety but also her confidence that one can rationally trust appearances. Her fears are seemingly real (the voice in the closet which has threatened murder) and unreal because they have 'no precise object'. This is linked to the wider, predominantly Enlightenment debate which is staged in the novel as a discussion on the role of the senses (seeing as believing) and the significance of religious faith (a different kind of belief).

Clara recounts how her own and Catherine's education stimulated a religious understanding which 'was the product of lively feelings, excited by reflection on our own happiness, and by the grandeur of external nature' (p. 21). This emphasis on 'external nature' relates to how Clara is used to develop ideas about the primacy of the senses that are, in part, drawn from John Locke's *Essay Concerning Human Understanding* (1689).[20] This leads her to argue, in true Lockean fashion, that 'evil' is based on false perception:

> The will is the tool of the understanding, which must fashion its conclusions on the notices of sense. If the senses be depraved it is impossible to calculate the evils that may flow from the consequent deductions of the understanding. (pp. 32–3)

This philosophically expressed view of the importance of the senses in guiding understanding differs from Theodore's more bookish approach to religious morality, in contrast to Clara and Catherine:

> In his studies, he preserved an austerer and more arduous path. He was much conversant with the history of religious opinions, and took pains to ascertain their validity. He deemed it indispensable to examine the ground of his belief, to settle the relation between motives and actions, the criterion of merit, and the kinds of properties of evidence. (pp. 21–2)

Theodore searches for the moral connections between people and precepts, and his austere approach to such matters is an effective continuation of his father's beliefs. His father's religious convictions led to self-destruction, as Theodore's will lead him to murder his family. The present is ghosted by the past and in political terms this suggests that post-revolutionary America is just as unstable and politically combustible as pre-revolutionary America. A relationship, perhaps an oblique one, can be discerned here with Walpole's moral for *The Castle of Otranto* relating to how the sins of the father become visited upon their children. Eric Savoy has noted of *Wieland* that:

> The sins of the fathers – their excesses, their violence and abuses, their predispositions toward the irrational – are visited upon their children, who, despite their illusions of liberty, find themselves in the ironic situation of an intergenerational compulsion to repeat the past.[21]

This irony should be understood in political rather than literary terms. It suggests that Clara and her family and friends have only a precarious grasp on various philosophical and religious ideas, and that their disabling attachment to the past pre-dates the arrival of the mischievous Carwin.

Carwin functions to make visible these latent pre-existing tensions by challenging the strength of their beliefs. Clara's faith in the need to see evidence is confounded by how she is tricked by Carwin's ventriloquism which had suggested that murderers were lurking in her bedroom closet. He, however, blames her for not properly realising this because, 'You were precipitate and prone to condemn. Instead of rushing on the impostors, and comparing the evidence of your sight with that of hearing, you stood aloof, or you fled' (p. 109). Likewise, Carwin tricks Pleyel, who has fallen in love with Clara, into believing that she is not worthy of him by ventriloquising a dialogue between her and Carwin that suggests that they are lovers. Pleyel is fooled by this because, so the novel implies, he neither trusts nor loves Clara enough to believe her protestations of innocence. Carwin thus brings to light what is already missing or only partially comprehended in their lives. However, Carwin does not take responsibility for impersonating the voice of God, which tells Theodore to sacrifice his wife and children and to attempt the killing of Clara. The reader cannot know if Carwin is telling the truth, or has been testing Theodore's faith. The novel suggests three possible explanations for Theodore's actions: Carwin has tricked him, God really has commanded him to sacrifice his family, or he is insane.

The novel inevitably heads towards uncertainty as the seemingly stable lives and good republican virtues of Clara and her associates become subject to their own metaphoric spontaneous combustions. However, it is important to consider the character of Carwin in this. In part he illustrates how a misplaced confidence in rationality is generated by an inner Gothic presence (implied by a certain type of religious observance and somewhat tense, emotionally solipsistic familial bonds). However, as a catalyst for this peculiarly American Gothic instability it becomes important to know something about him.

Much of Clara's anxiety about Carwin is related to her attempt to gauge his precise moral status. However, the problem is deeper than this because Carwin's actions suggest that any kind of 'reality' (let alone a moral truth) cannot be trusted. His seemingly mischievous playfulness is not apolitical but can be related to three specific issues: language, the idea of finding a voice, and Romanticism. Goddu has explored how Carwin's ventriloquism challenges a conservative adherence to principle and tradition and so undermines how contemporary dictionaries attempted to provide a secure basis for linguistic meaning. She notes that Webster's *An American Dictionary of the English language* (1828) represented a republican attempt to ideologically cleanse and fix language in the interests of a political vision of stability. In this ideological context Carwin's ability to project language, to unfix it, compromises such attempts at securing a model of 'reality' through destabilising linguistic meaning.[22]

On a related issue it could also be argued that Carwin's roving voice also represents an inability to generate a properly located national voice. Clara's Enlightenment principles are really European ones, as indicated in her return to Europe at the end of the novel. How to give voice to America, in anything other than ambivalent terms, represents one of the major, if latently expressed, anxieties within the novel.

Carwin, however, like Clara and her associates, possesses some pre-existing views which come from a European tradition even if they are fundamentally Romantic in essence. Brown appears to associate Romanticism with a form of moral instability that challenges any coherently established republican reality. This is clear from his incomplete novel *Memoirs of Carwin the Biloquist*, which was serialised in the *Literary Magazine* between 1803 and 1805. In the novel Carwin claims that he develops his own realities and scorns the kind of bookishness that contributed to Theodore's downfall, stating that 'It was easy to perceive, that books alone were insufficient to impart knowledge'.[23] Rather, Carwin trusts experience and finds in his ability to project and mimic voices a trait that in part defines him, noting that, 'My character had been, in some degree, modelled by the faculty which I possessed' (p. 276). His character is also modelled by his imaginative construction of the realties which this faculty enables him to generate, and his imagination is one which is, in contrast to the youthful Clara's, fundamentally Gothic: 'I was accustomed to despise danger when it presented itself in sensible form, but [. . .] goblins and spectres were to me objects of the most violent apprehensions' (p. 229). Whilst he acknowledges that this was a fault of his education, it nevertheless implies a Gothic Romanticism which, as in the use of his projected voice, generates, or stimulates, Gothic realities. Whereas the Wieland family were raised by a father with strict religious principles, for Carwin, 'A thousand superstitious tales were current in the family. Apparitions had been seen, and voices had been heard on a multitude of occasions. My father was a confident believer in supernatural tales' (p. 234). The claim that 'voices had been heard' indicates how Carwin's later ventriloquism is associated with an imagined Gothic.

In the *Memoirs* Carwin is befriended by a wealthy benefactor, Ludloe, who is interested in Carwin's character and attempts to encourage him to become morally self-reflexive and to make frequent confession to him. The incomplete nature of the narrative makes it difficult to see what Ludloe's ultimate purpose is, but it appears as though he wishes Carwin to play a role in a Utopian society which he hopes to establish on some isolated islands. First he encourages Carwin to try to marry a wealthy widow, Mrs Bennington, because although Ludloe regards marriage as a form of slavery, he sees it as a way of securing Carwin's financial future. Carwin's ability to destabilise reality by mischievously manipulating it is also implied in his attempts to conceal elements of his past from Ludloe.

Carwin's associations with a disembodied voice also hint at another suppressed narrative relating to the body and its desires, appetites, and needs. In *The Monk* sexuality and desire are the destabilising elements of the narrative. For Radcliffe repression, as a means of self-control, becomes a virtue, whereas for Lewis self-control, in his strictly male reading of desire, is not so easy. Carwin, however, sees himself as a sexual pragmatist (in what is arguably an alternative male reading of desire), and this emphasises the body's 'needs'. Carwin, for example, is not sure that he can pursue the widow Bennington because he is forced to 'acknowledge, with shame and regret, that I was accustomed to regard the physical and sensual consequences of the sexual relation as realities, and everything intellectual, disinterested, and heroic which enthusiasts connect with it, as idle dreams' (p. 271). This makes sense of why in *Wieland* he mockingly decides to damage Pleyel's romantic fantasies about Clara. Indeed he explains that he gained access to Clara's household through her servant Judith who was not, so Carwin claims, as 'innocent' as Clara thinks (p. 184). Carwin states that Judith comes from 'a family where hypocrisy, as well as licentiousness, was wrought into a system' (p. 184). Carwin 'was captivated by her charms' and notes that 'her principles' were 'flexible' (p. 184). However, Carwin also claims that his relationship with Judith was not tarnished by 'the iniquity of seduction' but was fundamentally pragmatic: 'Your servant is not destitute of feminine and virtuous qualities; but she was taught that the best use of her charms consists in the sale of them' (p. 185). For Carwin, and presumably Judith, the selling of her body can be isolated from her otherwise 'virtuous qualities' because sex is merely about appetite (for pleasure, for money).

Carwin in both *Wieland* and the *Memoirs* is an amoral agent of a Gothic Romanticism that takes its pleasures where it can find them. This kind of restlessness of the well-travelled sexually experienced Carwin is also suggested in the disembodied voices that projectively wander into other people's lives and transform them (the full title of the novel is *Wieland; or, The Transformation*).

It is important to appreciate that Carwin's actions should be read in political terms. The fundamental question posed by Brown concerns where authority (both moral and political) can be found.

As Goddu has noted, *Wieland* stages a debate about the instability of language, which can be explained in historical terms by reference to republican strategies intended to lexically fix meaning, strategies which reflect a wider attempt to secure notions of cultural order and political stability. This also represents a desire to find a 'voice', one which can give utterance to new, emerging, experiences. These texts also suggest the presence of a new kind of Romanticism that destabilises Enlightenment certainties. Carwin represents a mode of restlessness which by definition cannot be accommodated, but which should be seen in political terms because it represents a republican anxiety about the fragile nature of the political realities of post-revolutionary America.[24]

Brown's American Gothic is far removed from the British tradition developed by Radcliffe and Lewis. Both *Wieland* and the *Memoirs* are first-person narratives that place the emphasis on the individual and their sense of reality, which contrasts with the overview (the third-person narration) provided by Radcliffe and Lewis, where the focus shifts between different characters and narratives. The principal difference between these two traditions is because America has had a revolution, rather than is in fear of one. The basic problem addressed by Brown concerns whether the new post-revolutionary democracy exists in reality because society appears to be merely formed out of a series of loose, and so precarious, alliances between individuals.

The wider issue here is history. Radcliffe attempted to locate the roots of the middle class within an aristocratic genealogy. It represents an attempt to inscribe the middle classes into history as a means of concealing their mercantile origins and pre-emptively safeguarding the precariousness of any potential class fluctuations engendered by the new money-based society. However, Brown's writings suggest the inescapability of the past and imply the difficulties in establishing anything 'new' other than the amoral 'playfulness' of a Carwin, who represents the presence of an anti-social Gothic Romanticism that is inevitably part of the problem rather than grounds for a solution.

We shall see later how these specifically American concerns about the past, identity, and notions of 'realism' impact on the writings of Edgar Allan Poe and a twentieth-century writer such as Toni Morrison, who examines how 'other' histories relating to race and slavery played a part in shaping the nation. In Brown there is no real supernatural experience as there is in Walpole and Lewis. Poe's 'horrors' can also be explained away in historical and psychological terms. Brown therefore develops the Gothic in a way that invites a non-supernatural reading, an issue which, as we shall see, later writers in the American tradition would either develop or take issue with.

READING *FRANKENSTEIN*

Ann Radcliffe and Charles Brockden Brown respond to prevailing intellectual and philosophical trends. Radcliffe's version of subjectivity, for example, is in response to Romantic ideas about the intellect, the role of the imagination, and the place of the sublime. Brown's writings were influenced by Romantic notions of political justice derived from William Godwin's *An Enquiry Concerning Political Justice* (1793).[25] However, the early Gothic does not passively assimilate pre-existing concepts (about nature, justice, beauty, and the sublime) but actively interrogates these concepts.

That Mary Shelley would respond to Romantic ideas is unsurprising given that she was married to Percy Shelley and knew Byron, and that her parents, William Godwin and Mary Wollstonecraft (who died shortly after giving birth to Mary), were two of the foremost radical intellectuals of the time. However, in keeping with both *The Italian* and *Wieland*, Shelley debates such ideas rather than restates them, and this is achieved through a sceptical approach to Romantic idealism. Her interrogation of sublimity in *Frankenstein* provides us with a clear example of how a Gothic narrative mounts this kind of challenge.

Frankenstein addresses a central feature of Romanticism: the role of nature. For the Romantics, encounters with particularly dramatic aspects of nature are sublime because they stimulate the imagination and enable the subject to transcend the everyday world of duties and responsibilities, and so discover their place in a higher order of things. Immanuel Kant's 'The Analytic of the Sublime' is a key philosophical analysis of this moment, and he claims that in the sublime moment, phenomena (objects) become replaced by noumena (ideas).[26] For Kant, this also indicates that the mind comprises both the ability to imagine and a propensity for rationality (because we do not stay in a permanent noumenal state but return to a more terrestrial world of logic and order). What animates nature is key to understanding the sublime. Radcliffe finds God within nature; an atheist such as Percy Shelley discovers a secular creative force (see his poem 'Mont Blanc', 1817), for Kant the experience tells us how the mind works (its capacity for stimulation), whereas for Burke sublimity is linked to Terror. What constitutes the sublime suggests different things to different philosophers, poets, and novelists, and therefore what the sublime means was subject to some debate. Mary Shelley, however, takes the radical step in *Frankenstein* of suggesting that the sublime is little more than a culturally (or perhaps intellectually) constructed way of looking at the world. For her, accounts of the sublime rest on a false premise relating to the presence of meaning, and she makes this challenge by problematising the Romantic assertion that nature gives shape to that meaning.

The metaphysical status of Shelley's creature indicates how she challenges Romantic conceptions of nature. The creature is both natural (made up of human parts, and possessing a recognisably human inner life) and unnatural (because he has been stitched together from dead bodies). The fact that he is both real and unreal disturbs Victor Frankenstein's belief that the natural world is a transcendent one. This is clear when Victor meets the creature for the first time since he had created and abandoned him. The meeting takes place whilst Victor is grieving for his murdered brother, William (whom he knows has been killed by the creature). Victor attempts to gain some relief from his feelings of grief by seeking the kind of sublime transcendence that a visit to the Alps should, in a Romantic world, provide. Victor notes that in the presence of this 'imperial nature' the 'sublime and magnificent scenes afforded me the greatest consolation that I was capable of receiving. They elevated me from all littleness of feeling, and although they did not remove my grief, they subdued and tranquillized it'.[27] However, the scene symbolically illustrates Victor's egotism, an egotism which had led him to create the creature and turn his back on his family and fiancée (Elizabeth) in pursuit of scientific success. The scene ceases to be about nature but about Victor's egotism when he claims:

> I retired to rest at night; my slumbers, as it were, waited on and ministered to by the assemblance of grand shapes which I had contemplated during the day. They congregated round me; the unstained snowy mountain-top, the glittering pinnacle, the pine woods, and ragged bare ravine, the eagle, soaring amidst the clouds – they all gathered round me and bade me be at peace. (p. 142)

Victor imaginatively recasts nature so that he lies at its centre (indeed his creation of the creature suggests his 'mastery' over nature). Shelley develops this egotism by suggesting that it explains the latent hostility towards domesticity which his scientific endeavours imply. This is apparent in Victor's somewhat heartless claim that he has been distracted, even if only temporarily, from William's death in this concord with nature because, 'The sight of the awful and majestic in nature had indeed always the effect of solemnizing my mind and causing me to forget the passing cares of life' (p. 143). The scene leads Victor into contemplating the supposed benefits of living a simple, more natural life: 'Why does man boast of sensibilities superior to those apparent in the brute[?]' (p. 143). However, all of this sets the scene for the arrival of the creature. This short, very densely argued passage from the novel implies a relationship between egotism and the sublime, and dwells on the misconstruction of nature as a form of transcendence. Victor's account of the brute is then literalised by the sudden appearance of the creature, at the sight of which 'a mist came over my eyes, and I felt a faintness seize me' (p. 144). This blurring of vision is central to how the novel challenges Victor with the alternative idea of the sublime which is embodied in the 'monster'.

Shelley's argument, and other Gothic novels such as *The Italian* and *Wieland* are at some level concerned with intellectual argument, is that nature is seen as sublime but that this perception is a cultural rather than a natural one. How Victor sees the landscape tells us very little about it, but reveals a lot about him. Ultimately the novel asserts that 'seeing' itself is not natural because it is tainted by cultural factors. The sublime constitutes a moment of projection for Victor and this is crucial to understanding how the novel replaces the sublime with a key Gothic motif: the double. Such issues are focused by how the creature, initially, exemplifies ideas about the sublime that are drawn from Burke's *Philosophical Enquiry*, which was discussed in the Introduction. In *Frankenstein* the creature appears to embody Burke's theory of sublime Terror. It is a mode of sublimity which supplants the seemingly more innocent version of it that Victor hopes to discover on his journey to the Alps. Indeed the arrival of the creature disturbs his Romantic reveries, but it is important to note that the creature seems to be a part of the drama of the landscape that Victor contemplates. He is the Romantic brute made flesh and as such represents the dark, Gothic, side of the sublime. However, Shelley does not leave it there – she will also imply that even this Burkean model of sublimity rests on a false perception: one that construes the creature as a 'monster'.

Burke claims that it is the idea of death that constitutes a key element of the sublime, and the creature's composition from dead beings literalises the presence of death even as his supposedly terrifying appearance promises violence. If Victor's take on the sublime merely serves to mark out the sublime as little more than egotistical projection, the embodiment of Burke's sublime rests on a false perception of the creature as a terrifying monster. Shelley wants us to consider this by emphasising how 'sight' misperceives the creature. The novel is explicit about this when it contrasts the warmth with which the old, blind Mr De Lacey responds to the creature with the violent assault that Felix, his son, subjects the creature to. Victor also empathetically listens to the creature's sorry narrative of abandonment and rejection, in which:

> His words had a strange effect upon me. I compassionated him and sometimes felt a wish to console him, but when I looked upon him, when I saw the filthy mass that moved and talked, my heart sickened and my feelings were altered to those of horror and hatred. (p. 192)

The novel implies that the creature should be understood by his speech, not by his appearance. In the context of the sublime it suggests that the creature has been moulded through a Burkean discourse of Terror which falsely associates him with pain, terror, and death. However, the creature is a construction, built from dead bodies, whose view of the world has been intellectually stitched together from overhearing the language lessons given to Safie by the De Laceys. The creature cannot therefore be unproblematically identified as a natural object at all, and this challenges the idea that sublime perceptions are themselves natural. What is fundamentally artificial, the novel subtly claims, is a Romantic conception of nature which falsely sees meaning in nature and wrongly ascribes the terrors of monstrosity on the basis of a misperception. Suddenly nature does not look so natural after all, as neither the Alps nor the creature can finally be separated from culturally inflected ways of seeing.

Victor's first sight of the creature is when William's body is discovered and he discerns that someone is concealed in the nighttime gloom: 'A flash of lightning illuminated the object and discovered its shape plainly to me; its gigantic stature, and the deformity of its aspect, more hideous than belongs to humanity' (p. 123). The creature is illuminated within nature and given a terrifying appearance which evokes Burke's model of Terror. However, these associations are gradually eroded to the point where the sublime becomes meaningless and so undermines Victor's sense of a 'natural' order. At the end of the novel he acknowledges this transformation: 'I cannot believe that I am the same creature whose thoughts were once filled with sublime and transcendent visions' (p. 263). However, to understand Victor's despair it is important to consider what Shelley replaces the sublime with.

In Chapter 5 Victor recounts the moment when he brought the creature to life. The scene centres on a disjunction between theory and practice. Victor notes that 'His limbs were in proportion, and I had selected his features as beautiful': however, he is forced to accept that his pursuit of beauty has created ugliness (the unaesthetic whole being bigger than its parts). Victor, exhausted by his toils, falls asleep and has a richly symbolic dream in which:

> I thought I saw Elizabeth, in the bloom of health, walking in the streets of Ingolstadt. Delighted and surprised, I embraced her, but as I imprinted the first kiss on her lips, they became livid with the hue of death; her features appeared to change, and I thought that I held the corpse of my dead mother in my arms; a shroud enveloped her form, and I saw the grave-worms crawling in the folds of the flannel. (p. 106)

This dream has obvious Gothic associations which might seem to invite a psychoanalytical interpretation. However, such analysis can also be historicised, and in Shelley's case it is important to note that her formulation of an inner life is in direct contrast to Romantic misperceptions of the external world. The dream refers to how his act of creation has usurped the role of his dead (or now redundant) mother. The dream also illustrates how Victor's scientific endeavours are dependent upon his latent hostility towards domesticity.

His symbolic killing of Elizabeth with the kiss of death indicates that it is the bourgeois world of marriage and family ties that he finds stifling (and it is for this reason that he has not returned home after the formal completion of his studies). Victor may evidence some horror at this dream (it is, after all, a nightmare), but what will later become truly horrific is the acknowledgement of the painful truth that the creature represents, and acts upon, his covert hostility towards domesticity. As Mary Poovey notes, 'In *Frankenstein*, the monster simply acts out the implicit content of Frankenstein's desire; just as Frankenstein figuratively murdered his family, so the monster literally murders Frankenstein's domestic relationships'.[28] Victor's journey now becomes an increasingly inward one in which he is forced to accept that the creature functions as 'my own vampire' (p. 124), and that, after the creature has killed William, Justine, and Henry, 'I am the assassin of those most innocent victims; they died by my machinations' (p. 230).

The Romantic confidence in nature is replaced by an anxiety about the inner life. The sublime appeared to offer transcendence, but there can be no transcendence when you are confronted by another version of yourself. The creature, initially, appears to be a better (or more conformist) version of Victor, as he desires the kind of family bonds that Victor finds so circumscribing. This new emphasis on an inner life, one in which doubling functions to make explicit the apparent hidden depths of the psyche, can be seen in historical terms because it challenges historically specific Romantic conceptualisations of nature. This inner world is also one which has political affects. The wider issue addressed is how a particularly instrumentalist model of masculinity has created monstrosity by its refusal to engage with the allegedly more feminine world of domesticity. Indeed, Victor is not the only male character seemingly on the run from domesticity. Robert Walton, who sends the narrative 'home' to his sister, Margaret Saville, via a series of letters, is on a bizarre egotistical search for a tropical paradise at the North Pole. The staging of Victor's inner life has to be seen in relation to these issues of class and gender as they are the means through which Shelley articulates her highly politicised critique of what was typically constructed in ahistorical, depolitical, and transcendent terms: the sublime aspects of nature. Putting class and gender back into the picture will, as we shall see, become an important aspect of the development of the Gothic in the nineteenth century as it moves away from Romantic concepts and addresses the social and economic strains engendered by a maturing industrial society. However, so far we have considered the Gothic only as a prose form, and the next chapter will begin with a discussion of the relationship between poetry and the Gothic.

SUMMARY OF KEY POINTS

- The Gothic represents an anti-Enlightenment impulse.
- The Gothic is a critically self-reflexive form.
- There is a close, but sometimes critical, engagement with Romantic ideas.
- Explorations of 'evil' can help to identify a Gothic text's political outlook.
- The Gothic addresses nationally specific contexts.

QUESTIONS AND POINTS FOR DISCUSSION

- How does an understanding of national contexts influence our reading of Gothic texts?
- How does the Female Gothic contrast with the Male Gothic?
- How does the Gothic engage with ideas of 'revolution'?
- How does the Gothic respond to ideas of sublimity? Is there a Gothic sublime?

NOTES

1. Horace Walpole, *The Castle of Otranto*, ed. W. S. Lewis, intro. E. J. Clery (Oxford: Oxford University Press, [1764] 1998), p. 9. All subsequent references in the text are to this edition.
2. See Emma Clery, Introduction to *The Castle of Otranto*, ed. W. S. Lewis, intro. E. J. Clery (Oxford: Oxford University Press, [1764] 1998), and 'The genesis of "Gothic" fiction', in

The Cambridge Companion to Gothic Fiction, ed. Jerrold E. Hogle (Cambridge: Cambridge University Press, 2002), pp. 21–40; Robert Miles, 'The Gothic and Ideology', in *Gothic Fiction: The British and American Traditions*, ed. Diane Long Hoeveler and Tamar Heller (New York: MLA, 2003), pp. 58–65; James Norton, 'The first English Gothic novel: Walpole's *The Castle of Otranto*', in Hoeveler and Heller, pp. 90–8.

3. See Clery, Introduction to *Otranto*, p. xxiv, and 'The genesis of "Gothic" fiction', p. 26. For extracts from Hurd's *Letters on Chivalry and Romance*, see *Gothic Documents: A Sourcebook, 1700–1820*, ed. E. J. Clery and Robert Miles (Manchester: Manchester University Press, 2000), pp. 67–77.

4. Clery, Introduction to *Otranto*, pp. xxv–xxxiii; Robert Miles, 'Gothic and ideology', pp. 58–65.

5. The Whigs were opposed to the possibility of a Catholic monarchy in the seventeenth century, but were ardent supporters of the protestant Hanoverian settlement in the eighteenth century. However, at the time Walpole was writing *Otranto* they had started losing political clout.

6. Fred Botting, *Gothic* (London: Routledge, 1996), p. 64.

7. Ann Radcliffe, 'On the Supernatural in Poetry', in *Gothic Documents: A Sourcebook, 1700–1820*, ed. E. J. Clery and Robert Miles (Manchester: Manchester University Press, 2000), pp. 163–72, p. 168.

8. Ann Radcliffe, *The Italian* (Oxford: Oxford University Press, [1797] 1992), p. 63. All subsequent references in the text are to this edition.

9. Matthew Lewis, *The Monk* (Oxford: Oxford University Press, [1796] 1992), p. 7. All subsequent references in the text are to this edition.

10. See the scene with the vicar-general, p. 352.

11. Ellen Moers, *Literary Women* (London: Women's Press, [1976] 1978).

12. See also special issue of *Gothic Studies*, 6: 1 (May 2004) on 'The Female Gothic', ed. Andrew Smith and Diana Wallace, and special issue of *Women's Writing: The Elizabethan to Victorian Period*, 1: 2 (1994) on 'Female Gothic Writing', ed. Robert

Miles. See also Alison Milbank, *Daughters of the House: Modes of Gothic in Victorian Fiction* (Basingstoke: Macmillan, 1992); E. J. Clery, *Women's Gothic: From Clara Reeve to Mary Shelley*, Writers and Their Work series (Tavistock: Northcote, 2000); and Suzanne Becker, *Gothic Forms of Feminine Fiction* (Manchester: Manchester University Press, 1999).

13. Mary Wollstonecraft, *The Vindication of the Rights of Women*, ed. Miriam Brody (Penguin: Harmondsworth, [1792] 1991): see pp. 151–6.

14. Robert Miles, *Ann Radcliffe: The Great Enchantress* (Manchester: Manchester University Press, 1995), p. 164.

15. On this issue of class and Britain see Miles's *Ann Radcliffe*, pp. 149–73.

16. David Punter, *The Literature of Terror*, vol. 1 (London: Longman, [1980] 1996), p. 65.

17. Teresa A. Goddu, 'Historicizing the American Gothic: Charles Brockden Brown's *Wieland*', in *Approaches to Teaching Gothic Fiction: The British and American Traditions*, ed. Diane Long Hoeveler and Tamar Heller (New York: Modern Languages Association of America, 2003), pp. 184–9, p. 187.

18. Franklin's *Autobiography* was first published in French in 1791; the first English edition was published in 1793.

19. Charles Brockden Brown, *Wieland; or, The Transformation* and *Memoirs of Carwin the Biloquist*, ed. and intro. Emory Elliott (Oxford: Oxford University Press, [1798] 1998), pp. 1–224, p. 42. All subsequent references in the text are to this edition.

20. See Emory Elliott's excellent Introduction which helps to place the novel in the context of such philosophical and political ideas: *Wieland*, pp. vii–xxx.

21. Eric Savoy, 'The Rise of American Gothic', in *The Cambridge Companion to Gothic Fiction*, ed. Jerrold E. Hogle (Cambridge: Cambridge University Press, 2002), pp. 167–88, p. 172.

22. Goddu, 'Historicizing the American Gothic', p. 188.

23. Brown, *Wieland*, pp. 225–89, p. 252.

24. As with the writings of Radcliffe and Lewis, there is some ambivalence here. Savoy, for example, also suggests that *Wieland* indicates a republican horror that democracy guides people in such a manner that they no longer need to think for

themselves, meaning that the novel raises 'doubts about the ability of individuals to govern themselves in a full-fledged democracy' (p. 175).

25. See Brown, *Wieland*, p. viii.

26. Immanuel Kant, 'The Analytic of the Sublime', in *The Critique of Judgement*, trans. James C. Meredith (Oxford: Clarendon, [1790] 1986), pp. 90–203.

27. Mary Shelley, *Frankenstein; or, The Modern Prometheus* (Harmondsworth: Penguin, [1831] 1985), p. 142. All subsequent references to this edition are given in the text.

28. Mary Poovey, *The Proper Lady and the Woman Writer: Ideology as Style in the Works of Mary Wollstonecraft, Mary Shelley, and Jane Austen* (Chicago: Chicago University Press, 1984), p. 126.

CHAPTER 2

The Gothic, 1820–1865

GOTHIC MUTATIONS: POETRY

So far we have considered the Gothic as a predominantly prose form. However, the roots of the Gothic are to be found in earlier theatrical and poetic traditions. Radcliffe, for example, is heavily indebted to Shakespearean tragedy and in *The Italian* often begins her chapters with a quotation from his plays. However, her interrogation of Romantic concepts, such as the sublime and the role of nature, is firmly rooted in the poetry of the period. In addition the Gothic more generally owes some debt to the 'Graveyard Poetry' of the 1740s and 1750s. Edward's Young's *Night Thoughts* (1742–5), Robert Blair's *The Grave* (1743), James Hervey's *Meditations among the Tombs* (1745–7), Thomas Warton's *On the Pleasures of Melancholy* (1747), and Thomas Gray's *Elegy written in a Country Churchyard* (1751) all made a significant contribution to developing a Gothic ambience (by dwelling on feelings of loss), and provided an investigation into life and death that constituted a peculiarly Gothic metaphysic. The Gothic novel's link to Romantic poetry was noted by Sir Walter Scott when he proclaimed Radcliffe 'the first poetess of romantic fiction'.[1] The Romantic interest in exploring non-rational (anti-Enlightenment) states led many of the Romantic poets to write in the Gothic mode. This section explores how a Romantic Gothic tradition of poetry developed themes (concerning sexuality, art, and the imagination) which influenced a later poetic tradition here represented by Christina Rossetti's *Goblin Market* (1862). It is important to note that after the Gothic heyday of the late eighteenth and early nineteenth centuries, the Gothic does not disappear but subversively infiltrates other forms of writing, including poetry, and the realist Victorian novel. Wordsworth's collaboration with Coleridge on *The Lyrical Ballads* (1798) included Coleridge's Gothic allegory *The Rime of the Ancient Mariner*. At this time Coleridge seemingly had the Gothic much in mind, which is apparent from *Christabel* (1798–1801).[2] *Christabel* is set in a fantasised medieval world of castles and knights, but is less a tale about chivalry than demonic influence. The poem begins with Christabel's discovery of the apparently abducted Geraldine, whom Christabel carries into the castle of her father, Sir Leoline. During the night Geraldine seduces Christabel and in the morning supplants her in Sir Leoline's affections when she claims to be the daughter of an old friend, Lord Roland, from whom he has become estranged. Robert Miles has noted that the poem contains many different narratives, including Geraldine's tale of her abduction, the drama between Christabel and Geraldine, Sir Leoline's story of estrangement, and a dream narrative recounted by Bracy the Bard which allegorises the danger that Geraldine appears to represent (not only lesbian desire, but hints of vampirism).[3] This suggests that the poem's unevenness in tone is a consequence of its struggle to coherently express the subversive elements of the Gothic themes. As Miles notes, 'instability of tone, in this respect, is the measure of the poem's own assessment of its transgression' (p. 189). In order to appreciate this it is necessary to pay attention to the way that language is used to suggest the presence of incompletion (in what is an unfinished poem). This might seem only obliquely related to the poem's central drama, but the use of language is revealing.

The poem begins with ''Tis the *middle* of the night by the castle clock' (1.1, my italics), making the seemingly mundane point that the action takes place between night and morning: however, this language of in-betweenness, or liminality, is reiterated throughout the poem. When Christabel prepares the way for Geraldine's entry into the castle:

> A little door she opened straight,
> All in the *middle* of the gate. (ll. 125–6, my italics)

Geraldine seemingly faints and vampire-like is carried over the threshold, whereupon she promptly regains consciousness (this finds its echo in *Dracula* when Jonathan Harker is invited to enter the castle of his 'own free will'; the movements might be different but the effect is the same – the vampire's world is freely embraced).[4] Geraldine disrobes in Christabel's room and 'Behold! her bosom, and *half* her side – ' (1.252, my italics). This language of incompletion suggests that Christabel, true to the Female Gothic, is vulnerable because of an absent mother (who is dead, but spectrally present). Geraldine seems to promise fulfilment when she looks at Christabel and:

> Deep from within she seems *half-way*
> To lift some weight with sick assay. (ll. 257–8, my italics)

The first part of the poem culminates in Christabel's seduction and concludes with a moral that implies that the sleeping Christabel will be reborn in the morning.

The second part of the poem restates this language of in-betweenness by referring to the tolling of the bell for matins in which there is 'Between each stroke – a warning knell' (1.342). The sense of danger which inhabits these incomplete or in-between worlds is developed in Bracy the Bard's dream. The dream is between reality and fantasy, between consciousness and unconsciousness. It represents an attempt to reclaim this language of liminality for an allegorical purpose which reveals the truth about Geraldine's vampirism through a tale concerning a dove (Christabel) being attacked by a snake (Geraldine). Bracy states that:

> I stooped, methought the dove to take,
> When lo! I saw a bright green snake
> Coiled around its wings and neck,
> Green as the herbs on which it couched;
> Close by the dove's its head it crouched.

And with the dove it heaves and stirs,
Swelling its neck as she swelled hers! (ll. 548–54)

These images are reinforced by references to how Geraldine and
the post-lapsarian Christabel hiss like snakes. The predatory nature
of the snake suggests an eroticised vampirism in the image of the
swelling neck.

Looking closely at how Coleridge uses language enables us to see
how he establishes his Gothic vision through a language of inde-
terminacy, which illustrates how the emptiness of both Christabel's
life (she has lost her mother) and Sir Leoline's (he has lost not just
his wife, but also his friend Lord Roland) suggests emotional vul-
nerabilities which Geraldine can exploit. However, the poem's
demonisation of Geraldine implicates a particularly conservative
view of apparently transgressive sexuality. This issue of demonisation is central to Keats's poem *Lamia* (1820).[5]

The first part of *Lamia* focuses on how Lamia, a mythical figure
who, like Geraldine, has associations with serpents and vampires,
infiltrates the human world of ancient Corinth in order to seduce
Lycius. Keats uses classical mythology to construct a pagan world
that puts it beyond (or before) Christian moralising. Whereas in
Christabel Geraldine is a figure of destruction, Lamia is a force of
creativity. Indeed at one level she becomes a representative figure of
the poetic radicalism which was so important to the Romantics.
Like Geraldine she is a sexual predator, but her transformation of
Lycius's world is positive rather than negative. It is one in which
the human world and the mythical world are potentially merged, as
in the second part of the poem Lamia and Lycius intend to conse-
crate their relationship through marriage. Her links to Romantic
creativity are clear in the passage that refers to her decoration of the
room where the wedding feast is to take place. She is described as
controlling:

her viewless servants to enrich
The fretted splendour of each nook and niche.
Between the tree-stems, marbled plain at first,
Came jasper panels: then anon, there burst
Forth creeping imagery of slighter trees,

And with the larger wove in small intricacies.
Approving all, she faded at self-will. (II, ll. 136–42)

Lamia's control over nature marks out her creativity. An idealised image of the artist, she introduces beauty and colour into the world. Keats therefore refuses to demonise Lamia, and instead identifies scientific knowledge as a force of destruction because it takes away the magic that is conjured by the artistic imagination. Lycius's philosophy tutor, Apollonius, appears as an uninvited guest at the wedding, and his rationalistic view of the world threatens to destroy the magic that is associated with Lamia. The poem notes that:

There was an awful rainbow once in heaven:
We know her woof, her texture: she is given
In the dull catalogue of common things.
Philosophy will clip an Angel's wings,
Conquer all mysteries by rule and line,
Empty the haunted air, and gnomed mine –
Unweave a rainbow, as it erewhile made
The tender-person'd Lamia melt into a shade.
(II, ll. 231–8)

The allusion to a scientific understanding of the rainbow refers to Isaac Newton's work on optics (Newton was a bogeyman figure for the Romantics), and Keats therefore demonises the kind of rationality which the Enlightenment typically associated with progress. Whilst the Gothic is often ambivalent about the Enlightenment (because irrationality is rarely wholeheartedly seen as a good thing), Keats's poem is clear in its support of the creative imagination.

In *Christabel* Geraldine is associated with the vampire; that Lamia is also vampiric is implied in how she is destroyed by Apollonius's heartless rationalistic gaze, in which 'the sophist's eye / Like a sharp spear, went through her utterly' (II, ll. 299–300). In trying to save Lycius from Lamia he kills him by killing her because he dies, seemingly of grief, shortly after.

Gender issues are central to this drama. Miles claims that Apollonius's impaling of Lamia represents 'an aggressive male gaze' which pierces 'a feminine body' (p. 197) and so illustrates 'the philosopher's misogyny' (p. 198). Whilst the poem appears to radicalise the idea of monstrosity because Lamia is represented in a positive way, nevertheless the conflict within the poem between rationality and creativity depends upon conventional notions of gender identity. Rationality is masculine, creativity possibly feminine ('possibly' because of Lamia's apparent dominance over the somewhat passive Lycius). In *Christabel* Sir Leoline's castle is a patriarchal space which functions as an extension of his authority. In both poems gender influences the approach to issues about invasion, seduction, and threatened transformation.

Gender issues are also central to Christina Rossetti's *Goblin Market* (1862).[6] Rossetti was the niece of John Polidori (the author of *The Vampyre*, 1819) and sister to Gabriel Rossetti, a key figure in Pre-Raphaelite art, and although she is writing some time after the Gothic heyday, her poem illustrates how the Gothic infiltrated ostensibly non-Gothic poetic forms. On a superficial level *Goblin Market* appears to be addressed to children. Its tale of strange Goblin men who entice unwary maidens into buying their fruit (they then waste away and die) is, at one level, a tale of sisterly love as Lizzie helps to save her sister Laura, who has eaten some of the forbidden fruit. The issue of salvation can be seen in Christian terms as Laura goes through a process of redemption after she has sinned (because Eve-like she ate the fruit). However, once we contextualise the poem different readings emerge. Dorothy Mermin has noted how the poem's imagery corresponds to a Pre-Raphaelite aesthetic and that in the representation of the brotherhood of Goblins, Rossetti critiques the male-orientated art world.[7] Mermin also notes that the poem echoes a mid-nineteenth-century perception of Keats which reinforced the association between 'imaginary worlds, sexuality and art' (p. 147). Ellen Moers discusses the poem in the context of the Female Gothic, arguing that the Goblins 'are not lovable little hobbits, but true monsters', familiar from a Gothic tradition of animal-like monsters.[8] She also notes that the Goblins are brothers, and that this is a very different world from that of the sisters, because Goblins are 'a separate breed' (p. 102).

In order to bring out this Gothic presence it is, as was the case with *Christabel*, necessary to consider how language is used. Typically the Gothic employs images of transgression in a displaced way. Monsters are not straightforwardly just monsters, for example (as we saw in *Frankenstein*): rather they illustrate the presence of certain cultural anxieties that are indirectly expressed through apparently fantastical forms. In other words, as in *Otranto*, the Gothic develops its arguments in a disguised way. In *Goblin Market* Rossetti draws attention to this process by emphasising how the use of a comparative language illustrates how images are constructed in a displaced way (and so invites us to examine the poem more closely). Laura, seduced by the presence of the Goblins, is described in these terms:

> Laura stretched her gleaming neck
> Like a rush-imbedded swan,
> Like a lily from the beck,
> Like a moonlit poplar branch,
> Like a vessel at the launch
> When its last restraint is gone. (ll. 80–6)

Whilst at some level this is meant to be purely descriptive, at a more sophisticated level it emphasises how Laura is really none of these things – she is 'like' many images here, but it is only a likeness rather than the reality. We need, as so often with the Gothic, to get beneath the surface language to find the hidden narrative. In some respect this is gestured to in the final lines that indicate that it is Laura's inability to exercise self-restraint that is the problem. Later, when Lizzie confronts the Goblins and tries to buy fruit from them, she withstands their physical assault when they attempt to force her to eat the fruit in front of them:

> White and golden Lizzie stood,
> Like a lily in a flood, -
> Like a rock of blue-veined stone
> Lashed by tides obstreperously, -
> Like a beacon left alone
> In a hoary roaring sea. (ll. 417–22)

Elizabeth K. Helsinger has argued that the poem refers to prostitution, with the goblin men representing the clients who attempt to seduce innocents such as Laura and Lizzie.[9] The market referred to in the title can therefore be read as referring to a male-controlled trade in women. Christina Rossetti had an active interest in trying to help the plight of 'fallen' women, and Lizzie's return to Laura when Laura licks the fruit juices from her represents an attempt to redeem a 'fallen' woman. Again, the language plays an important role in this. Lizzie is like an immovable force surrounded by violent men who try to make her eat the fruit, so that she is in danger of being consumed by 'a hoary (whorey) roaring sea' of men. Lizzie, however, stands there 'Like a royal virgin town' (l. 427) and resists the assault.

Looking at how Rossetti uses language thus provides us with a key to how we need to approach the poem. It is like a fairy tale, but actually it is a Christian tale concerning the dangers of pre-marital sex, a moral warning which exists uneasily alongside the images of lesbianism that ghost the exchanges between Laura and Lizzie.

The poem makes its moral clear when it refers to Jeanie, who also ate the Goblins' fruit:

> Jeanie in her grave,
> Who should have been a bride;
> But who for joys brides hope to have
> Fell sick and died. (ll. 311–14)

The poem does not demonise desire per se, only premature desire. The poem concludes with the two sisters now married with children; however, this seems like an inadequate conclusion. Critics such as Moers and Mermin have noted that men are excluded from the poem because the emphasis is on the sisters, but, as in *Christabel*, images of lesbian desire play a crucial role. Laura and Lizzie live in a domestic idyll which is threatened by the goblin men. When Lizzie returns to Laura and effects a homeopathic cure by having her lick the juices from the crushed fruit on her, she says:

> Come and kiss me.
> Never mind my bruises,

> Hug me, kiss me, suck my juices
> Squeezed from goblin fruits for you,
> Goblin pulp and goblin dew.
> Eat me, drink me, love me;
> Laura, make much of me. (ll. 475–81)

The poem notes that Laura:

> Shaking with anguish fear, and pain,
> [. . .] kissed and kissed her with a hungry mouth.
> (ll. 500–1)

That the Christian moralising cannot contain this lesbian narrative is implied in the concluding stanza of the poem, where the synopsis of the virtues of sisterly love notes:

> For there is no friend like a sister
> In calm or stormy weather:
> To cheer one on the tedious way. (ll. 572–4)

The reference to the 'tedious way' can be read as a critique of the domestic responsibilities that go with motherhood, which means that the ostensible celebration of family life with which the poem concludes is compromised by a typically Gothic ambivalence, precisely because it is an image of family life which cannot accommodate the earlier images of lesbian desire. This points to the covert Gothic narrative which is hidden within a language of comparison.

The Gothic has a close relationship to poetry. One root of the Gothic is to be found in the 'Graveyard Poetry' from the mid-eighteenth century; in addition, Romanticism and the Gothic share many anti-Enlightenment impulses. By looking at how the language is used in such poems we gain an insight into the reasons for their hesitations, complexities, and contradictions.

As we shall see, the Gothic of mid-nineteenth-century Britain develops in quite a different way from that of America, which will be addressed in the following section.

EDGAR ALLAN POE AND THE AMERICAN GOTHIC

Poe is a writer over whom there has been considerable critical debate. First, it is important to acknowledge the versatility of Poe's writing, which includes short stories, poems, essays, and the novels *The Narrative of Arthur Gordon Pym* (1838) and *The Journal of Julius Rodman* (1840). Poe's avowed preference was for work that could be read in one sitting, which is why he generally favoured the shorter format. Not only did he write in a number of forms, but also in a number of literary modes. Many of his tales are obviously Gothic, but many are humorous (and indeed his Gothic tales often possess a rather dark humour), some are close to science fiction, and he wrote some highly influential detective stories (discussed here for their Gothic content).

The critical reception of Poe illustrates how two approaches, the psychoanalytical and the literary-historical, have generated contrasting readings. Poe has been of particular interest to psychoanalytically minded critics since the publication of Marie Bonaparte's *The Life and Works of Edgar Allan Poe: A Psycho-Analytic Interpretation* (1933), which was published with a foreword written by Freud.[10] Bonaparte's Freudian approach treated Poe's tales as if they functioned like dreams (see her analysis of 'The Fall of the House of Usher', for example) or as if they could be understood as like the words uttered by a patient on the psychoanalyst's couch (which is relevant to her reading of 'The Murders in the Rue Morgue', explored here).

For Freudians the patient reveals their subconscious desires in a displaced way. A dream, for example, might appear to be constituted from a range of seemingly inexplicable and surreal images, but once we know something of the dreamer then these images begin to make sense. By linking such images to the patient's past the dramas of the patient's subconscious life are clarified. Bonaparte reads many of the tales as if they were like dreams: as cryptic representations of Poe's real-life dramas which can be explained by reference to biographical facts.

'The Murders in the Rue Morgue' (1841) centres on the seemingly inexplicable murders of Madame L'Espanaye and her daughter. A number of people overheard the murders and gave evidence concerning the likely national identity of the killer, despite their unfamiliarity with the 'language' which they had heard. Dupin, Poe's amateur detective, solves the case by revealing that the killer was an escaped orang-outang whose grunts had been misinterpreted as a variety of foreign languages. The tale concludes with Dupin and the narrator meeting the owner of the orang-outang, and his eye witness account confirms Dupin's version of events. [11] Bonaparte reads this strange tale of an orang-outang's killing of two women in a Paris apartment as indicative of Poe's feelings about his parents, as a consequence of his likely witnessing of the primal scene (in which the child first sees, or overhears, their parents in a sexual act). For Bonaparte the primal scene would alarm the child because it would appear as though the father was violently assaulting the mother. Also this moment symbolically stages the castration of the mother by the father so that the child perceives that the mother has been castrated (because she lacks male genitals) and that this has been effected by the father's penetration. This is represented in the tale, according to Bonaparte, by how the ape penetrates Madame L'Espanaye's body 'with the phallic razor' (p. 448), and her subsequent near decapitation with the razor symbolically represents her castration. That the primal scene is an especially disturbing experience for the child is, for Bonaparte, captured by the ferocity of the orang-outang's murderous assault. This assault takes on the sexual colouring of the primal scene and has a specific association with Poe's mother (and Poe's sister) concerning some speculation as to whether Poe's sister was conceived as the result of an extra-marital affair. This means, according to Bonaparte, that the primal scene's violence is linked to illegality (or illegitimacy) because it represents the sexual immorality of Poe's mother. In this instance the ape's placing of the daughter's body up the chimney symbolises the violent impregnation of Poe's mother, the chimney here representing the womb which now contains a child. This leads Bonaparte to speculate, somewhat grandly, whether Dupin, 'venerable ancestor of Sherlock Holmes and the whole race of detectives', was 'merely created to solve, for Poe's unconscious, the riddle of who was his sister's father' (p. 455).

This reading of Poe has been highly influential, not only in terms of Poe but also on the Gothic in general. Poe's work would later be taken up by Jacques Lacan, a quite different psychoanalyst from Bonaparte (and so also Freud), which indicates the central place that Poe has in psychoanalytical discussions of literature (at least as it is practised by psychoanalysts).[12] However, literary critics of the Gothic, such as Teresa A. Goddu, have emphasised the importance of historicising Poe so that we appreciate that 'the terror of Poe's tales are not of the soul but of society', which means resituating Poe within a tradition of American literature (which includes the twentieth-century mode of Southern Gothic) from which he had been excluded 'as an aberrant figure'.[13] Poe's contribution to the development of an American Gothic tradition cannot be underestimated, and the central critical issue (indeed controversy) with which he is associated relates to race.

Toni Morrison, whose novel *Beloved* (1987) will be discussed in Chapter 4, claimed in her *Playing in the Dark: Whiteness and the Literary Imagination* (1992) that 'no early American writer is more important to the concept of American Africanism than Poe'.[14] There has been considerable discussion about Poe's attitudes to race in an attempt to gauge whether he was overtly or covertly racist, or whether his often ironic tone subtly but tellingly subverts such images. The critical positions taken on 'Rue Morgue' illustrate how the tale can be read in light of certain Southern attitudes towards race and helps to situate Poe within an American Gothic tradition.

Critics have noted how images of race in the early American Gothic tradition are often covertly developed. Carwin in *Wieland*, for example, has seemed to some critics to possess an outsider status which suggests a symbolically black experience of white middle-class mores (represented by the Wieland family and their friends).[15] Poe's representation of the orang-outang has also received some critical focus that suggests that the ape represents Southern fears concerning the possibility of black insurrection.

What is noticeable in the tale is how the prefatory material relating to the psychology of deduction is undermined by how Dupin solves the case. Dupin realises that the grip on the neck of Mademoiselle L'Espanaye is too broad to be human, and, by referring to a passage from Georges Cuvier's *The Animal Kingdom*

(1834), he makes the association with an orang-outang. The tale suggests that in Cuvier's book the orang-outang is characterised by its 'gigantic stature [. . .] prodigious strength and activity [. . .] wild ferocity, and [. . .] imitative propensities'.[16] John Carlos Rowe has noted that in fact Cuvier describes these apes as fundamentally passive and close to human because they can successfully imitate human behaviour.[17] Mark Jancovich has also noted that Thomas Jefferson in *Notes on the State of Virginia* (a book on a slave-owning state, first published in 1781, that Poe and many of his Southern readers would have been familiar with) claimed that in the 'Great Chain of Being' (a pre-Darwinian hierarchy of species) the orang-outang was the creature below the black man.[18] Thus Cuvier's idea of the imitative 'humanity' of the ape reflects, through Jefferson, a model of black experience which implies that such subjects are less than human.

The idea that the orang-outang could be seen as emblematically black is also reinforced in the implication that he is like some kind of runaway slave. The ape is the possession of a sailor who had caught him in Borneo, a country that was popularly regarded at the time as the place where the missing link between the animal and the human might be found. The reference to Borneo also implies that the orang-outang has been transplanted, like a slave, from his place of origin for the purpose of raising money, as the sailor's 'ultimate design was to sell it' (p. 165).

Jancovich amongst others has read the tale as illustrating Southern white fears concerning slave insurrection.[19] In 1831 there had been just such an insurrection in Virginia, led by Nat Turner, that resulted in the death of sixty whites. The insurrection was violently put down but led to widespread fears concerning possible future uprisings. Jancovich notes that in the tale the ape 'uses the weapons of the Parisian mob – a reference to the guillotine. Furthermore, he wraps himself in the tricolour, the revolutionary flag': 'at a time of slave riots in the South such details would have been highly charged' (p. 38). The tale contrasts the ferocity of the killings with the coolness of Dupin's rationality, and this emphasises that the orang-outang represents irrational, mindless violence and therefore a kind of insurrectionary slave mentality. Lindon Barrett, for example, argues that:

Dupin's duel [. . .] with principles of unreason [is] articulated through subtle markers of race. As much as the offending orang-utan represents a principle of unreason, it also connotes in nineteenth-century cultural parlance signifiers of race: linguistic, anatomical, physiognomic, geographic.[20]

However, it is important not to simply dismiss Poe as a racist writer. Some critics, such as Terence Whalen, have examined Poe's non-fiction which appeared in the *Southern Literary Messenger* and have plausibly demonstrated that Poe did not write one of the more notably racist book reviews (the Paulding-Drayton review) which has been ascribed to him. Whalen suggests that Poe was no more racist than many of his contemporaries in the South, and that he sought to keep extreme racist views out of the journal. However, Whalen's idea that Poe possessed an 'average racism' or perhaps 'circumstantial racism' still grates to the modern mind, even whilst one could accept that what makes Poe interesting is how his writings illustrate how Southern attitudes were developed in the period.[21]

However, this view is also problematic. Some critics have noted that Poe's writings actually seem to destabilise the whole notion of a black–white binary divide. Leland S. Person, for example, has explored how covert images of black revenge on white narrators are imaged in a number of tales. Typically, given the Gothic's ambivalence, such tales 'reveal complicated patterns of racism and antiracist sympathy, a recognition on Poe's part that racial signifiers are inherently unstable, while racism and racist efforts to ascribe fixed racial identities lead inevitably to revenge'.[22] In this sense Poe's writings interrogate racism, rather than are actually racist. J. Gerald Kennedy, in an analysis of the closing pages of Poe's *The Narrative of Arthur Gordon Pym* (in which the notion of whiteness is rendered oddly mysterious, in a novel which has up until that point emphasised the 'savagery' of non-white races), claims that 'in puzzling yet unmistakable ways, Poe works against the grain of his own racial prejudices, producing a novel that enforces and subverts conventional white attitudes about race'.[23] To appreciate how this might be reflected in 'Rue Morgue' we need to shift the focus from the orang-outang to Dupin and explore what kind of 'whiteness' he represents.

Dupin's associations with logic appear to suggest that he is a superior rationalist because he is a superior psychologist, and this superiority is related to his social status. The narrator informs us that Dupin was from 'an illustrious family' but has now 'been reduced to such poverty that the energy of his character succumbed beneath it' (p. 143). Like Roderick Usher in 'The Fall of the House of Usher' (1839) he appears to be the last of his line. The fact that Dupin is no longer part of society, 'We existed within ourselves alone' (p. 144), suggests his aristocratic distance from the rest of society. This distance in turn implies that because Dupin is outside (or above) society he can effect the necessary detachment to 'see' through its problems. In effect the tale tries to implement, as does 'The Purloined Letter' (1845), the restoration of an aristocratic social and intellectual elite. However, this idea of the special character of Dupin is challenged within the tale in a variety of forms: socially, intellectually, and morally – so that the very factors which appear to confirm his superiority are subtly turned against him, and this enacts the kind of compromising of whiteness that critics have noted.

On a social level it should be noted that Dupin's apparent superiority actually appears to generate social isolation, one in which his presence has been erased through social amnesia. As the narrator notes, 'it had been many years since Dupin had ceased to know or be known in Paris' (p. 144), which implies not so much social superiority as social irrelevance. One could claim that this represents Southern white fears concerning their possible racial overthrow, but the dynamics of the tale suggest that it is Dupin's social spectrality that enables him to stand outside of society's problems and so solve them. However, this seems to depersonalise Dupin and this relates to his supposed intellectual superiority, which is dramatised at the beginning of the tale in the lengthy preamble on how to effect certain types of psychological deduction (the preamble might be 'written' by the narrator, but it is clearly intended as a summary of Dupin's views). In the preamble there is a discussion about how to win at games such as draughts and cards. The process of outwitting your opponent occurs when:

> the analyst throws himself into the spirit of his opponent, identifies himself therewith, and not unfrequently sees thus,

at a glance, the sole methods (sometimes indeed absurdly simple ones) by which he may seduce into error or hurry into miscalculation. (p. 142)

Dupin's apparently eccentric but powerful sense of individuality is compromised by this ability to become other people by entering into their thoughts. The narrator notes that when Dupin effects this kind of analysis, 'His manner at these moments was frigid and abstract; his eyes were vacant in expression' (p. 144). Dupin, at the very moment when he exercises his superiority, seems to disappear. If we examine him within discussions about race it is possible to see just how precarious his identity is, and this precariousness is not due to an external threat but appears to be self-generated (rather as the implied incest in 'Usher' causes the end of the family line). As we saw, Barrett suggests that Dupin's associations with reason imply his white, intellectual superiority over the symbolically black and unreasoning ape. However, it could be argued that what is dehumanising is Dupin's attachment to reason. Dupin seems to be socially, intellectually, and psychologically lost, and in addition his adherence to reason suggests that he is morally lost. He informs the narrator that they should investigate the case because Le Bon, a banker's clerk (who had once helped Dupin on another matter), had been falsely arrested on suspicion of the murders and because 'An inquiry will afford us amusement', prompting the observation from the narrator that 'I thought this an odd term so applied' (p. 153). Indeed for Dupin the solving of the 'murders' appears to bear equivalence to winning at draughts, chess, or cards. The coolness of his intellect is not just in contrast with the ape's ferocity, it also contrasts with the violent deaths suffered by Madame L'Espanaye and her daughter. Dupin's lack of moral empathy with the victims arguably aligns him with the non-human ape.

How to discuss race in Poe is a complex issue, not least because Poe extends the mimicry of the ape to the tale itself, which apes a detective tale without really being one (or at least not the one that we expect to get). Dupin solves the case by knowing about the size of the grip of an orang-outang, not because he can get inside its mind. In reality there are no 'murders' at all, so that even the title of the tale is a hoax. This complicates the issue of race in Poe because it looks like a strategy to lampoon images of social, racial, and intellectual superiority by subtly emphasising their moral vacuity, one which in the end makes Dupin no better, morally speaking, than an ape. As always in the Gothic, ambivalence is the central issue. However, it is important to note that Poe begins a debate about race which plays a significant role in future writings within the American Gothic tradition, which will be discussed in the following two chapters.

GOTHIC MUTATIONS: PROSE

Poe's writings address predominately American concerns, and his fascination with irrationality and how to rationalise it away (as in his detective stories), or his focus on emotionally disturbed states (as in most of his other tales), aligns him with American Romanticism. In America, Romanticism was developed in the writings of the transcendentalist movement in the 1830s and 1840s (including Emerson and Thoreau, amongst others) and historically occurred later than European Romanticism. As we have seen, the Gothic represents one form of Romanticism, and whilst European Romanticism's heyday is not usually regarded as extending beyond the 1820s in Britain, it still has a vestigial presence in ostensibly 'realist' modes of writing. By exploring Emily Brontë's use of Romanticism in *Wuthering Heights* (1847) we can see how the Gothic is transformed during the period. In addition an account of sensation fiction (arguably *the* new and most popular form of writing in the 1850s and 1860s) illustrates how the Gothic shaped a later literary form.[24]

Anne K. Mellor has suggested that *Wuthering Heights* can be regarded as a type of Romantic poem because, like much Romantic poetry (especially that of Blake), it explores the tensions between conflicting ideas and feelings (tensions which are, as we have seen, central to Keats's *Lamia*).[25] Further, Sandra M. Gilbert and Susan Gubar have argued that the tensions in the novel are a consequence of a clash between the Romantic narrative (concerning the 'passions' of Heathcliff and the first-generation Catherine) and the domestic narrative associated with Nelly Dean and the 'home-building' of the second-generation Catherine. They claim that at the end of the novel, with Heathcliff and Catherine dead and the Heights presided over by the domesticated figures of Hareton and the second Catherine, 'the nineteenth century can truly begin, complete with tea-parties, ministering angels, governesses, and parsonages'.[26] How the Gothic infiltrates the novel, requires an exploration of three factors: the role of Nelly Dean, Romanticism, and ghosts.

A considerable amount of criticism on the novel has addressed the role of Nelly. At one level she appears to be the voice of (domestic) order and rationality whose view of the world is coloured by her enthusiasm for an abstract notion of the well-integrated family unit – abstract, because her experiences at the Heights actually suggest that family rivalries and animosities ultimately destroy any meaningful family life. Nelly therefore upholds a set of bourgeois family virtues which is contradicted by her experience of how families really behave. She attempts to establish a 'norm' that demonises certain types of behaviour by using the Gothic as a language to exclude those who threaten to disrupt her notion of domestic harmony. Heathcliff, for example, has what Gilbert and Gubar refer to as 'undeniable monster potential' (p. 293), and Nelly uses language in order to emphasise his 'otherness'. She refers to his eyes as 'black fiends' and 'devil's spies' (p. 49), thinks of him as 'an evil beast' (p. 93), and twice refers to him as 'a goblin' (pp. 95 and 281), and although she will modify the premise of her question, she does ask 'Is he a ghoul or a vampire?' (p. 281). This indicates that Nelly regards Heathcliff as a dangerous outsider, but it also reveals how, as in *Frankenstein*, this type of language is employed to exclude, rather than to understand. As in *Frankenstein*, it is necessary to get beneath the surface tensions in order to identify how the story's narration helps to establish 'norms', and as Gilbert and Gubar note, 'in its use of technique, *Wuthering Heights* might be a deliberate copy of *Frankenstein*' (p. 249). Nelly's use of language thus underlines her refusal to accommodate Heathcliff to the family (because he is not a biological member of it) and explains her inability to see the relationship between Heathcliff and the first-generation Catherine as anything other than wilful and undisciplined. Her type of rationality, in other words, is unable to account for the rebellious qualities of the Romantic passions that are represented by Heathcliff and

Catherine, so that she censures without understanding (rather like Victor Frankenstein). However, it is important to move beyond this and address what it is that Heathcliff and Catherine represent that could so unsettle bourgeois norms. Terry Eagleton has noted that Heathcliff functions as both a bourgeois and an anti-bourgeois figure, and in that respect he articulates a specifically Gothic ambivalence. The crucial moment is when Heathcliff disappears for two years and returns as a gentleman. However, Heathcliff's actions (especially after Catherine's death, when he becomes particularly vindictive) serve to make visible just how viciously a money-based society goes about its 'business'.[27] As in *Frankenstein*, the norm generates its monsters who reflect back upon, and so demonise, the norm. Heathcliff addresses this in his account of why Catherine is dying; crucially he claims that it is because of social pressures rather than organic disease. He says to Nelly about her illness and Linton's ministrations:

> You talk of her mind being unsettled. How the devil could it be otherwise in her frightful isolation? And that insipid, paltry creature attending her from *duty* and *humanity*! From *pity* and *charity*! He might as well plant an oak in a flowerpot, and expect it to thrive, as imagine he can restore her to vigour in the soil of his shallow cares! (p. 133)

This makes it clear that Heathcliff and Catherine not only represent the Romantic elements in the novel, but that Heathcliff has turned this into a manifesto. Mellor has noted how their claim for social rebellion coincides (in the time-scheme used in the novel) with the American and later French Revolutions (the action broadly spanning 1776–1802, the period covered by the American Revolution to the rise of Napoleon). Mellor also argues that, 'Heathcliff begins with a fierce sexual passion and love of freedom, but finally distorts that energy into a reign of terror' (p. 199). The central paradox in the novel is therefore whether it condones a conservative reading of a rebellious Romanticism or whether it exonerates such rebellion by suggesting that it provides an antidote to a stultifying bourgeois domesticity. In other words, the novel contains two contrasting, and competing, monsters: Nelly and

Heathcliff. However, whilst Heathcliff might become monstrous this is because, as Eagleton has noted, he comes to exemplify the brutality of an economic system which underpins the bourgeois world that Nelly so unquestioningly supports.

So far the Gothic operates at two levels, as an aspect of Nelly's moralising and as an element of Romanticism (with all the threatened social overthrow that it implies). The novel therefore incorporates the type of tensions between order and threatened disorder that are central to the Gothic tradition. Indeed the novel's suggestion that Nelly's moralising is peculiarly dehumanising (whereas Heathcliff and Catherine represent the importance of feeling) creates a tension between doctrinaire moral beliefs and emotions that was central to *Lamia*. However, *Wuthering Heights* moves beyond this by suggesting the presence of the supernatural when it implies the presence of ghosts. We first see this when Lockwood's sleep is disturbed by what appears to be the ghost of Catherine in the guise of a child requesting admission to his room. Lockwood attempts to release himself from the child's grasp: 'I pulled its wrist on to the broken pane, and rubbed it to and fro till the blood ran down and soaked the bedclothes: still it wailed "Let me in!" ' (p. 67). Lockwood is not sure if this is part of his nightmare, but he is struck by the apparent reality of the child and her seeming indestructibility, and this indicates that the ghosts articulate another order of reality which, in this instance, cannot be either literally or ideologically accommodated within a domestic space. Lockwood's appalled response implies that what is truly disturbing is that this seemingly unreal encounter is due to his misunderstanding of what 'life' at the Heights is really about. Lockwood inhabits ideologically, if not socially, the same world as Nelly, and it is an incomplete one because of its conceptual limitations. Ghosts are not just spectral beings: they also function as political entities, and the Gothic therefore maintains its seemingly radical possibilities – this is made clear at the end of the novel in the suggestion that the ghosts of Heathcliff and Catherine haunt the moor, in what is a telling critique, of a culture's inability to accept their rebellious Romanticism. They do not die, but remain as a constant reminder of the limitations of a bourgeois culture, and their spectral presence implies that the radicalism is still there, waiting, because it has not *quite* been laid to rest.

Wuthering Heights is not a Gothic novel in any obviously conventional sense: it is not, for example, a Gothic novel in the way that *The Monk* or *Dracula* is. However, it does reveal how the Gothic infiltrated other forms of writing. In terms of specific types of fiction during the mid-nineteenth century, the Gothic's clearest continuing presence can be seen in sensation fiction, which dominated the popular market at the time.

Prominent writers of sensation fiction include Mary E. Braddon, Wilkie Collins, and Charles Reade (amongst many others). The form typically relied upon identifiable Gothic themes and characterisations, including the presence of ancestral secrets, malevolent plotters, and insanity. Winifred Hughes has noted that this new mode of writing possessed a 'general affinity with the eighteenth-century Gothicism of Ann Radcliffe and "Monk" Lewis, the historical romance of Sir Walter Scott, [and] the oriental tales of Byron'.[28] Hughes also notes the form's indebtedness to popular melodrama, in which certain 'types' of characters were often used to allegorise 'Good and Evil' (p. 7), although sensation fiction often subtly developed this in its focus on complex constructions of identity (in which characters are often not as they appear to be).

If sensation fiction is both indebted to, but also complicates, popular stage melodrama, it also, as Alison Milbank has argued, complicates an earlier tradition of Gothic writing. Milbank's discussion of Wilkie Collins locates him within both Male and Female Gothic traditions. For Milbank, Collins's work is characterised by an 'interest in the destabilisation of female identity, and in the secularisation of the domestic house, combined with a social and quasi-religious determinism', which ostensibly links him to Matthew Lewis.[29] However, she also notes that Collins's writings lack 'the heavy sense of a particularly masculine guilt' (p. 53), which excludes him from the Male Gothic. Milbank acknowledges that many critics, including Walter Phillips and David Punter, have commented on Collins's associations with Radcliffe's Female Gothic, and Milbank has explored how Collins reworks specific elements of Radcliffe's Gothic, which raises gender-related questions about a male writer's recycling of elements of the Female Gothic tradition.[30] To make this clear it is necessary to look at the structure and themes of *The Woman in White* (1860).

The Woman in White was one of the major publishing sensations of its time (it became a popular play and a dance was named after it, as were a certain type of bonnet and a perfume).[31] The main themes of the novel, typical of sensation fiction, revolve around identity, the law, gender, class, money, insanity, and family secrets. One of the curious aspects of the novel is that its 'Preamble' tells us how to 'read' the novel (this has some superficial associations with Walpole's second preface to *Otranto*: superficial because in Collins's case it is not developed into a literary manifesto).

The preamble asks us to imagine that we are hearing evidence from a range of witnesses (the novel is composed of a series of eye witness accounts from different narrators), and 'As the Judge might once have heard it, so the Reader shall hear it now'.[32] The reader is therefore asked to sift through the evidence to get at the truth, which suggests a Gothic world of hidden secrets (one of Collins's earlier novels was titled *The Dead Secret*, 1857) which will be rationally explained. This might suggest the triumph of order, but Collins subjects the processes of deduction to considerable scepticism and scrutiny, and in particular this conditions his approach to issues concerning identity.

The novel centres on Walter Hartright's attachment to Laura Fairlie and the attempts that are made to disinherit her by her villainous husband, Sir Percival Glyde (who is ably supported by the charismatic Count Fosco). Marian Halcombe, a relative of Laura's, helps Walter and Laura, and after a complex series of plot resolutions Walter and Laura are free to marry at the end when the villains have all been punished (indeed are dead). However, Walter is not obviously the hero-detective of the novel at the beginning, and this is implied in his economic and gender disempowerment (he is a not very wealthy drawing-master to wealthy young ladies). The drama begins late one night when, whilst walking to London, he encounters the mysterious Anne Catherick. He recalls:

There, in the middle of the broad, bright high-road – there, as if it had that moment sprung out of the earth or dropped from the heaven – stood the figure of a solitary Woman, dressed from head to foot in white garments. (p. 47)

This 'extraordinary apparition' (p. 47) asks him for help, and although he states that 'the grossest of mankind could not have misconstrued her motive in speaking' (p. 48), this nevertheless suggests that he does indeed entertain the idea that she could be a prostitute. This encounter with the spectral Catherick initiates the mystery of the novel. Its effect on Walter is revealing because he is struck by the apparent unreality of the encounter, leading him to question 'Was I Walter Hartright?' (p. 50), a question provoked in a consideration of *her* identity. The issue of identity is further complicated by two other factors: the structure of the novel and gender.

Alison Milbank has noted that the novel divides the typical Radcliffean heroine between Laura (heiress, beauty), Marian (intelligence), and Anne Catherick (the 'bearer . . . of secrets'); in addition the Radcliffean villain is divided between Sir Percival (aristocratic plotter) and Fosco (dangerously powerful).[33] This structural displacement of identifiable Gothic identities is further complicated by the representation of gender. This is illustrated in the famous passage in which Hartright recounts his first meeting with Marian:

> She had a large, firm, masculine mouth and jaw; prominent, piercing, resolute eyes; and thick, coal-black hair, growing unusually low down on her forehead. Her expression – bright, frank, and intelligent – appeared, while she was silent, to be altogether wanting in those feminine attractions of gentleness and pliability, without which the beauty of the handsomest woman alive is beauty incomplete. (pp. 58–9)

This raises two issues: first, Hartright will need to free himself of his prejudices if he is going to be able to see 'objectively' (so he can function as a detective), and second, he needs to become more like Marian, that is, more 'masculine'. This suggests a conventional link between masculinity and rationality, but the novel ironises this when Walter (having been dismissed by Marian because of his socially inappropriate attachment to Laura) is sent on a perilous journey to South America where his adventures turn him from effete drawing-master into a man of action. Collins produces a strange double narrative in which the novel superficially appears to corroborate the prevailing gender scripts, whilst at a more sophisticated level it parodies gender stereotypes. This is implicit in Walter's consideration of his portrait of Laura, in which he notes that it captures her beauty, but little else, and that alongside:

> her sweet expression, and her winning simplicity of manner, was another impression, which, in a shadowy way, suggested to me the idea of something wanting. At one time it seemed like something wanting in *her*: at another, like something wanting in myself, which hindered me from understanding her as I ought. (p. 76)

The painful truth that Walter cannot quite acknowledge is the possibility that Laura really is like his two-dimensional representation of her, because her conformity to conventional gender scripts compares unfavourably with the resourceful and energetic Marian.[34] With sensation fiction the Gothic becomes reworked in conjunction with aspects of stage melodrama. This reworking is not a passive process (an aspect of the Gothic we have noted before): rather, it indicates how the Gothic explores particular issues. *The Woman in White*, like *Wuthering Heights*, raises questions about class, money, and gender, issues which have their roots in an earlier Gothic tradition, but which took on an increasing urgency in the maturely developing industrial society of mid-nineteenth-century Britain. The Gothic is no longer just about aristocratic milieux: it has now moved on to critique the type of bourgeois codes of conduct suggested in the figure of Heathcliff and the idea of gender divisions which underpinned the establishment of new social and economic identities. Both *Wuthering Heights* and *The Woman in White* indicate that new ways of understanding identity will become a prerequisite for understanding social change – an issue made clear in *Jane Eyre*.

READING *JANE EYRE*

This chapter has in part explored how in the nineteenth century the Gothic came to inhabit ostensibly non-Gothic modes of writing, including the seemingly 'realist' novel (such as *Wuthering Heights*) and fairy-tale influenced poetry (such as *Goblin Market*). We have also observed how nationally inflected debates about race appear in the Gothic (Poe) and examined how issues relating to gender and sexuality are interrogated in a range of Gothic texts (Keats, Coleridge, and Collins). What unites these otherwise disparate writings is a fascination with identity, with how it is shaped by desire, race, class, and gender: issues which play a central role in Charlotte Brontë's *Jane Eyre* (1847).

How to read *Jane Eyre* for its Gothic elements involves identifying the formal scenes (such as descriptions of the vampiric Bertha Mason, or Jane's incarceration in the red-room, for example) which are clearly indebted to the Gothic. However, the novel's use of the Gothic is more sophisticated than that, because it structures how Jane's struggle for social and economic visibility is staged within a Gothic drama which challenges certain readerly expectations of the romantic novel. That the novel's ostensible love story is challenged by a scepticism about what 'love' means (and obligates one to) indicates the presence of a radicalism which some conservatively minded contemporary reviewers found deeply troubling. Elizabeth Rigby in 1848 wrote in *The Quarterly Review* that Brontë's narrator 'is throughout the personification of an unregenerate and undisciplined spirit', and went on to claim that 'The tone of mind and thought which fostered Chartism and rebellion is the same which has also written *Jane Eyre*'.[35] According to the novelist Margaret Oliphant, writing in 1855, *Jane Eyre* effected 'the most alarming revolution of modern times' in changing the direction of the novel of romantic love.[36] This revolutionary aspect of the novel is closely related to how Brontë uses the Gothic. It also, however, relates to how the novel compromises what was understood as literary realism at the time. In *Wuthering Heights*, its ostensible construction of a realistic world is challenged by a Gothic narrative which exposes what the claims for realism tend to conceal – in this instance an unaccommodated language of rebellion.

Jane Eyre is written in the realist mode to the degree that it unfolds as a kind of autobiography in which retrospective sense is made of earlier experiences. However, in one important scene, the opening paragraph to Chapter 11, the text's claims to realism are undermined by a self-conscious literary moment, when the narrator begins: 'A new chapter in a novel is something like a new scene in a play; and when I draw up the curtain this time, reader, you must fancy you see a room in the George Inn at Millcote'.[37] This literary self-consciousness suggests that although until this point the reader may have been beguiled by the apparent realism of Jane's tale, they now need to engage with the fundamentally fictive, and therefore inherently symbolic, nature of the text. This symbolic level, of course, pre-dates this moment, but it is noteworthy that the text registers its fictionality and so places an additional demand on the reader – that they should not read the novel 'literally' or 'realistically'. The symbolic moments that we are directed to are, as we shall see, in the main generated by the Gothic subtexts. In order to appreciate this a few crucial scenes from the novel will be explored: Jane's early reading, Jane's dream of Bertha on the eve of her marriage to Rochester, and Rochester's account of Bertha.

The novel opens with Jane, as a child, reading Bewick's *History of British Birds* (published in two parts, in 1797 and 1804). In response to the socially hostile environment that she experiences within the Reed family, she occupies a window seat in a breakfast room where she can draw the curtain and obtain some privacy. This secret reading implies Jane's attempt to escape from the oppressive atmosphere of the house, and to some degree the book mentally provides this with its accounts of 'Lapland, Siberia, Spitzbergen, Nova Zembla, Iceland, Greenland' (p. 40). However, such places reinforce one of the themes of the novel concerning how ice and fire represent two aspects of Jane's self, and the book therefore reflects Jane's sense of emotional isolation.[38] Jane also notes that the book is full of images of desolation, images which reflect her unhappiness. In addition, Bewick's oddly titled book is full of Gothic illustrations, including representations of dancing demons and animated skeletons. Jane initially observes these with some revulsion 'The fiend pinning down the thief's back behind him, I passed over quickly: it was an object of terror. So was the black, horned thing seated aloof on a rock, surveying a distant crowd surrounding a gallows' (p. 40). However, she also acknowledges that 'Each picture told a story; mysterious often to my undeveloped understanding and imperfect feelings, yet ever profoundly interesting' (pp. 40–1). Jane's early, indeed formative, encounter with literature emphasises that she inhabits a Gothic world and indicates that her imagination is constructed *by* the Gothic. She will later interpret experiences in a Gothic way (such as the link she makes between Bertha and vampirism, for example), so that the novel becomes a Gothic reader's view of the world. Jane's encounter with the seemingly blandly titled *History of British Birds* is not an innocent one: it contains tales of horror which fascinate her, but which also reflect on her position within the Reed household. This connection is given a powerful emphasis when John Reed takes the book from her and throws it at her so that 'I fell, striking my head against the door and cutting it' (pp. 42–3). The book influences her mind but is responsible for physically damaging her head. The later love plot is shaped by this Gothic imagination which tinges the love story with the kinds of danger and anxiety that Bewick's book provokes, but it also, perhaps paradoxically, helps to produce an insight into how 'love' is not an innocent, or danger-free, emotion.

The scene with the book is also about cultural ownership. As John Reed tells Jane before launching the book at her, 'I'll teach you to rummage my book-shelves: for they *are* mine' (italics in original, p. 42). Ownership of culture is thus dependent upon class and gender factors – an issue that later conditions Jane's experiences as a governess. Jane's (and presumably the reader's) sense of injustice is further developed when Jane is admonished for her physical attack on John Reed and sent to the red-room, a much critically discussed scene which serves to emphasise her isolation. Gilbert and Gubar note of the incident that 'Jane's pilgrimage consists of a series of experiences which are, in one way or another, variations on the central, red-room motif of enclosure and escape' (p. 341). However, Jane is not quite alone in the novel, and in order to appreciate this we have to consider the relationship between her and Bertha Mason.

The parallels between Jane and Bertha have received considerable critical attention. Bertha appears to represent a world of rebellion and sexual freedom which has been circumscribed by her incarceration within Rochester's house. This theme of incarceration therefore refers back to Jane's incarceration in the red-room. Also, Bertha is described as racially 'other' (although technically a

Creole), and this notion of otherness is linked to Jane's 'otherness'. Jane's 'outsider' status, which is later dramatised in her socially awkward role of a governess (as an 'upper' servant who is not part of the family), is only alleviated when she accidentally (or perhaps providentially) discovers members of her family who admit her into their home when she is close to starvation after leaving Rochester. The book is written from the point of view of the mature Jane, who describes her childhood self in terms that echo the later perceptions of the 'mad' Bertha. She notes that whilst with the Reeds: 'I was a discord in Gateshead Hall; I was like nobody there' and that she was looked upon as 'a heterogeneous thing, opposed to them in temperament, in capacity, in propensities; a useless thing, cherishing the germs of indignation at their treatment, of contempt of their judgement' (p. 47). Also, Jane's first encounter with Bertha takes place after a telling dream she has concerning Rochester on the eve of their (first) marriage.

In recounting the dream to Rochester, Jane states that she felt the presence of 'a strange, regretful consciousness of some barrier dividing us' (p. 309). For Jane this appears to be connected to a small child for whose welfare she is responsible. She notes of this child: 'I might not lay it down anywhere, however tired were my arms – however much its weight impeded my progress, I must retain it' (p. 312). For Gilbert and Gubar this represents Jane's inability to leave behind her orphaned childhood, and until she can do this she will be unable to properly develop as an adult.[39] However, the dream also suggests Jane's horror at the burdens of motherhood and functions as a pre-emptive critique of the role she will be expected to play as Rochester's wife. The novel has no obvious positive representations of motherhood, and Jane's craving to belong to some kind of family should be seen as one of the impulses that characterise the Female Gothic (a search for origins which in Jane's case is in part met when she encounters the Rivers family, to whom she is related). However, because images of motherhood are so resolutely excluded from the narrative it is understandable that Jane should view the role with some misgivings. This is especially so given that Jane has to care for Adèle, Rochester's child, a product of a brief liaison with Céline Varens, a 'French opera-dancer' (p. 172). Jane's dream proceeds to implicate Rochester as a negligent father when Jane, left with the child, 'heard the gallop of a horse at a distance on the road; I was sure it was you; and you were departing for many years, and for a distant country' (p. 310). These images of burden and abandonment set the scene for the appearance of Bertha (who is both a burden to Rochester and, despite his claims to the contrary, is, in his attempt to bigamously marry Jane, being abandoned by him).

Jane awakens from the dream and tells Rochester of the figure that confronted her, a figure who is racially othered in Jane's references to 'thick and dark hair', her 'savage face', the 'fearful blackened inflation of the lineaments!', 'the lips' which 'were swelled and dark' and 'the black eyebrows . . . raised over the bloodshot eyes' (p. 311). This vision stands in front of Jane's mirror wearing Jane's wedding veil, but Jane's search for an explanation leads her to claim that she was 'the foul German spectre – the vampire' (p. 311). Again, it is Jane's grounding in Gothic literature which both introduces a Gothic element into the narrative *and* uses the Gothic to identify the hidden world that Rochester has concealed (relating to female sexuality). Bertha functions as the Gothic element within the narrative to the degree that she is associated with racial otherness, insanity, and sexual promiscuity. However, such associations with 'otherness' are consistently undermined because of the covert link between Bertha and Jane – which implies that the ostensible 'norm' is tinged with a Gothic presence, a typical characteristic of the form. Thus Bertha does not come to frighten Jane, but to warn her about what marriage to Rochester entails, and Jane notes that the figure takes off the veil and 'rent it in two parts, and flinging both on the floor, trampled on them' (p. 311).

Jane's dream and her subsequent encounter with Bertha illustrate the danger that Jane, at this point, faces from Rochester: that she too could become a burden and be abandoned. Bertha may seem like a vampire (and she does bite and suck blood from her brother, Mason), but she represents what a culture is compelled to demonise because it cannot accommodate, an issue which is made clear in Rochester's explanation about Bertha after his failed attempt to bigamously marry Jane.

As we saw with Poe, race can be exploited in the construction of 'otherness'. In *Jane Eyre* race is linked to a debate concerning irrationality and rationality. Rochester has been manipulated into marrying Bertha for financial reasons, but realises he has been duped when he discovers the presence of insanity in the family. For Rochester she is both mentally enfeebled and sexually voracious: as he puts it 'What a pigmy intellect she had, and what giant propensities! How fearful were the curses those propensities entailed on me!' (p. 334). However, this idea of the too passionate Bertha becomes transferred from her to the West Indies itself, so that Rochester recalls how, listening to the 'yells' of the now incarcerated Bertha:

> The air was like sulphur-streams – I could find no refreshment anywhere. Mosquitoes came buzzing in and hummed sullenly round the room; the sea, which I could hear from thence, rumbled like an earthquake – black clouds were casting up over it; the moon was setting in the waves, broad and red, like a hot cannon-ball – she threw her last bloody glance over a world quivering with the ferment of tempest. (p. 335)

The West Indies represents hell in its association with sulphur, heat, and blood. It is a version of hell which seems an entirely appropriate locale for Bertha with her 'demon-hate' in which 'no professed harlot ever had a fouler vocabulary than she' (p. 335). In case we miss the point, Rochester actually states that 'This life [. . .] is hell: this is the air – those are the sounds of the bottomless pit' (p. 335). This emphatic demonisation of the West Indies leads Rochester to contemplate suicide; however, at that moment, 'A wind fresh from Europe blew over the ocean and rushed through the open casement: the storm broke, streamed, thundered, blazed, and the air grew pure' (p. 335). This scene contrasts the 'hellish' West Indies with the calm and coolness of Europe. Indeed, Rochester perceives in this freshening wind the presence of 'Hope' which tells him in god like fashion to 'live again in Europe: there it is not known what a sullied name you bear, nor what a filthy burden is bound to you'. This voice of reason also suggests that he should lock up Bertha ('the maniac') in his English residence, Thornfield Hall, so enabling him to 'travel [. . .] to what clime you will, and form what new tie you like'. Unsurprisingly Rochester notes, 'I acted precisely on this suggestion' (p. 336).

The scene illustrates how the Gothic permeates the novel by turning commonplace phenomena (the weather) into symbolic realities (hell versus reason) which in this instance speak (literally) to the characters. However, it is also important to note that such issues are inevitably touched by ambivalence because Bertha represents the type of person that the too passionate Jane could have become. The novel thus employs images of race in order to develop tensions between allegedly irrational and rational states (moral, sexual, and cultural), but Bertha also functions to register the dangers of female confinement within marriage. That Jane learns from this is clear when, on the day before the marriage, she contemplates with some anxiety the new clothes which Rochester has bought for her to wear on their honeymoon. She notes that they constitute 'wraith-like apparel' which gave off a 'most ghostly shimmer'. Jane senses that her identity is compromised in this, that she will become insubstantial or ghost-like. She notes of this 'Mrs Rochester' that 'She did not exist; she would not be born till tomorrow' (p. 303), and as many critics have noted, Jane needs to find and so know herself before anything other than an unequal marriage can take place.

To read *Jane Eyre* for its Gothic elements requires an exploration of how the novel's complex symbolism is rooted within a Gothic tradition (here made emblematically present by the seemingly innocuous Bewick's *History of British Birds*). In the opening lines of chapter 11 we are covertly invited to read the novel for such symbolic presences as the claims to literary realism become strategically undermined. Reading *Jane Eyre* in this way illustrates how the Gothic came to permeate apparently non-Gothic forms of writing. It also reveals that new psychological tensions appeared in literature during the period, tensions which were given clear prominence in the Gothic of the second half of the nineteenth century, which will be explored in the next chapter.

SUMMARY OF KEY POINTS

• The Gothic becomes incorporated within the 'realist' novel in nineteenth-century Britain.
• Sensation fiction reworks elements of the Gothic.

- The Gothic often represents 'tabooed' sexuality.
- Racial issues are often exploited to create images of 'otherness'.

QUESTIONS AND POINTS FOR DISCUSSION

- What are the differences, if any, between Gothic prose and Gothic poetry?
- How is sexuality represented?
- Compare and contrast how Edgar Allan Poe and Charlotte Brontë use racial imagery.
- To what ends does the Gothic infiltrate and subvert literary realism?

NOTES

1. *Sir Walter Scott on Novelists and Fiction*, ed. Ioan Williams (London: Routledge, 1968), p. 103.
2. Samuel Taylor Coleridge, *Christabel*, in *The Portable Coleridge*, ed. I. A. Richards (Harmondsworth: Penguin, 1980), pp. 106–27. All subsequent references in the text are to this edition.
3. Robert Miles, *Gothic Writing, 1750–1820: A Genealogy* (Manchester: Manchester University Press, [1993] 2002). All subsequent references in the text are to this edition. See pp. 185–6.
4. Bram Stoker, *Dracula* (Oxford: Oxford University Press, [1897] 1996), p. 15.
5. John Keats, *Lamia*, in *Keats: Complete Poetical Works*, ed. H. W. Gorrod (Oxford: Oxford University Press, 1970), pp. 161–78. All subsequent references in the text are to this edition.
6. Christina Rossetti, *Goblin Market*, in *A Choice of Christina Rossetti's Verse* (London: Faber and Faber, 1989), pp. 13–28. All subsequent references in the text are to this edition.
7. Dorothy Mermin, 'Heroic Sisterhood in *Goblin Market*', in *Victorian Women Poets*, ed. Tess Cosslett (London and New

York: Longman, 1996), pp. 145–57, p. 147, p. 155.

8. Ellen Moers, *Literary Women* (London: Women's Press, 1976), p. 101. Moers locates the poem within a tradition that includes Lewis Carroll, Charles Kingsley, Jean Ingelow, Herman Melville, and H. G. Wells (p. 102).

9. Elizabeth K. Helsinger, 'Consumer Power and the Utopia of Desire: Christina Rossetti's "Goblin Market"', in *New Casebooks: Victorian Women Poets*, ed. Joseph Bristow (Basingstoke: Macmillan, 1995), pp. 189–222.

10. Marie Bonaparte, *The Life and Works of Edgar Allan Poe: A Psycho-Analytic Interpretation*, trans. J. Rodker (London: Imago, 1949). All subsequent references in the text are to this edition.

11. For a reading of the tale which examines the relationship between Gothic and detective fiction, see Benjamin F. Fisher's 'Blackwood Articles à la Poe: How to Make a False Start Pay', *Revue des Langues Vivantes* 39 (1973), revised in *Perspectives on Poe*, ed. D. Ramakrishna (New Delhi: APC, 1996), pp. 63–82.

12. See Jacques Lacan, 'Seminar on "The Purloined Letter"', *Yale French Studies*, 48 (1972), 39–72. For an analysis which follows Bonaparte's line of enquiry, see Daniel Hoffman's *PoePoePoePoePoePoePoe* (New York: Vintage, [1972] 1985), pp. 106–18.

13. Teresa A. Goddu, 'Historicizing the American Gothic: Charles Brockden Brown's *Wieland*', in *Approaches to Teaching Gothic Fiction: The British and American Traditions*, ed. Diane Long Hoeveler and Tamar Heller (New York: MLA, 2003), pp. 184–89, p. 189, p. 184.

14. Toni Morrison, *Playing in the Dark: Whiteness and the Literary Imagination* (Cambridge, MA: Harvard University Press, 1992), p. 32.

15. See Emory Elliott, Introduction to Brown's *Wieland and Memoirs of Carwin the Biloquist* (Oxford: Oxford University Press, 1998), pp. xvii–xviii.

16. Edgar Allan Poe, 'The Murders in the Rue Morgue', in *The Complete Tales and Poems of Edgar Allan Poe* (Harmondsworth: Penguin, 1965), pp. 141–68, p. 162. All subsequent references in the text are to this edition.

17. John Carlos Rowe, 'Edgar Allan Poe's Imperial Fantasy and the American Frontier', in *Romancing the Shadow: Poe and Race*, ed. J. Gerald Kennedy and Liliane Weissberg (Oxford: Oxford University Press, 2001), pp. 75–105.

18. Mark Jancovich, *Horror* (London: Batsford, 1992): see pp. 38–9. All subsequent references to this edition are given in the text.

19. See also Rowe, 'Edgar Allan Poe's Imperial Fantasy and the American Frontier', p. 99.

20. Lindon Barrett, 'Presence of mind: detection and radicalization in "The Murders in the Rue Morgue"', in Kennedy and Weissberg, *Romancing the Shadow*, pp. 127–76, p. 173.

21. Terence Whalen, 'Average Racism: Poe, Race, and Contemporary Criticism', in Kennedy and Weissberg, *Romancing the Shadow*, pp. 3–40, p. 4, p. 34.

22. Leland S. Person, 'Poe's Philosophy of Amalgamation: Reading Racism in the Tales', in Kennedy and Weissberg, *Romancing the Shadow*, pp. 205–24, p. 220.

23. J. Gerald Kennedy, ' "Trust no man": Poe, Douglass, and the Culture of Slavery', in Kennedy and Weissberg, *Romancing the Shadow*, pp. 225–57, pp. 243–4.

24. Emily Brontë, *Wuthering Heights* (London: Dent, [1847] 1993). All subsequent references in the text are to this edition.

25. Anne K. Mellor, *Romanticism & Gender* (London and New York: Routledge, 1993), pp. 190–1.

26. Sandra M. Gilbert and Susan Gubar, *The Madwoman in the Attic* (New Haven and London: Yale University Press, [1979] 2000), p. 302.

27. Terry Eagleton, *Myths of Power: A Marxist Study of the Brontës* (Basingstoke: Macmillan, [1975] 1988), pp. 104–5.

28. Winifred Hughes, *The Maniac in the Cellar: Sensation Novels of the 1860s* (Princeton: Princeton University Press, 1980), p. 7.

29. Alison Milbank, *Daughters of the House: Modes of Gothic in Victorian Fiction* (Basingstoke: Macmillan, 1992), p. 52.

30. See Milbank, *Daughters of the House*, p. 64.

31. See Tamar Heller, *Dead Secrets: Wilkie Collins and the Female Gothic* (New Haven: Yale University Press, 1992), p. 111.

32. Wilkie Collins, *The Woman in White* (Harmondsworth: Penguin, [1859] 1985), p. 33. All subsequent references in the text are to this edition.

33. Milbank, *Daughters of the House*, pp. 72, 76–7.

34. See also Andrew Smith, *Victorian Demons: Medicine, Masculinity and the Gothic at the Fin de Siècle* (Manchester: Manchester University Press, 2004), pp. 126–7, where I also discuss *The Woman in White* in similar terms.

35. Elizabeth Rigby, *The Quarterly Review*, 84 (December 1848), 173–4, quoted in Gilbert and Gubar, *Madwoman in the Attic*, p. 337.

36. Margaret Oliphant, *Blackwood's Magazine*, 77 (May 1855), 554–68, quoted in Gilbert and Gubar, *Madwoman in the Attic*, p. 337.

37. Charlotte Brontë, *Jane Eyre* (Harmondsworth: Penguin, [1847] 1979), p. 125. All subsequent references in the text are to this edition.

38. See Gilbert and Gubar, *Madwoman in the Attic*, pp. 361–6.

39. See Gilbert and Gubar, *Madwoman in the Attic*, pp. 357–8.

CHAPTER 3

Gothic Proximities, 1865–1900

HIDDEN IDENTITIES: GHOSTS

When exploring the Gothic it is difficult to isolate psychological factors from social issues. In a form which focuses so closely on complex models of identity it is not surprising that a range of different issues are addressed. However, arguably one of the most telling characteristics of the Gothic from the 1790s to the 1890s concerns the progressive internalisation of 'evil'. It would be dangerous to generalise about this trend, but it would nevertheless be true to say that a new focus on psychology indicates that a predominantly secularised version of 'monstrosity' began to appear. Monsters are not, as they were with Walpole's animated giants, or Lewis's demons, externally manifested sources of danger. Instead, by the mid-nineteenth century such horrors had largely been internalised. The roots of this can be discerned in *Frankenstein* in the doubling between Victor and his creature, but it is given fresh impetus in the mid-nineteenth century Gothic, as indicated by the emergence of the ghost story as a popular form from the 1840s onwards. Typically in the ghost story the 'monster' lives with you, invading your domestic spaces, so that 'evil' acquires a proximity to the self which it did not necessarily have in the earlier Gothic.[1] This new departure is a matter of emphasis rather than a revolutionary break. The roots of this internalisation of evil are to be found in much of the Romantic Gothic, whilst their mature development can be observed within the later Victorian Gothic. To appreciate this it is necessary to return to an issue touched upon in the Introduction. In Burke's *Philosophical Enquiry* he developed, as we also saw in the discussion of *Frankenstein*, a theory of sublime terror which is stimulated by our more dangerous encounters with the world. Burke attempts to explain this within a philosophical language which is dogged by an empiricist view of the world, which is why he is so systematic in his itemisation of causes and effects. However, we can also say that Burke is addressing psychological issues within a philosophical approach which cannot properly account for the origins of 'terror' as an emotion. As discussed in the Introduction, Burke does not have a language of psychology with which to explore unconscious or subconscious factors because, historically speaking, this language was unavailable to him.

If Burke's *Philosophical Enquiry* represents an attempt to account for new types of emotional experience, then Freud provides a more person-centred, critically nuanced account of the self which helps us to explore such changes as they appear in the Gothic tradition. This may seem like a historically perverse claim (that the Victorian Gothic which pre-dated Freud can be historically explained in Freudian terms), but it relates to an essential quality of the Gothic which has been addressed throughout: that it is an interrogative rather than intellectually or culturally passive form. As the Romantic Gothic treated Burkean ideas with scepticism, so that scepticism generated a new version of the self which was more complex than Burke's empiricism would allow. Indeed it developed a version of the self which appears to be strangely Freudian before Freud. This relationship is not a tenuous one, as evidenced by the fact that Freud's essay 'The Uncanny' gains most of its conclusions from a reading of E. T. A. Hoffmann's short story 'The Sand Man' (1816).

As outlined in the Introduction, for Freud, the key terms of the uncanny relate to the home. The home is a place of family, domesticity, and therefore safety. However, Freud famously notes that linguistically the two terms of his argument – *heimlich* (homely) and *unheimlich* (unhomely, or uncanny) – merge, leading him to conclude that '*unheimlich* is in some way or other a subspecies of *heimlich*'.[2] This is not just because of some lexical slippage between the terms, it is because for Freud the home *is* a sinister place. In keeping with his theory of the Oedipus complex (which underpins his reading of 'The Sand Man'), the home becomes a dangerous place because it is the site where sexual secrets are harboured and propagated. The child's feelings about their parents influence infantile sexual development, meaning that the home is not a safe, or innocent, place to be.

Because the home can become the place which generates sexual anxieties it is therefore no surprise that the Gothic of the late nineteenth century also suggests, in the ghost story, that the home is a dangerous place. Trauma, however, should not be solely seen in psychological terms because, as we shall see, the ghost story also references an anxiety about the 'wealth' invested in the home and middle-class concerns about who really 'owns' such places. Dickens's *A Christmas Carol* (1843), J. H. Riddell's *The Uninhabited House* (1875), and Henry James's *The Turn of the Screw* (1898) help to clarify these issues.

Dickens wrote a number of long ghost stories which he referred to as 'my little Christmas Books', indicating that he saw them as seasonal winter's tales intended as light entertainment.[3] However, these 'Christmas Books' often contain quite sinister narratives concerning loneliness, anxiety, despair, and poverty. The best-known of these books is *A Christmas Carol*, and although it was written in 1843 it nevertheless gives a good sense of the kinds of issues which typified the ghost story (and by extension the Gothic) during the middle of the nineteenth century and onwards.

Scrooge's lodgings can be read in terms of the uncanny. This is apparent by how he lives in his chambers – a wealthy man living in self-imposed poverty (in which he is not properly 'homed') – and in the more obvious sense that his home is subject to ghostly visitations. These two aspects of the tale are closely related and illustrate the complex way in which the uncanny operates in such texts during the period.

As discussed in the Introduction, Freud claims that feelings of uncanniness are generated by the intimated presence of 'spirits and ghosts' (p. 364). In ghost stories the dead are not quite dead but then Scrooge is not, so the tale implies, really 'alive' because his emotional distance from the world underlines his inability to empathise with others (which in turn makes him the 'inhuman' Gothic figure of the first part of the tale).

The invasion of Scrooge's chambers by ghosts represents a direct invasion into his life. The ghost of Jacob Marley illustrates not only what he could become (a soul tormented) but also what he is (a spectral 'inhuman' figure). The point is to make Scrooge realise that in order to change his fate he has to change who he is, and this is effected by bringing Scrooge 'back to life' (or back to the present). The three ghosts which confront Scrooge all illustrate certain points of his history, past, present, and future, and thus the ghosts have an inherent connection to Scrooge, rather than appear as external manifestations of 'evil' (indeed they are there to help him).

A Christmas Carol relies on the uncanny in its representation of ghosts *and* in how the ghosts are used to illustrate the workings of Scrooge's inner life. Whilst this effects a psychological transformation in Scrooge, this psychological factor should not be separated from social issues. Uncanniness might appear to be a purely psychological phenomenon but it represents a model of anxiety which needs to be seen within the social context that gives rise to it. In Scrooge's case the context clearly concerns anxieties over money.

The tale was written in the 1840s during a period of economic depression known as 'the hungry forties'. Scrooge is a miser who contributes to the presence of poverty because he hoards his wealth. At the end of the tale he buys Christmas presents and this suggests that he is putting money back into circulation. The conclusion therefore contains a paradox, because it implies that Scrooge needs to become a better capitalist, one who uses money when, arguably, it was capitalism which caused the problem in the first place.

The issue of money is important because ghost stories often foreground concerns about class and wealth. However, given that they are also about invaded domestic spaces (which are also economic spaces) it is understandable that many women writers produced major collections of ghost stories, novellas, and novels in the period. Amelia B. Edwards published many significant ghost stories in the 1860s and wrote the important long tale *Monsieur Maurice* in 1873. Mary E. Braddon in the 1870s and 1880s produced many influential tales, as did E. Nesbit in the 1890s and onwards. Vernon Lee (real name Violet Paget) wrote the novella *A Phantom Lover* (1886), and her collection of tales *Hauntings, Fantastic Stories* (1891) addresses the conjunctions between gender and various forms of social and economic power.

One prominent ghost-story writer of the time, although one now somewhat neglected, is J. H. Riddell (or Charlotte Riddell). Like other women writers in the ghost-story tradition she examined the relationship between class and gender (a theme that is implicit in Dickens's account of money). She also wrote several non-Gothic texts which testify to her interest in financial matters. Her best-known novels set in the financial sector are *City and Suburb* (1861), *Mitre Court* (1885), and *The Head of the Firm* (1892). She also produced a series of Gothic novellas, *Fairy Water* (1873), *The Uninhabited House* (1875), *The Haunted River* (1877), and *The Disappearance of Mr. Jeremiah Redworth* (1878), as well as the collection of tales *Weird Stories* (1884), which includes many ghost stories.

The Uninhabited House initially seems to lampoon the kind of materialism that we find in Dickens as it focuses on the legal practicalities of letting out River House, which is reputedly haunted. The owner of the house loses her case against her tenants who claim that they had not been informed about the ghost when they rented the property. A clerk who is involved in the letting of the house, and who narrates the story, stays in the house in hope of explaining the mystery. It transpires that it is haunted by the previous owner, Mr Elmsdale, a wealthy but unscrupulous money-lender who, for a variety of reasons, wished to financially ruin a Mr Harringford, who owed him money and who subsequently murdered him. The novella moves beyond the largely psychological issues later suggested by Freud in 'The Uncanny' by implying that money is uncanny because it appears to possess a vitality (a life) which either enhances or destroys the people it touches. The ghost of Mr Elmsdale is like a version of Scrooge. One witness recounts seeing 'a man...seated counting over bank-notes. He had a pile of them before him, and I distinctly saw that he wetted his fingers in order to separate them'.[4] The ghost of Mr Elmsdale is, like Jacob Marley's, still attached to the business world. When Mr Harringford murders the wealthy Elmsdale the curse of financial success is passed on to him, as he notes 'From the hour I left him lying dead in the library every worldly plan prospered with me', however, 'I had sold my soul to the devil' (p. 104). His wife and children die and he becomes lame and prematurely aged. The moral appears to be simple enough – money come by dishonestly makes you inhuman. Money, like the ghost, is both present and absent because it represents both a material reality and a moral emptiness. As in *A Christmas Carol*, the solution appears to lie in the proper redistribution of wealth, which occurs when Harringford dies and bequeaths his wealth to Elmsdale's daughter, who then marries the narrator.

This seemingly bizarre tale of ghosts and ill-begotten wealth illustrates again the essentially middle-class anxieties of the form. The anxiety is that a class could, under certain circumstances, gain and lose everything within a generation.[5] In addition Riddell's adoption of a male narrator does not disguise the fact that the poverty with which he is threatened, unless he makes a financially advantageous marriage, in reality captures the experience of many women at the time.

Both Dickens and Riddell therefore address issues about money and class, and in Riddell's case gender. Their narratives indicate that ghosts are not quite so otherworldly after all, indeed they seem to be more *heimlich* than *unheimlich* in the prosaic class-bound anxieties that they articulate.

Riddell's tale is not just about money and it would be untrue to suggest that all such stories are focused on money and power. However, Riddell's love plot is intimately related to financial concerns because they govern the expectations that characters have about their chances of marrying.

Love, money, ghosts, and suggestions of insanity are central issues in Henry James's *The Turn of the Screw* (1898), which can be read as a *fin de siècle* version of *Jane Eyre*, centred upon a governess's feelings for her employer. James's novella made an important contribution to the ghost story because it casts doubt on whether the ghosts are 'real' or merely projections of the governess's somewhat overwrought imagination.

The novella begins in a kind of ghost story competition in which Douglas, the narrator, presents the governess's story. If love in Riddell's novella is in part conditioned by certain financial expectations, in James it is associated with a possible delusion that controls the plot. This is indicated in Douglas's response to a question about the governess, 'Yes, she was in love. That is, she *had* been. That came out – she couldn't tell her story without its coming out.'[6] Douglas also goes on to note, 'The story *won't* tell ... not in any literal, vulgar way' (p. 6).

James's syntactically complex novella bears stylistic testimony to this oblique approach in which the governess's perception of the ghosts of Quint and Jessel is central because their very existence is open to question. Whilst Dickens's and Riddell's ghosts fulfil a purpose because their presence is meant to create a better life (for Scrooge) or because they result in economic advancement (for Riddell's narrator), James's ghosts appear to represent the projections of the love-struck and anxious governess.

The governess's unrequited feelings for her employer become dramatised in the relations between the spectral Quint and Miss Jessel, who also appear to have been involved in a doomed relationship. In addition, the governess's perception of the children, Flora and Miles, is influenced by her anxiety that Quint and Jessel could represent an immoral influence over them. This means that all the characters, real and spectral, are forced into a series of relationships forged by the governess. Miles, for example, because of some undisclosed problems at school, appears to the governess as a potential Quint, and so she attempts to protect him from Quint's influence. However, Mrs Grose, the pragmatic housekeeper, undermines the governess's claims about the presence of the ghosts. In one scene the governess points at Jessel, but Mrs Grose responds with 'Where on earth do you see anything?' (p. 105), a view supported by Flora: 'I see nobody. I see nothing. I never *have*' (p. 106). The governess rationalises away such claims (at least to her own, if not necessarily the reader's, satisfaction), but this means that the novella operates at two levels: as a tale about ghosts *and* as a tale about the governess's projection of her feelings about possible rejection.

The narrative develops some of the aspects of the uncanny which relate to doubling. The problem is that the governess is necessarily unable to see that the ghosts are (or at least can be read as) projections of herself. *The Turn of the Screw* thus dramatises the interior (emotional, psychological) origins of the types of horror that an earlier, less secular, Gothic tradition located externally.

These three stories of ghosts are quite different in emphasis and in their development of uncanniness. It is important to note that the ghost story has often posed problems for critics because their very structure, in which a survivor tells or focalises the tale, signals in advance that any 'horrors' are likely to be overcome. However, in James's complex tale of psychological influence and spectrality (a theme he also developed in the short story 'The Friends of the Friends', 1896), the surviving governess arguably does not overcome the trauma of what happens because she is the principal agent in its generation.[7] However, when reading ghost stories it is also important to consider how they express class-bound issues, because ghost stories, with their accounts of haunted middle-class houses, are also articulating class anxieties which obliquely touch upon the perils of home ownership.

James's novella explores issues about projection and doubling which appear in other Gothic tales. How the 'other' functions as a means of awakening is, as we shall see, a central aspect of Robert Louis Stevenson's tale of doubling, *The Strange Case of Dr Jekyll and Mr Hyde* (1886), and is a feature of many mid-nineteenth-century Gothic tales which touch upon sexuality.

GOTHIC DOUBLES

The Gothic's use of doubling is a clear indication of the internalisation of 'evil'. Indeed in the new, predominantly secularised context of the mid- to late nineteenth-century Gothic, 'evil' seems a misnomer because such 'inner' narratives can be explained in psychological *and* social, rather than strictly theological, terms. In the Introduction we saw that Freud in 'The Uncanny' initially regarded the double as indicating the emergence of our adult conscience. However, this 'conscience', which has a positive role in regulating behaviour, turns into a dangerously powerful form of censorship that, for Freud, stifles the development of the self so that the double becomes 'the uncanny harbinger of death' (p. 357) because it psychologically kills (or represses) the self. This version of the double has its roots in Descartes's famous dictum 'I think therefore I am', which implies that the self can reflect upon its own processes. For Freud this self-reflection indicates the presence of a child-like 'old surmounted narcissism' (p. 357), so that maturation is dogged by self-regarding infantile urges. This view of the double as a harbinger of death, as a liberator from censorship, and as a mode of repression can all be witnessed in Sheridan Le Fanu's *Carmilla* (1872) and Stevenson's *The Strange Case of Dr Jekyll and Mr Hyde*.

The roots of the double can be found in Coleridge's *Christabel*. Chapter 2 explored how the language used in Gothic poetry displaces and so covertly develops images of a tabooed lesbian desire. By paying close attention to how Coleridge and Rossetti used language it is possible to see how it enabled them to both articulate *and* conceal notions of sexual awakening. Both *Christabel* and *Goblin Market* represent images of lesbianism and in their different ways struggle to both show and disguise this (perhaps more so in Rossetti, but it is there in Coleridge's attempt to allegorise such desire in Bracy's dream). It is not just the issue of lesbian desire which is important but also the representation of fragile, because permeable, models of subjectivity. Geraldine might appear as an external threat but she effects an inner awakening. Laura and Lucy are sisters but iconically lovers because the Goblins also bring about a (premature) sexual awakening – the antidote to which transfers the awakening from men to women.

This Gothic strand links lesbianism with sexual discovery, and sexual discovery in a wider sense is an issue in the Gothic during the period, as well as being central to Freud's account of subject formation. Le Fanu's *Carmilla* is a good example of a text from the period which explores lesbianism, sexual awakening, and national identity, all within an account of the self and its vampiric desires.

Le Fanu, an Irish writer of mixed Protestant and Catholic descent (although a graduate of the Protestant Trinity College, Dublin), was a well-known novelist famous for *Uncle Silas* (1864), *Wylder's Hand* (1864), and *Guy Deverell* (1865), as well as an influential Gothic short-story writer. *Carmilla* was published in the collection *In a Glass Darkly* (1872), which contained a number of Gothic short stories, including 'Green Tea', 'The Familiar' and 'Mr Justice Harbottle'. The prologue to *Carmilla* claims that the tale has been subject to some scientific scrutiny by Doctor Hesselius

(Le Fanu's investigator into paranormal activity), who had concluded that the 'case' represented 'some of the profoundest arcana of our dual existence' (p. 72).

Laura, who lives with her English father in Styria, narrates the tale. Her mother has died, and this, typically a feature of the Female Gothic, leaves her peculiarly vulnerable. Their world is transformed when they are asked to look after Carmilla, a young woman who has been involved in a carriage accident on their estate. Laura seems to recollect Carmilla from a childhood dream, a dream that Carmilla also recalls and which establishes an apparent psychic link between them. The two are drawn to each other, whilst in the neighbourhood there are a number of mysterious deaths of young women (who seem to have died from vampire bites). Laura also appears to become a victim of these assaults, but then Carmilla disappears. A General Spielsdorf, who some time before had seemingly lost his daughter to a vampire that resembled Carmilla, arrives and helps track Carmilla to her tomb, where she is staked and decapitated.

The crucial moment concerns the dream that Laura had concerning Carmilla when she was six years old:

> I saw a solemn, but very pretty face looking at me with a kind of pleased wonder ... she caressed me with her hands, and lay down beside me on the bed, and drew me towards her smiling. I was wakened by a sensation as if two needles ran into my breast very deep at the same moment, and I cried loudly.[8]

The claim that Laura was awoken by the attack suggests that this was not a dream. Victor Sage has explored this moment in depth, concluding that 'The question of whose dream we are in (and whether life is 'dream' or not) is a crux in the narrative'.[9] For Sage, Laura's father's insistence that this was only a nightmare (a view supported by the servants) represents a denial of the reality of Laura's experience. Twelve years later, when Carmilla returns, Carmilla recounts her version of the 'dream' which appears to corroborate Laura's sense that it was a real waking experience, and therefore, as Sage notes, 'Carmilla seizes the dream, and in doing so, possesses Laura's reality' (p. 182). Ownership of Laura is thus staged as a battle between her father and Carmilla, a battle which arguably has its roots in *Christabel*.

Conflict in *Carmilla* is related to dramas about love. The tale suggests that a father's love and lesbian love are incompatible. Laura is caught between these different models of love and in part she registers her unease through ambivalent feelings for Carmilla: 'I felt rather unaccountably drawn towards the beautiful stranger. I did feel, as she said "drawn towards her", but there was also something of repulsion' (p. 87). Carmilla tells her:

> I live in your warm life, and you shall die – die, sweetly die – into mine. I cannot help it; as I draw near to you, you in your turn, will draw near to others, and learn the rapture of that cruelty which yet is love. (p. 89)

Laura is torn between liberating feelings of sexual awakening and a concern that there is an element of coercion in this. The reader, following Sage, can see that Carmilla in owning the 'dream' is exercising considerable influence over Laura. 'Love' becomes a conduit for infiltration and infection even whilst it seems to promise an awakening. The emphasis on Laura's ambivalent feelings indicates her vulnerability. Carmilla masquerades as a force for good, but in fact is a vampire. Carmilla is not Laura's lost other half but merely, as Sage has noted, pretends to be so: what Laura 'thinks of as warm and close and self-confirming – a true acknowledgement of her self – is merely cold and dead' (p. 187).

Questions about the ownership of the self are central to *Jekyll and Hyde*, but in *Carmilla* this has added significance because of a debate about national identities. Earlier chapters have touched on how 'evil' in the Gothic is often asserted as a foreign, invasive presence, but in *Carmilla* it is Laura and her father who are alien to the area. Laura's English father has worked for the Austrian Service and has a generous pension which enabled him to buy a castle as the family home. Laura states, 'My father is English, and I bear an English name, although I never saw England' (p. 72). Laura and her father speak English 'partly to prevent its becoming a lost language among us, and partly from patriotic motives' (p. 73). Later she claims of the castle, 'It is not too stately to be extremely comfortable; and here we had our tea, for with his usual patriotic leanings he insisted that the national beverage should make its appearance' (p. 83). It is subsequently revealed that Carmilla is a Karnstein and therefore a member of a family with long established ties to the region (although the family had died out a hundred years before). Carmilla, or Countess Karnstein, thus has a greater claim on the area than Laura and her father, who are the alien, foreign, invasive presence.

This confusion of typical Gothic roles references how notions of 'civilisation' (here constituted as a kind of Englishness) were compromised at the time by anxieties concerning possible moral, social, and psychological degeneration. Theories of degeneration, which originated with Bénédict Augustin Morel's work on 'Cretinism' in France in the 1840s, were developed by the Italian criminologist Cesare Lombroso in the 1870s as a means of identifying criminal types. In the 1890s such theories underpinned Max Nordau's *Degeneration* (1892), which sought to explain cultural decline through an analysis of supposedly degenerate writers such as Oscar Wilde, emile Zola, and Henrik Ibsen (amongst many others).[10] Edwin Lankester in *Degeneration: A Chapter in Darwinism* (1880) developed the theory that a peaceful, overly refined, society would be prone to collapse because it was no longer invigorated by the battle against natural enemies.[11] These later theories, at quite different levels, expressed concerns that civilisation could merely be a prelude to a wider social, economic, and cultural fragmentation. A chief anxiety was that sexual 'degeneracy' both enabled and indicated the spread of this decline. Sexual behaviour (and its 'healthy' manifestations) was therefore subject to some considerable scrutiny. Medical developments helped to support and monitor this because sexual behaviour became regarded as the site of least resistance through which the spread of all kinds of diseases (moral as well as physical) could be spread.[12] *Carmilla* also expresses these concerns, which later commentators would read as indicators of degeneracy. *Carmilla* thus represents a very fragile notion of a civilised 'Englishness', fragile because Laura is open to the sexual ministrations of the 'degenerate' Carmilla, whose repeated associations with languor are, in this context, suggestive of a sexual exhaustion which anticipates those writings on degeneracy concerned with sexual health.

Bram Dijkstra has explored at length the connotations of female languor in a range of paintings and texts produced at the *fin de siècle*. Such images of languor drew upon popular pseudo-scientific ideas that claimed that blood depletion was caused by too much sexual activity because energy, and so blood, was exhausted in coitus. Although this relates to both sexes, Dijkstra specifically examines how women were typically figured as a vampiric drain upon the blood (or energy) of others (usually men) in order to symbolically replenish their own blood.

Dijkstra notes the strange doubling in *Carmilla* observing that Carmilla appears as 'the photographic negative of Laura'.[13] However, Carmilla also develops images of languor which Dijkstra argues were associated with female sexual degeneracy (the sexually exhausted woman). Laura notes that although Carmilla appears to be in robust health, 'her movements were languid – *very* languid' (p. 88, italics in original). Their relationship is characterised by a form of masculine courtship in which Laura acknowledges that 'I could boast of no little attentions such as masculine gallantry delights to offer' (p. 91). However, this playing with gender roles is ultimately challenged by the presence of this 'weak', languid female body, which prompts Laura to record that 'there was always a languor about her, quite incompatible with a masculine system in a state of health' (p. 91). In Dijkstra's terms Carmilla, the vampire, symbolically needs blood to replace that expended through (lesbian) sexual activity. At the end of the tale, after Carmilla has seemingly caused the deaths of many local peasant women, she is discovered in her coffin awash with blood: 'the leaden coffin floated with blood, in which to a depth of seven inches, the body lay immersed' (p. 134). When they decapitate Carmilla 'a torrent of blood flowed from the severed neck' (p. 134).

Carmilla parasitically feeds her appetites and as a vampire she is a classic Gothic monster, although this is compromised by Laura's ambivalent feelings for Carmilla: 'I was conscious of a love growing into adoration, and also of abhorrence. This I know is paradox, but I can make no other attempt to explain the feeling' (p. 90). In part this is because of the apparent doubling between the two.

As mentioned earlier, anxieties about degeneration provide a cultural context for the tale. Laura's attempt to retain a nationally inflected model of civilisation (in the tale largely associated with English tea-drinking rituals) is what makes her vulnerable. The suggestion that civilisation cannot quite be trusted because it harbours discontents and is under threat by visceral pleasures which lurk beneath its surface (and which always threaten to tear such a surface apart), is a key aspect of how images of doubling are represented in Stevenson's *Jekyll and Hyde*.

In the Gothic tradition 'evil' is often defined by the threat it poses to 'civilisation'. *Jekyll and Hyde*, like *Carmilla*, problematises this by raising questions about the origins of 'evil' *within* civilisation. The novella can easily be caricatured as merely being about warring factions within Dr Jekyll, but a closer examination reveals that Stevenson emphasises that any notion of conflict needs to be seen within the context of what constitutes civilisation. The novella opens with an account of the weekly walk taken around London by Utterson and his distant relative Enfield. Utterson is a lawyer and therefore ostensibly associated with a respectable bourgeois profession, but a closer look reveals the presence of a Gothic mood. He is described as 'a man of rugged countenance, that was never lighted by a smile; cold, scanty and embarrassed in discourse; backward in sentiment: lean, long, dusty, dreary', and although this is qualified with 'and yet somehow lovable', this 'somehow' suggests that the grounds for the claim are unclear.[14] It is then noted of Utterson and Enfield that:

> It was reported by those who encountered them in their Sunday walks, that they said nothing, looked singularly dull, and would hail with obvious relief the appearance of a friend. For all that, the two men put the greatest store by these excursions, counted them the chief jewel of each week. (p. 30)

The opening of the novella thus implies that a meaningless attachment to middle-class rituals (here the Sunday walks) empties experience of pleasure and significance. It is out of this emptiness that Hyde is generated. This specifically middle-class emptiness is apparent in the isolated and lonely lives of all the main characters who are 'successful' members of bourgeois professions such as medicine and the law. As in some theories of degeneration, the precarious nature of social bonds indicates a crisis within notions of civilisation. Hyde might appear to be a Darwinian throwback with his 'ape-like tricks' (p. 96), but there is at least, so the novella implies, a vitality about him which is sadly lacking in the other characters, and thus Hyde becomes the double of them all. 'The Uncanny' with its analysis of dangerous doubles provides one critical approach to the text. Hyde, seen within the context of a seemingly moribund civilisation, can also be interpreted as an evolving creature. Hyde physically becomes bigger as the novella develops, and this coming into being is also apparent in the language that Jekyll employs in his seemingly explanatory narrative, 'Henry Jekyll's Full Statement of the Case'. Jekyll's first-person account slips into a third-person narrative voice – 'Henry Jekyll stood at times aghast before the acts of Edward Hyde' (p. 82) – which indicates a struggle for control within the narrative; later the view that 'Jekyll was now my city of refuge' (pp. 91–2) suggests that Hyde is narrating. The final sentence claims that 'I bring the life of that unhappy Henry Jekyll to an end' (p. 97), which is also ambivalent because we cannot be sure if Jekyll has killed Hyde or Hyde has killed Jekyll.

Jekyll and Hyde, like *Carmilla*, is ostensibly about doubled selves, but it never loses sight of the social conflict that Jekyll and Hyde represent. Jekyll and Hyde are associated with different classes and in this respect dramatise the social tensions which characterised London at the time. The idea of leading a double life has also suggested to Elaine Showalter that the novella incorporates a covert narrative relating to homosexual relations between Jekyll and Hyde, in which Hyde blackmails his socially superior 'lover'.[15] Such images can also be discerned in Wilde's *The Picture of Dorian Gray* (1891), which plots the development of a secret life within an apparently respectable society. The complexities of these Gothic narratives lend themselves to many different readings and theoretical approaches. Theories of degeneration have a predominately European flavour to them and provide one way of looking at how these texts generate models of identity. How identity was explored in the American Gothic during the period helps develop a critical counterpoint to this British tradition.

RACE AND HISTORY: POST-BELLUM GOTHIC

We have seen that an analysis of place and context reveals how texts exhibit nationally specific anxieties. The tales of Edgar Allan Poe, for example, can be related to some ambivalent ideas about race in America during the 1830s and 1840s. Racial otherness and its particular Gothic inflection as a category of Gothic otherness was also clear in the representation of Bertha Mason in *Jane Eyre*. In Britain at the *fin de siècle*, as we shall see in the reading of *Dracula* which concludes this chapter, concerns about racial otherness were closely tied to anxieties about imperial decline. In America after the Civil War (1861–65) such issues were constituted in quite different terms. Whilst Britain was nervously looking out at threats to its empire, the United States was going through a period of colonial expansion in Cuba (1895–9) and the Philippines (1899–1902). However, this was combined with a certain amount of soul-searching relating to the legacies of slavery, which the Civil War had ostensibly helped to eradicate. Late nineteenth-century America was still ghosted by the past of slavery, and this plays a powerful role in a strand of American Gothic in the period. Whilst, of course, it is important to acknowledge the contribution made to the American Gothic by writers as diverse as Ambrose Bierce, Charlotte Perkins Gilman, and Edith Wharton, it is also necessary to consider how the Gothic addresses racial issues in what had been until quite recently, difficult to obtain but nevertheless culturally significant Gothic tales.

Jerrold E. Hogle has noted that a useful context for the discussion of race in the American Gothic is provided by freed women slaves, which also highlights how gender considerations shaped racial representations. Memoirs written by African American women, including Harriet E. Wilson's *Our Nig* (1859) and Harriet Jacob's *Incidents in the Life of a Slave Girl* (1861) provide very useful contextual information, as does Frederick Douglass's earlier *Narrative of the Life of Frederick Douglass* (1845). It is also important to consider, as Hogle notes, how white representations of African Americans, on both the pro- and anti-abolitionist sides, 'so readily combine the attractive and the repulsive, the deeply familiar and the unfamiliar [...] in one symbol'.[16] This fundamentally

Gothic ambivalence informs such tales as Charles W. Chesnutt's 'The Sheriff's Children' (1899) and 'Po' Sandy' (1899), George Washington Cable's 'Jean-Ah Poquelin' (1879), and Kate Chopin's 'Désirée's Baby' (1893).

Charles W. Chesnutt was of mixed race and had slave-owning white grandfathers. He combined a successful legal career with writing fiction. 'The Sheriff's Children' was published in the collection *The Wife of His Youth and Other Stories of the Color Line* in 1899. Charles Crow has noted that in Chesnutt's fiction the frequently bland or occasionally cheerful narratives voices are 'always to be distrusted' because, as in the case of 'The Sheriff's Children', 'ominous, dissonant voices can be heard in the background almost from the first sentence'.[17] The tale is set some time after the Civil War in Troy, a small isolated village, where Tom, a young man of mixed race, has been arrested for the murder of Walker, a former Confederate captain. The local townspeople decide to lynch Tom (who is actually innocent of the crime although he did steal a coat from Walker, which implicates him) and march on the prison, where Campbell, the sheriff (a former Confederate colonel who lives with his daughter), refuses to hand Tom over and promises to defend him. The mob leave and Campbell, who is momentarily distracted, has his pistol taken by Tom, who states that he intends to shoot the sheriff and escape. Campbell tries to reason with Tom, who reveals that he is his son, the result of relations that Campbell had with Cicely, one of his slaves from before the war with whom he quarrelled and in a moment of anger had sold. Her new owner had whipped Cicely to death and Tom expresses his anger and resentment about the circumstances in which he was raised. Campbell's daughter has, however, entered the gaol and overhears only the part where Tom indicates that he will kill Campbell, and she shoots Tom as he is about to carry out this threat. Tom is wounded and overpowered, but in the morning Campbell finds that he has torn off his bandages in order to bleed to death.

The tale emphasises that the horrors of slavery, and the dramas of the Civil War have a continuing presence even within a town situated in the highly isolated Branson County, where many of its inhabitants fought in the war on the Confederate side, but where the war did not penetrate: 'all along the seaboard the war had raged;

but the thunder of its canon had not disturbed the echoes of Branson County'.[18] However, the war has a more insidious influence as it shaped the mentalities of the people involved in it. Campbell comes from a wealthy landowning and slave-owning family, but he is a liberal by education and inclination: both well travelled and well educated he had been 'an ardent supporter of the Union', but late in the war he gave in 'at last to the force of circumstances' and 'served with distinction in the Confederate army' (p. 353). Campbell becomes a formally representative figure of law and order who initially perceives Tom as possessing an irrationality which suggests links to Gothic images of madness: 'if the man was not mad, he was in a state of mind akin to madness, and quite as dangerous' (p. 356). When Tom reveals who he is and that he intends to shoot Campbell, Tom indicates that he has no compassion because:

> What father's duty have you ever performed for me? Did you give me your name, or even your protection? Other white men gave their colored sons freedom and money, and sent them to the free states. *You* sold *me* to the rice swamps. (p. 357)

Tom initially says that he will not shoot Campbell as long as he promises not to attempt to recapture him until the following morning. This is a crucial moment in the text because it indicates just how far the otherwise liberal-minded Campbell has been tainted by racist ideologies:

> The sheriff hesitated. The struggle between his love of life and his sense of duty was a terrific one. It may seem strange that a man who could sell his own child into slavery should hesitate at such a moment, when his life was trembling in the balance. But the baleful influence of human slavery poisoned the very fountains of life, and created new standards of right. The sheriff was conscientious; his conscience had merely been warped by his environment. (pp. 357–8)

Campbell's commitment to an abstract notion of duty thus suggests that he too finds it difficult to conceive of his son in human terms.

Morally this makes him little better than the lynch mob who 'had some vague notions of the majesty of the law and the rights of the citizen, but in the passion of the moment these sunk into oblivion; a white man had been killed by a negro' (p. 351).

The wounded Tom does, however, spark Campbell's conscience, and he vows to discover Walker's murderer and help Tom to improve his life. However, Tom's death ends any such optimism. 'The Sheriff's Children' might not seem to be a demonstrably Gothic tale because it lacks any supernatural elements. However, it does exploit Gothic images of 'madness', law and order, racial otherness, family secrets, and incarceration – all of which are used to represent the horror of slavery which cannot quite be laid to rest. The lingering presence of slavery is given supernatural development by Chestnutt in 'Po' Sandy'.

'Po Sandy' was published in *The Conjure Woman* (1899) and forms part of a series of stories known as 'John and Julius' tales in which Julius, a former slave, anecdotally relates a number of incidents which occurred during the time of slavery. These tales are recounted to his employer, John, who in turn narrates the tales as they were told to him. On a journey with John and his wife, Annie, they stop at a cottage and the noises coming from a nearby sawmill prompt Julius's recollections of Sandy. Sandy was a slave who, because of his hardworking nature, was frequently lent to other plantation owners when they needed extra help. This annoys Sandy because it results in protracted separation from his wife, Tenie. However, it transpires that Tenie is a sorceress (or conjure woman) and she agrees to turn Sandy into a tree on their plantation so that she can visit him and turn him back into his human form when nobody is around (his owner assuming that Sandy has escaped). Sandy agrees to this, but Tenie is then called away to another plantation and when she returns she discovers that the tree has been cut down and taken to the sawmill. She tries to stop the mill-hands from cutting up the tree, but they assume that she is mad, and as Julius recounts:

tied her arms wid a rope, en fasten' her to one er de posts in de sawmill; en den dey started de saw up ag'in, en cut de log inter bo'ds en scantlin's right befo' her eyes. But it wuz mighty

hard wuk; fer of all de sweekin', en moanin', an groanin', dat
log done it w'iles de saw wuz a-cuttin' thoo it. De saw wuz one
er dese yer ole-timey, up-en-down saws, en hit tuk longer dem
days ter saw a log 'en it do now. Dey greased de saw, but dat
didn' stop de fuss; hit kep' right on, tel fin'ly dey got de log all
sawed up.[19]

Tenie is thus forced to watch her husband carved up into planks of
wood that are used to help build a kitchen that becomes haunted by
Sandy's groans. Tenie becomes permanently deranged after this
scene. At one level this appears to be a tall tale, but on a symbolic
level the death of Sandy captures the reality of an experience in
which slaves became depersonalised and disposed of at will by their
owners. Tenie's horror and Sandy's pain become all the more
poignant because they are incommunicable to others. This seemingly outlandish tale thus, in a typically Gothic fashion, hints at a
historical truth in a highly displaced and symbolic way. As Crow has
noted, we need to pay attention to John's and Annie's different
responses to the tale:

'What a system it was', she exclaimed, when Julius had fin-
ished, 'under which such things were possible!'
'What things?' I asked, in amazement. 'Are you seriously
considering the possibility of a man's being turned into a tree?'
'Oh, no,' she replied quickly, 'not that'; and then she mur-
mured absently, and with a dim look in her fine eyes, 'Poor
Tenie!' (p. 349)

As Crow notes, for John this tale is a 'transparent fiction...easily
exposed by northern common sense', whereas for Annie the tale 'is
Gothic to her, and most readers now will have no difficulty seeing
who has a greater understanding of Julius's, and Chesnutt's, fable'
(p. 343). Annie perceives that the tale needs to be read symbolically
to understand how it addresses the horror of life (and death) as a
slave. John's incomprehension is also horrifying because it indicates
that he has failed to grasp the reality of the conditions of slavery.
The tale is therefore just as much an indictment of the present as it
is of the past.

This failure of compassionate understanding plays a crucial role in how Creole experience is represented in George Washington Cable's 'Jean-Ah Poquelin' (1879). The tale refers to a Gothic mansion which 'stood aloof from civilization' and which is inhabited by Jean Marie Poquelin, his brother Jacques, and an old mute African slave, a legacy from the days when the family were slave owners.[20] The tale is set in Louisiana in 1803 and is a good early example of Southern Gothic. Despite the dating within the tale, it draws parallels, as Crow comments, with post-war reconstruction.[21] The tale concerns the unsympathetic administration of a French-speaking district by an American government intent on taking over and exploiting the land for commercial purposes. In the process the Creoles are driven out by this apparent progress. Poquelin has become a recluse, having seemingly lost his brother on an expedition some time before, and his isolation leads to the townspeople superstitiously associating him with many of the ills which periodically befall them. It is then revealed that his reclusiveness is meant to conceal the fact that his brother still lives in the house, but is ill with leprosy, which was contracted in Africa (which becomes another way of symbolically representing the curse of slavery). Images of 'otherness' which have accrued to Poquelin over the years are thus visibly turned into a marker of his exclusion. At the end Poquelin dies, and his brother 'as white as snow' and the mute African take the coffin and 'without one backward glance upon the unkind human world, turning their faces toward the ridge in the depths of the swamp known as Leper's Land, they stepped into the jungle, disappeared, and were never seen again' (p. 372). In this instance the Creoles have become racially othered (Jacques is a mocking parody of whiteness) and aligned with the black mute – silenced, rejected, and unable to be accommodated, all to the shame of the community which has been responsible for Jean Marie Poquelin's demonisation.[22]

One common issue in these tales concerns the problematisation of 'evil'. Labelling certain forms of behaviour as 'evil' enables us to identify a text's political leanings. However, in the more complex Gothic tales (as in *Frankenstein* and *Jekyll and Hyde*, for example) the concept of 'evil' is subjected to a radical scepticism which challenges the 'norm'. The tales of Chestnutt and Cable also focus discussion about 'evil' in terms which unsettle models of normality by linking them either to mob rule (the lynch mob in 'The Sheriff's Children', and a mob which threatens to descend on Poquelin's house in 'Jean Ah-Poquelin') or to how such issues subtly implicate figures who appear, perhaps only at first, to be outside of the main story, such as Campbell, and John in 'Po Sandy'. Such a position is a consequence of focusing on how the horrors of the present have been generated by the resentments formed in the past. This is an issue given a new twist by Kate Chopin in 'Désirée's Baby' (1893).

Kate Chopin is perhaps best remembered for what was at the time a highly controversial novel, *The Awakening* (1899), which explored female entrapment within marriage. The theme is also developed in 'Désirée's Baby', which centres on Désirée's marriage to Armand, a slave owner. Initially the marriage is a happy one and Désirée has a son, the effect of which is to soften Armand's brutality to the slaves. However, after a few months the baby develops a colouration which suggests that he is of mixed race and Armand attributes this to Désirée because of her mysterious past (she was found abandoned as a child) which must, for him, have included a black forefather. Armand sends her away and she kills herself and their baby. Later, when clearing out Désirée's old love letters to him, Armand discovers a letter written by his mother to his father, an extract from which closes the tale: 'night and day, I thank the good God for having so arranged our lives that our dear Armand will never know that his mother, who adores him, belongs to the race that is cursed with the brand of slavery'.[23] It is unclear whether Armand knew of this and his rejection of Désirée was therefore an attempt to conceal *his* heritage. The tale also refers to the child of a slave woman, La Blanche, and Désirée first contemplates that her own child might have a black heritage when she notes the similarity between the two children. However, an alternative explanation for this is that La Blanche's son is the result of an affair with Armand, which implies a theme of unacknowledged kinship between slaves and plantation owners which runs through much literature on slavery at the time.[24] Even if Armand had been aware of his background he nevertheless treated the slaves in an inhuman fashion, and this inhumanity is emphasised in the banishment of

Désirée. The conclusion of the tale implies that it is the system of slavery which is inhuman, and the revelation of Armand's slave background has the effect of both compromising his position as a slave owner *and* of further implicating him in the history of slavery. This highly ambivalent ending, in which Armand is ideologically a part of the process of slavery and biologically a product of its history, suggests tensions which would destroy him. Disclosure would in all possibility socially harm him, but keeping the secret would damage him on an emotional level. In some regards this is speculative, but what is important to note is that Armand at the end is both a Gothic monster and a victim of the horrors of slavery, a conundrum that powerfully illustrates both the presence of irresolvable racial tensions and an urgency that racial categories of 'otherness' need to be transcended.

To critically read narratives such as these it is crucial to explore the specific cultural contexts which generated them. They all provide important evocations of the horrors of slavery and indicate how the Gothic conditions such representations. They also play an important part in shaping later Gothic texts which explore similar themes, such as Toni Morrison's *Beloved* (1987), which will be discussed in the following chapter. As mentioned earlier, the Gothic in Britain develops ideas of racial and national 'otherness' in quite a different way than in America: a reading of *Dracula* helps to illustrate this.

READING *DRACULA*

In previous chapters the concluding sections have advanced ways in which specific texts can be read. *Dracula*, however, raises particular problems because it is a novel which can be read in so many different, sometimes conflicting, ways. The novel has been subjected to a range of critical approaches including various psychoanalytical, Marxist, and cultural materialist readings. There have also been important studies of the novel that have addressed its representation of gender, race, and nation within the context of the *fin de siècle*. The edition of *Dracula* published by St. Martin's in their series 'Case Studies in Contemporary Criticism' includes essays which explore the novel in terms of gender criticism, psychoanalytic criticism, new historicism, and deconstruction, and concludes with an essay on 'Combining Perspectives'.[25] This illustrates the available theoretically inflected approaches to what is a highly complex novel. One feature that is shared by many of these disparate approaches is a concern about what vampirism signifies. In order to give a sense of these different approaches this section will examine how certain scenes in the novel can be read for representations of class, degeneration, doubling, sexuality, and empire.

Franco Moretti in *Signs Taken for Wonders* reads vampirism as a conceit for the workings of the capitalist system which seeks to bleed its workers dry.[26] Read in this way the Count's seemingly socially 'superior' class credentials place him above the predominantly middle-class vampire hunters, and this dramatises the distance between capitalist and worker (or vampire and their prey). However, such a reading requires us to reinterpret a feudal (that is, pre-capitalist) Count as a representative figure of an economic system which has more obvious associations with the good bourgeois professionals who in the main (the exception being the aristocratic Holmwood) constitute the vampire hunters. Read in symbolic terms the Count has associations with capitalism, but if he is read as a feudal agent then the issue of money suggests alternative ways of exploring class tensions.

Whilst at Castle Dracula, Jonathan Harker recounts his exploration of the Count's room (effected by forcing a window). To his surprise he finds that 'The room was empty!', but not quite:

> The only thing I found was a great heap of gold in one corner
> – gold of all kinds, Roman, and British, and Austrian, and
> Hungarian, and Greek and Turkish money, covered with a
> film of dust, as though it had lain long in the ground. None of
> it that I noticed was less than three hundred years old.[27]

Money reappears when the vampire hunters confront the Count, pursued to his final lair in London. Harker lunges at the Count with a knife which tears a slit in the Count's clothing, through which 'a bundle of bank-notes and a stream of gold fell out' (p. 306). The Count leaps out of a window and Seward records, 'I could hear the "ting" of the gold, as some of the sovereigns fell on the flagging' (p. 306). In Moretti's terms such a scene symbolises the link between capitalism and vampirism in which the Count appears to bleed money. However, an alternative way of reading this scene suggests that it reveals the Count's inability to adapt to the modern world and its economic practices. The pile of coins that Harker discovers at Castle Dracula indicates that the Count is a hoarder of wealth, because as a feudal aristocrat his wealth is inherited. Whilst the different nationalities referred to by the coins might indicate the presence of money accumulated through trade, the dust which covers them suggests that it is unused, or inert, capital. The later scene in London implies that the Count cannot necessarily be assured that he can hold on to this wealth. Van Helsing comments 'he fear want' (p. 307) as he proceeds to literally pocket the money.

The Count's desperate attempt to hold on to his money contrasts with the vampire hunters who, in typical capitalist fashion, use money as a weapon (one which enables them to bribe locksmiths and customs officials). Jonathan Harker notes of one potential problem that 'Judge Moneybag will settle this case' (p. 334). Later, Mina Harker in reflecting on the bravery of the vampire hunters, notes:

> it made me think of the wonderful power of money! What can it not do when it is properly applied; and what might it do when basely used! I felt so thankful that Lord Godalming is rich, and that both he and Mr Morris, who also has plenty of money, are willing to spend it so freely. (p. 356)

The vampire hunters put money into circulation (a capitalist notion of speculating in order to accumulate), whereas the Count is unable to adapt to this money-based economy because he is defined as an aristocratic hoarder of wealth.

By looking at how money is represented we can see how the use or misuse of money is related to the class clashes between the middle classes and the historically (and economically) redundant Count. The vampire hunters maintain a modern approach to keeping records, referenced through the presence of the phonograph, Kodak cameras, and notes recorded in shorthand. This modern world finally manages to lay the past to rest. However, although the bourgeoisie may emerge triumphant a question persists - how and why would they have been threatened by such a feudal remnant in the first place? In other words, how was it possible that *Dracula* could convince a reader of the novel in the 1890s that its terrors were plausible? One answer lies in the novel's repeated references to degeneration.

The novel explicitly refers to theories of degeneration when Mina Harker claims that 'The Count is a criminal and of criminal type. Nordau and Lombroso would so classify him' (p. 342). Mina's observation is an overdetermined model of degeneracy because it elides the distinctions between Lombroso's theory of criminality and Nordau's account of degenerate art. An explicit link is made to Lombroso's criminological writing of the 1870s in Harker's detailed description of the Count's physiognomy:

> His face was a strong – a very strong aquiline, with high bridge of the thin nose and peculiarly arched nostrils; with lofty domed forehead, and hair growing scantily round the temples, but profusely elsewhere. His eyebrows were very massive, almost meeting over the nose, and with bushy hair that seemed to curl in its open profusion. The mouth, so far as I could see it under the heavy moustache, was fixed and rather cruel-looking, with peculiarly sharp white teeth: these protruded over the lips, whose remarkable ruddiness showed astonishing vitality in a man of his years. For the rest, his ears were pale and at the tops extremely pointed; the chin was broad and strong, and the cheeks firm though thin. The general effect was one of extraordinary pallor. (pp. 17–18)

Leonard Wolf has noted that this lengthy description samples Lombroso's account of the physiognomical attributes of the 'archetypical' criminal.[28] The Count, because he is a criminal type, is therefore beyond redemption. However, the novel's representation of a degenerate throwback is not without ambivalence. Daniel Pick in *Faces of Degeneration*, for example, has noted that many of the male vampire hunters, such as Godalming, Van Helsing, and Harker, are prone to hysterical fits which would, certainly for

Nordau, have marked them out as emotionally degenerate types.[29] Also, whilst Pick claims that *Dracula* 'at once sensationalised the horrors of degeneration and charted reassuringly the process of their confinement and containment', he also acknowledges that 'degeneration remained a problem in this text' (p. 174).

The central problem is indicated by the references to both Nordau and Lombroso. Nordau was more interested than Lombroso in claiming that deviation from prevailing gender scripts indicated degeneracy. In a discussion of the 'mental stigma of degenerates' he refers to the presence of an 'emotionalism' which prompts the male degenerate to 'laugh until he sheds tears' so that he 'weeps copiously without adequate occasion', because 'a commonplace line of poetry or of prose sends a shudder down his back'.[30] Nordau's caricature implies that under certain circumstances the middle-class male could become infected with a deviant effeminacy. Although Nordau stipulates that this relates to art, the idea was central to Edwin Lankester's claim that an adherence to a notion of 'civilisation' renders men weak. *Dracula* develops this anxiety by suggesting that the socially upwardly mobile Jonathan Harker (a lawyer) needs to become a man of action. *Dracula* thus suggests that an adherence to middle-class mores (implied in Harker's profession and in his desire for domestic security with his intended marriage to Mina) generates the grounds under which degeneration could occur even whilst, paradoxically, it appears as if it is those very social values which the Count threatens. This refers to one of the essential ironies of the novel: that in order to become more 'manly' the vampire hunters need to ape the attributes of the warlike Count because the Count possesses the type of manliness that they need to emulate in order to defeat him.

This is an irresolvable ambivalence in the novel. Its presence should be seen as the consequence of specific historical tensions in Britain at the *fin de siècle*, when many types of seemingly 'deviant' behaviour were read as indicating the signs of degeneracy.

An alternative way of reading this ambivalence is suggested by how the ghost story was approached at the start of this chapter. The ghost story during the period indicates how 'evil' was progressively internalised in the Gothic. In *Dracula* the idea that a threatened middle-class degeneracy can be overcome by aping the putative signs of criminal degeneracy (as they are mapped onto the Count), suggests the presence of a mode of doubling which Freud saw as a key element of the 'uncanny'. For Freud, uncanniness is typified by a return of the dead and the full title of Stoker's novel is *Dracula; or, The Dead Undead*. As in the uncanny, one anxiety is that the dead are not really dead but merely demonic, degenerate versions of ourselves.

The clearest representation of doubling exists between the Count and Van Helsing. The Count's foreignness aligns him with Van Helsing, and Van Helsing's descriptions of the Count imply that Dracula is, intellectually speaking, like an early version of himself. Van Helsing notes of the Count, 'He had a mighty brain, a learning beyond compare, and a heart that knew no fear and no remorse...there was no branch of knowledge of his time that he did not essay.' (p. 302). The first letter from Van Helsing indicates that it is from 'Abraham Van Helsing, M.D. D.Ph. D.Litt etc., etc...' (p. 112). Van Helsing, a doctor of medicine, philosophy, and the law, can be read as a highly professionalised version of the Count. In part this explains why Van Helsing is so concerned about the Count's potential to adapt to, and so control, their world: 'In some faculties of mind he has been, and is, only a child; but he is growing, and some things that were childish at the first are now of man's stature' (p. 302). This creeping into knowledge is the biggest threat which he poses. The covert doubling between the Count and Van Helsing softens the differences between the vampire hunters and the vampires. Even Van Helsing's first letter to Seward includes a reference to an implied vampirism when it mentions 'that time you suck from my wound so swiftly the poison of the gangrene' which he had acquired after an accident (p. 112). Blood sucking is thus not just the preserve of the vampire, and this is clear in the representation of Lucy Westenra's the blood transfusions, which will be discussed below.

So far this section has sketched a number of ways of reading the novel. By exploring *Dracula* in relation to theories of degeneration a specific historical narrative emerges, although one which leaves space for a psychoanalytical approach. Whilst *Dracula* generates many different critical readings it is noteworthy that purely psychoanalytical interpretations of it have been challenged by more robustly historicist critics who take issue with how such a Freudian approach develops ahistorical symbolic readings.

The blood transfusions interpreted in a Freudian approach appear to be little more than thinly coded expressions of the male vampire-hunters' desire for Lucy. It should be noted that Seward, Morris, and Holmwood have all proposed to Lucy. Also, in Harker's account of the three female vampires at Castle Dracula he says of the fair-haired vampire, 'I seemed to know her face and to know it in connection with some dreamy fear' (p. 37), which we can later see as a reference to Lucy and which implies his sexual feelings for her. The blood transfusions seem to take on an erotic quality because they refer to ownership of Lucy's body (and its fluids). The transfusions read in Freudian terms imply a symbolic relationship between blood and semen, in which the former appears as a disguised version of the latter. The vampire hunters (with the exception of Mina and Jonathan) give their blood to Lucy. Seward's account of his transfusion suggests feelings of sexual love: 'No man knows till he experiences it, what it is to feel his own life-blood drain away into the veins of the woman he loves' (p. 128). That the transfusions do not function as strictly medical procedures is suggested in Van Helsing's warning that Seward should conceal his blood transfusion from Holmwood because it would 'enjealous him' (p. 128). Seward complains that Van Helsing did not take as much blood from him as he had from Holmwood; Van Helsing replies that this is because Holmwood is 'her lover, her *fiancé*' (p. 128), implying that Holmwood has a privileged right of access to Lucy's body. Later, when Lucy seems to be dying, Quincey Morris, the American frontiersman, provides blood with Van Helsing acknowledging its potency: 'A brave man's blood, is the best thing on earth when a woman is in trouble. You're a man, and no mistake' (p. 149). The symbolic sexual relationships are reiterated at Lucy's funeral, when Seward comments on Holmwood's view that his blood transfusion 'made her truly his bride': to this Van Helsing replies, 'then what about the others?' (p. 176), and claims that this makes Lucy 'a polyandrist' and him a 'bigamist' (p. 176).

Such a reading forges connections between sex and blood. However, Robert Mighall and William Hughes have argued that vampirism does not have to be conceived of in solely sexual terms.

Hughes, for example, has noted that blood depletion and the expenditure of semen had a place within medical discourse at the time, which invites us to consider that the botched blood transfusions can be read in relation to various ailments pertaining to hysteria.[31] For Mighall, Freudian readings of the novel support the cliché that the Victorians were sexually repressed (only able to entertain sexual images in coded symbolic forms). Mighall notes that the sexological writings of Richard von Krafft-Ebing illustrate how images of vampirism were often used in medicalised contexts to reinforce representations of pathology.[32] Such a strategy therefore constitutes an attempt to contain 'abnormal' behaviour within recognisable images of otherness. In this view vampirism is not necessarily related to sexual repression. How to read blood is therefore not as straightforward as a Freudian approach suggests, or as Hughes puts it: 'Blood is an item of multidiscursive significance, a cultural concept as much as a literal physiological substance'.[33] However, by reading the novel with sensitivity to its multiple symbolism we come to another major theme: colonialism.

To read the novel for its colonial narrative requires, in part, a reassessment of the role of blood. Stephen D. Arata has noted how the vampire hunters' donation of blood to Lucy is sequenced in terms of class and national significance. Blood is donated in turn by Holmwood, Seward, Van Helsing, and Morris, which traces a hierarchy of aristocratic, bourgeois, European, and American blood that illustrates how central the revitalisation of a threatened Britishness is to the novel.

Theories of degeneracy suggested the potential for national decline, which had a specific resonance in Britain. However, whilst the Count represents an invasion of Britain, this also needs to be seen within the context of an ambivalent doubling that is covertly developed throughout. Arata has noted that the Count's imperial ambitions (in which he would turn the British into a race of subordinate vampires) reflects Britain's imperialistic endeavours. Arata states: 'In Count Dracula, Victorian readers could recognise their culture's imperial ideology mirrored back as a kind of monstrosity' (p. 129).[34] Thus the real blood-sucking parasites are the British, not the Count. The revitalisation of the nation, stimulated by the banishment, pursuit, and killing of the Count therefore serves to make visible the forms of violence that were inherent to British colonialism.

Dracula is a highly ambivalent novel, and such ambivalence needs to be understood within the context of *fin de siècle* Britain. The novel contains images of emasculation and imperial decline, but its solution to such issues merely compounds the problem because it turns the vampire hunters into degenerate, violent colonisers. The complexities of the novel have provoked a variety of critical approaches which testify to the extraordinary ambivalence with which the novel represents contemporary fears. Trying to critically locate the novel requires us to acknowledge that its contradictions are a consequence of *fin de siècle* hysteria, a hysteria which can be read in psychoanalytical and culturally informed ways in order to gain an insight into Stoker's eccentric summation of what it meant to be white, British, middle-class, and male at the end of the nineteenth century.

SUMMARY OF KEY POINTS

- 'Evil' becomes progressively internalised during the nineteenth century.
- Ghosts in Gothic writing often reflect social and economic anxieties.
- The Gothic landscape becomes increasingly an urban one.
- In Britain, the *fin de siècle* Gothic is influenced by theories of degeneration.
- A strand of American Gothic addresses issues of race and the history of slavery.

QUESTIONS AND POINTS FOR DISCUSSION

- How does the uncanny relate to representations of 'evil'?
- How is desire represented in Gothic fiction?
- What do ghost stories reveal about class anxieties?
- How do Gothic texts compare and contrast images of race and/or empire?

NOTES

1. Although Coleridge's *Christabel* provides a good example of how the 'other' completes already empty lives.
2. Sigmund Freud, 'The Uncanny' in *Art and Literature: Jensen's Gradiva, Leonardo Da Vinci and Other Works*, trans. James Strachey, ed. Albert Dickson, Penguin Freud Library, 14 (Harmondsworth: Penguin, 1985), p. 347. All subsequent references given in the text are to the edition.
3. Charles Dickens, *A Christmas Carol*, in *The Christmas Books*, vol. 1, ed. Michael Slater (Harmondsworth: Penguin, 1985), p. xxix.
4. J. H. Riddell, *The Uninhabited House*, in *Five Victorian Ghost Novels*, ed. E. F. Bleiler (New York: Dover, 1971), pp. 1–118, p. 31. All subsequent references in the text are to this edition.
5. See David Punter, *The Literature of Terror: A History of Gothic Fictions from 1765 to the Present Day* (London: Longman, [1980] 1996), vol. 2, pp. 201–2.
6. Henry James, *The Turn of the Screw*, in *The Turn of the Screw and The Aspern Papers* (Hertfordshire: Wordsworth, 1991), pp. 1–128, p. 5. All subsequent references in the text are to this edition.
7. Henry James, 'The Friends of the Friends', in *The Oxford Book of English Ghost Stories*, ed., Michael Cox and R. A. Gilbert (Oxford: Oxford University Press, [1986] 2002), pp. 150–71.
8. Sheridan Le Fanu, *Carmilla* in *The Penguin Book of Vampire Stories*, ed. Alan Ryan (Harmondsworth: Penguin, 1987) pp. 71–137, p. 74. All subsequent references in the text are to this edition.
9. Victor Sage, *Le Fanu's Gothic: The Rhetoric of Darkness* (Palgrave: Basingstoke, 2004), p. 178. All subsequent references in the text are to this edition.
10. For an excellent account of the historical development of such theories, see Daniel Pick, *Faces of Degeneration: A European Disorder, c.1848–c.1918* (Cambridge: Cambridge University Press, [1989] 1996).
11. Edwin Lankester, *Degeneration: A Chapter in Darwinism* (London: Macmillan, 1880).

12. For an account of how sexuality was 'policed' during the period, see Michel Foucault, *The History of Sexuality: An Introduction*, vol. 1, trans. Robert Hurley (Harmondsworth: Penguin, [1976] 1984).

13. Bram Dijkstra, *Idols of Perversity: Fantasies of Feminine Evil in Fin-de-Siècle Culture* (Oxford: Oxford University Press, 1986), p. 341.

14. Robert Louis Stevenson, *The Strange Case of Dr Jekyll and Mr Hyde* (1886), in *The Strange Case of Dr Jekyll and Mr Hyde and Other Stories*, ed. Jenni Calder (Harmondsworth: Penguin, 1984), p. 29. All subsequent references in the text are to this edition.

15. Elaine Showalter, *Sexual Anarchy: Gender and Culture at the Fin de Siècle* (Harmondsworth: Viking, 1990). See 'Dr. Jekyll's Closet', pp. 105–26.

16. Jerrold E. Hogle, 'Teaching the African American Gothic: from its multiple sources to *Linden Hills* and *Beloved*', in *Approaches to Teaching Gothic Fiction: The British and American Traditions*, ed. Diane Long Hoeveler and Tamar Heller (New York: Modern Languages Association of America, 2003), pp. 215–22, p. 216. Hogle also notes that such representations therefore have associations with uncanniness. For further discussion of race see Teresa A. Goddu, *Gothic America: Narrative, History, and Nation* (New York: Columbia University Press, 1999).

17. Charles Crow (ed.), *American Gothic: An Anthology, 1787–1916* (Blackwell: Oxford, 1999), p. 343. See also Crow's 'Under the upas tree: Charles Chesnutt's Gothic', in *Critical Essays on Charles Chesnutt*, ed. Joseph R. McElrath Jr (New York: G. K. Hall, 1999), pp. 261–70.

18. Charles W. Chestnutt, 'The Sheriff's Children', in *American Gothic*, ed. Crow, pp. 349–59, p. 350. All subsequent references in the text are to this edition.

19. Charles W. Chestnutt, 'Po' Sandy', in *American Gothic*, ed. Crow pp. 343–9, p. 348. All subsequent references in the text are to this edition.

20. George Washington Cable, 'Jean-Ah Poquelin', in *American Gothic*, ed. Crow, pp. 360–72, p. 360. All subsequent references

in the text are to this edition.
21. See Crow, *American Gothic*, p. 360.
22. It could also be argued that the story is about the construction of 'whiteness' in relation to 'Africanness'. At another level it dramatises issues about being white in the South or America at large. The liberal, sympathetic, character is, of course, named White. I am grateful to Charles Crow for raising these issues in our correspondence.
23. Kate Chopin, 'Désirée's Baby', in *American Gothic*, ed. Crow, pp. 339–42, p. 342.
24. I am grateful for advice on this from Charles Crow, who in correspondence outlined this theme of kinship which impacted on the lives of Frederick Douglass and Booker T. Washington (who both had white fathers that they never knew) and Charles W. Chesnutt (who did not know the identity of his two white grandfathers).
25. See Bram Stoker, *Dracula*, ed. John Paul Riquelme, *Case Studies in Contemporary Criticism* (Boston: Bedford/St. Martin's, 2002).
26. See Franco Moretti, *Signs Taken for Wonders* (London: Verso, 1983).
27. Bram Stoker, *Dracula* (Oxford: Oxford University Press, [1897] 1996), p. 47. All subsequent references in the text are to this edition.
28. Leonard Wolf, *Annotated Dracula* (London: N. Potter, 1975), p. 300.
29. Daniel Pick, *Faces of Degeneration: A European Disorder, c.1848–c.1918* (Cambridge: Cambridge University Press, [1989] 1996), p. 170.
30. Max Nordau, *Degeneration* cited in *The Fin de Siècle: A Reader in Cultural History c.1880–1900*, ed. Sally Ledger and Roger Luckhurst (Oxford: Oxford University Press, 2000), p. 16.
31. William Hughes, *Beyond Dracula: Bram Stoker's Fiction and its Cultural Context* (Basingstoke: Macmillan, 2000): see pp. 139–77.
32. Robert Mighall, *A Geography of Victorian Fiction: Mapping History's Nightmares* (Oxford: Oxford University Press, 1999): see pp. 210–47. Also see his 'Sex, History and the Vampire', in

Bram Stoker: History, Psychoanalysis, and the Gothic, ed. William Hughes and Andrew Smith (Basingstoke: Macmillan, 1998), pp. 62–77.

33. Hughes, *Beyond Dracula*, p. 139.
34. Stephen D. Arata, 'The Occidental Tourist: *Dracula* and the Anxiety of Reverse Colonization', *Victorian Studies*, 33 (1990), 621–45. Reprinted in *Dracula: A Casebook*, ed. Glennis Byron (Basingstoke: Macmillan, 1999), pp. 119–44, p. 129.

CHAPTER 4

Twentieth Century

THE GHOST STORY AS THE END OF GOTHIC?

It was argued in the previous chapter that the ghost stories of Dickens, Henry James, and J. H. Riddell illustrate how 'evil' was internalised in the Gothic. Their writings also address social and political considerations relating to money, class, and gender. How to gauge the political vision of the ghost story in the early part of the twentieth century appears to be more difficult. Much of the criticism on the form is coloured by a response to the writings of M. R. James, whose highly influential ghost stories were published in collected form between 1904 and 1931. James's writings bear an imprint on the ghost stories of E. F. Benson, his brother A. C. Benson, Edmund Gill Swain, A. N. L. Munby, and Richard Malden, who had contact with James at Cambridge University; many of them were present there when James read out his tales in his college rooms at Christmas. However, other writers in the period, such as Algernon Blackwood and May Sinclair, produced tales in a slightly different, less heavily stylised, key. This section explores some selected writings of M. R. James, Blackwood, E. F. Benson, and Sinclair. How some of these writers can be linked to modernism provides a closing context in which a reconsideration of the ghost story's apparent formalism can be re-evaluated.

The ghost story has posed a problem for scholars working on the Gothic. In its unsettling of the relationship between the living and the dead the ghost story ostensibly raises some radical, putatively metaphysical, questions about identity. However, the structure of the ghost story often appears less unsettling, as its conventionality and easy-going fireside ambience creates, at least in the late nineteenth and early twentieth centuries, a mood which is antithetical to grand metaphysical debate. David Punter in *The Literature of Terror* argues that during the early part of the twentieth century the ghost story entered 'a highly mannered phase'[1] which culminated in 'the shockingly bland tones of M. R. James' (p. 68). Indeed, for Punter, James's settings are often little more than 'Gothic stereotypes' (p. 89), and although his formulaic constructions might possess a certain Gothic style, they are fundamentally devoid of radical content: 'They *work* well, but they *mean* almost nothing' (p. 90, emphasis in original). For William Hughes, 'James's tales construct an almost idyllic late-Victorian and Edwardian world' consisting of the quiet 'College Combination Room, the library, or the cathedral close'.[2] Even the Gothic's fascination with extreme mental states is absent because, as Julia Briggs claims, in James's tales 'psychology is totally and defiantly excluded'.[3]

This version of James implies that his writings are dominated by a narrative mannerism which excludes any troubling Gothic elements, or political or cultural conflicts. This has led Clive Bloom to argue that James's tales refer to 'a world both slower and more stable' than the 'modernistic' period in which he was writing.[4] This issue of the retrospective nature of James's writing and how it relates to modernism will be returned to. However, the idea that James's tales represent stable worlds is difficult to reconcile with the prevalence of death, abduction, and demonic hauntings which so often characterise them. The past is a dangerous place in his tales, but, as we shall see, this is related to a response to modernism which relocates its apparent amorality within the seemingly urbane narratorial voices.

M. R. James was provost of King's College, Cambridge, and provost of Eton, a classical scholar and a medievalist historian. This academic background plays a crucial role in his tales, which so often revolve around scholarly discoveries which bring the past back to life. That this background informed his tales is clear from the title of his first collection of ghost stories, published in 1904, *Ghost*

Stories of an Antiquary, which was followed in 1911 with *More Ghost Stories of an Antiquary*. Three further collections were published, *A Thin Ghost and Others* (1919), *A Warning to the Curious* (1925), and *Wailing Well* (1928), before a collected edition was published in 1931.

James's tale 'The Mezzotint' (1904) describes how a group of Cambridge dons observe an unfolding narrative concerning the abduction of a baby from a country house, which is recounted on a mezzotint engraving being considered for purchase for their museum. Historical research reveals that the mezzotint was engraved by Arthur Francis and the tale illustrated by the mezzotint relates to an incident involving his family. The tale concerns how the ghost of a figure named Gawdy, who had been executed for killing one of Francis's gamekeepers, enacts his revenge by abducting and then murdering Francis's only child. This chilling narrative is at odds with how the dons respond to it. Theirs is a cosy, cloistered world which is only temporarily upset by this narrative. Their conversation revolves around middle-class sporting activities, and in one instance 'tea was taken to the accompaniment of a discussion which golfing persons can imagine for themselves'.[5] Later, over Sunday morning breakfast, 'Hardly a topic was left unchallenged, from golf to lawn-tennis' (p. 44). These comments illustrate the moral vacuity of the lives of the dons who unconsciously understand that their vacuity is, at a symbolic level, generating the horror which is manifested in the mezzotint: as one of them notes, 'it looks very much as if we were assisting at the working out of a tragedy somewhere' (p. 46). The tragedy is turned inwards because what is really tragic, so the tale implies, is their inability to empathise with the human drama staged by the mezzotint.

M. R. James is more complex than critics have allowed, and his tales can be read as a critique of blandness, rather than as an exercise in narrative form. He was to return to these issues in the later 'The Haunted Dolls' House' (1925).[6] In the tale a Mr Dillet purchases an antique dolls' house which is a mocked-up version of Horace Walpole's Gothic folly, Strawberry Hill. At one o'clock every morning it stages the murder of an old man, and his subsequent ghostly return and murder of two young children. Some research reveals that the dolls' house was made by James Merewether, who had murdered the old man (his father-in-law) because he intended to exclude the family from his will; the murdered children were Merewether's. Dillet suffers an emotional breakdown but such is the structure of the tale (in which the tale is heavily mediated through the narrator) that the reader is kept at a distance from Dillet's private drama, and this curiously places the reader as a passive voyeur of his despair and forces the reader to occupy the same amoral position as the dons in 'The Mezzotint'.

Both tales implicitly address a horror of an emerging amorality which, as we shall see, can be linked to a somewhat conservative view of modernism. However, M. R. James's ghosts are fundamentally malign figures and are thus different from the ghosts of Dickens and Riddell. The earlier ghosts made various social and economic issues visible, whereas these later ghosts suggest a metaphysical horror about the dangers inherent to existence, especially an existence characterised by moral emptiness. The idea that the world is fundamentally malign is also apparent in the writings of Algernon Blackwood, who was interested in various mystical beliefs which were pantheistic in origin, although the Gods which inhabited his version of nature were rarely benign. He wrote many novels and tales, not all of which concerned the supernatural, with the most important collections of ghost stories being *The Empty House* (1906), *The Listener* (1907), and *John Silence, Physician Extraordinary* (1908), which recounts the findings on occult phenomena of his eponymous scientific investigator, a figure somewhat in the mould of Le Fanu's psychic detective, Dr Hesselius.[7]

In 'The Willows' (1907) the narrator describes how a canoe journey undertaken with a fellow adventurer down the Danube results in their becoming trapped on an island which is in danger of being swamped by the rising water level of the river. Whilst on this island they sense that they are being watched and then their equipment interfered with by strange malign beings whose existence they can intuit but not see. The tale is unconventional in that it suggests that the world is 'ghosted' by other creatures. The narrator and his companion sense that the creatures mean to sacrifice them and they are only spared because they find another person to kill in their stead. Blackwood implies a world which bears some similarity to contemporary spiritualist concerns (which were very popular during the period) about the proximity of another plane, but here not so much an astral one, as a place inhabited by other creatures who claim their territorial rights. The narrator notes:

> we ought by rights to have held some special kind of passport to admit us [. . .] we had, somewhat audaciously, come without asking leave into a separate little kingdom of wonder and magic – a kingdom that was reserved for the use of others who had a right to it, with everywhere unwritten warnings to trespassers for those who had the imagination to discover them.[8]

This feeling of dispossession implies a form of disempowerment – a theme which Blackwood returned to in 'The Wendigo' (1910), in which a primeval spirit selects its victims when they enter its territory.[9] Like 'The Willows' it concerns an expedition which is threatened by this malign presence. The abduction of one of the party and his subsequent return to them, when he has been physically damaged and emotionally traumatised, is caused by their invasion into this primeval world. Blackwood was particularly interested in the projected presence of territorially minded mysterious beings. A more conventional ghost story, 'The Empty House' (1906), relates how Shorthouse accompanies his Aunt Julia on a visit to a notoriously haunted house. The tale emphasises that the two have trespassed into a world which does not belong to them. Like the characters in 'The Willows' they find themselves potentially trapped by their surroundings, in which 'the influences against them, whatever these might be, were slowly robbing them of self-confidence, and the power of decisive action'.[10] The tale emphasises that Shorthouse needs to control his fears (and those of his aunt):

> Instinctively, by a sort of sub-conscious preparation, he kept himself and his forces well in hand the whole evening, compelling an accumulative reserve of control by that nameless inward process of gradually putting all the emotions away and turning the key upon them [. . .] Later it stood him in good stead. (p. 279)

In these tales a form of manliness (familiar to some degree from *Dracula*) is tested by encounters with apparently arbitrarily malign forces. How to preserve your sanity in these moments is the primary concern, a task mainly achieved by not drawing attention to yourself. This issue of malign spirits is given an unusual twist in the work of E. F. Benson.

Benson, although one of M. R. James's auditors at Cambridge, developed a quite different model of the ghost story. Benson often used explicit imagery which referred to spiritualism (which is not to say that he was therefore a 'believer'). Spiritualism was a popular movement in Britain (and America) in the late nineteenth and early twentieth centuries, one that took on a particular significance during and immediately after the First World War. Writers including Kipling (whose son was killed in the war) and Conan Doyle (who lost a son and a brother in the war) were drawn towards the spiritualist movement (although Conan Doyle's tale 'The Parasite', 1894, suggests a scepticism about mediums). Benson's writings, like Blackwood's, focus on whether the world is ghosted by a spiritual domain; however, Benson is often satirical about spiritualism and his tales frequently have a tongue-in-cheek quality to them. 'Mr. Tilly's Séance' (1922) concerns how Mr Tilly, whilst on his way to a séance, is run over and killed by a traction engine and how 'he perceived his own crushed remains, flat as a biscuit, lying on the roadway'.[11] Tilly's spirit then proceeds to the séance presided over by the medium Mrs Cumberbatch in her 'chair which had once belonged to Madame Blavatsky' (p. 164), a famous medium and co-founder of the Theosophical Society. Tilly notes that Mrs Cumberbatch uses phosphorous sticks and the conjuring of strange noises to beguile her clients into believing that she is conversing with spirits. However, she is a genuine medium and brings Tilly into the séance and manipulates his presence to satisfy the expectations of her clients. Tilly, appalled by the highly stylised conventions of the séance, never returns. The tale mocks spiritualism but affirms the presence of spirits; it also debunks a medium who is genuine although she has no spirits to commune with.

The jocular tone of the story is a feature of an earlier tale, 'How Fear Departed from the Long Gallery' (1911), which opens with the lines 'Church-Peveril is a house so beset and frequented by spectres, both visible and audible, that none of the family which it shelters under its acre and a half of green copper roofs takes psychical phenomena with any seriousness'.[12] The family in question, the Peverils, have many ancestral, eccentric, but harmless ghosts. However, the tale becomes increasingly sinister, recounting the presence of ghosts of twin babies murdered in 1602. They rarely appear and only in the Long Gallery, and bring death to any who see them, but only if they inspire negative emotions such as fear (or, in one instance, derision). This changes when a house guest, Madge Dalrymple, encounters the ghosts and feels compassion for them and is saved by the redemptive power of positive emotions. Benson's ghosts may not appear to be malign, and a comment in 'Caterpillars' (1912) could stand as a synopsis of the form as influenced by James: 'Most ghosts, when all is said and done, do not much harm; they may perhaps terrify, but the person whom they visit usually gets over their visitation'.[13] However, the tales after the First World War are often much darker than those that preceded it (Benson had an interest in the war, writing *The Outbreak of War, 1914*, 1933, and *The Kaiser and English Relations*, 1935). 'The Face' (1924) recounts how Hester Ward's domestic idyll is destroyed when she is carried off by the ghost of the villainous Sir Roger Wyburn.[14] Hester has dreamt about this abduction from an early age and when it occurs there is no logical explanation for it. There is simply the inexplicable return of the past (one which does not belong to Hester), and Sir Roger's motivation is unclear. The arbitrariness of Hester's selection is the principal chilling aspect of the tale which unconsciously glosses what was for many the inexplicable killings in the war. Benson reworks elements from the pre-war 'The Room in The Tower' (1912), in which the narrator also has a prophetic dream concerning a family where the mother dies and pursues him, again for arbitrary reasons.[15] The ghost might be terrifying (if it is a ghost: there are suggestions that it may be a vampire), but the narrator, unlike Hester, escapes in the end. Inexplicable acts and arbitrary punishments represent a new and not always developed trend in Benson's post-war writing, which is characterised by a perception that the modern world is inherently impersonal (a feature to be found in M. R. James). As the narrator notes in 'Expiation' (1923), on hearing the explanation of a ghost story told by a vicar: 'his communication was very impersonal. It was just a narrating voice, without identity, an anonymous chronicle'.[16] It is this impersonality, or emptiness, which suggests links to modernism.

There was a relationship between modernism and the Gothic. T. S. Eliot, for example, in *The Waste Land* (1922) makes a specific reference to *Dracula* (1897):

> A woman drew her long black hair out tight
> And fiddled whisper music on those strings
> And bats with baby faces in the violet light
> Whistled, and beat their wings
> And crawled head downward down a blackened wall
> And upside down in air were towers
> Tolling reminiscent bells, that kept the hours
> And voices singing out of empty cisterns and exhausted
>   wells.[17]

The lines refer to Jonathan Harker's sight of the Count crawling head first down one of the towers at Castle Dracula. They also refer to the insistent presence of images of maternalism in the novel, although here such imagery is pathologised in its association with vampirism. Eliot's use of the Victorian Gothic within his account of modern decay suggests the continuing significance of the apparently 'low' Gothic form within the 'high' modernist text, in which the Gothic provides a model of instability (both social and psychological) that illustrates an aspect of the fragmented modernist self.[18] James Joyce in *Ulysses* (1922) makes a more jocular reference to *Dracula*, writing, 'He comes pale vampire, through storm his eyes, his bat sails bloodying the sea, mouth to her mouth's kiss. Here. Put a pin in that chap, will you?'[19]

The demands which such modernist texts place upon the reader require them to undertake a complex semiotic journey through revitalised mythologies that dwell on the emptiness (consider Eliot's 'The Hollow Men', 1925) and moral confusion of modern life. The Gothic is resurrected in modernist texts in a way which bears some similarity with James's use of the Gothic in 'The Haunted Dolls' House'. There James uses a Gothic drama to address contemporary concerns about amorality and modern waste lands *and* places a special demand on the reader in suggesting their complicit voyeurism. As in modernism, the Gothic provides a focus for a debate about the loss of value (moral and social), a debate which has its roots in the discussions about golf in 'The Mezzotint' and which culminates in the voyeurism of 'The Haunted Dolls' House'. James's alleged 'blandness' is thus misleading; he is not bringing the Gothic to an end by containing its subversive or transgressive energies through his self-conscious narrative formalism, but rather using the Gothic as the counterpoint against which a modern (bland) amorality appeared to be developing.

An alternative response to modernism can be found in the ghost stories of May Sinclair. Sinclair was a short-story writer and novelist as well as the author of a biographical study of the Brontës; indeed her tale 'The Intercessor' (1911) reworks aspects of *Wuthering Heights* with, as David Seed has noted, elements of the ghost story derived from Henry James.[20] Sinclair, like Henry James, was a member of the Society for Psychical Research, and this influences her tales, which take such matters more seriously than E. F. Benson did. Her important contribution to the ghost story can be found in, although it is not confined to, the collection *Uncanny Stories* (1923).[21] David Seed and David Glover have both discussed Sinclair's tales in a modernist context, arguing that her interest in psychical or non-material experience implies an allegiance to a modernist sensibility which sees in the world not the amoral emptiness that characterises M. R. James, but the hidden complexities which lie within experience.[22] This is clear in 'Finding the Absolute', which centres on an after-death encounter between Spaulding, a metaphysical philosopher who has spent his life dedicated to the pursuit of absolute truth, and Immanuel Kant.[23] It is set in heaven, where Kant shows Spaulding how past, present, and future become endlessly recycled and so constitute the kind of absolute experience that Spaulding has been searching for. However, the tale is ambivalent about this because heaven, in this eternal repetition of time, suggests that they are trapped in a type of hell in which no new experience can be generated.

This type of spiritual investigation also accords with the quasi-scientific discourse employed in reports submitted to the Society for Psychical Research, and this is suggested in the title of another tale from *Uncanny Stories*, 'The Nature of the Evidence'. The tale revolves around Edward Marston's inability to consummate his second marriage with Pauline because of the intervention of the ghost of Rosamund, his much-loved first wife. The focus is on how Marston, who is attracted by the superficial charms of the vampish Pauline, can rejoin Rosamund in sexual congress. Pauline's sexual physicality, 'her gross flesh and blood', is contrasted with Rosamund, 'the heavenly discarnate thing'.[24] Marston explains that Pauline's idea of passion does not compare with the passion that he enjoys with the ghost of Rosamund, which the narrator of the tale sees as 'some terrible and exquisite contact. More penetrating than sight or touch. More – more extensive: passion at all points' (p. 234). This passionate meeting of souls suggests a distrust of the body, an issue central to Sinclair's tale 'The Villa Désirée' (1926).

Diana Wallace sees this tale as a version of the Female Gothic because it examines 'the otherness of male sexuality'.[25] The story recounts the anxieties experienced on her honeymoon by Mildred Eve, who is waiting for her new husband, the sinister Louis Carson, to join her in France. She discovers the room she is to sleep in was occupied by Carson's previous wife, who had died there alone after suffering a seizure. On her first night Mildred receives a spectral visitation from a figure who resembles Carson and which struggles into being. She notes how this form:

> stood a little in front of her by the bedside. From the breasts downwards its body was unfinished, rudimentary, not quite born. The grey shell was still pregnant with its loathsome shapelessness. But the face – the face was perfect in absolute horror. And it was Louis Carson's face.[26]

This figure seems to presage a sexual assault in which this growing being can, as Wallace claims, be read as a hardening phallic presence, which suggests a horror about the threatened violence of male sexuality (one in which Carson's earlier wife's encounter with it meant that she had died of fright).[27] For Wallace the tale 'is a brilliantly economical Modernist version of the Bluebeard tale'.[28] It suggests a horror of physicality that was suggested in 'The Nature of the Evidence' and addresses similar issues touched on by Benson in 'The Face'.

How to read these tales requires us to be sensitive to the complexities of the period and to how writers responded to the intellectual trends associated with modernism. The modernist cry for innovation subtly influenced the development of the ghost story. The new technical innovations of radio and film in the period were also to provide opportunities for the development of the Gothic.

RADIO AND FILM

Throughout the book we have noted in passing how the Gothic's resilience is indicated by the many different narrative modes that it comes to inhabit: the novel, novella, drama, poetry, and the short story. The twentieth century's new media, film, radio, and television, became vehicles for the continuing presence of the Gothic.

Richard J. Hand in *Terror on the Air! Horror Radio in America, 1931–1952* explores the popularity of horror on the radio, which provided the major domestic output for horror in the pre-television age.[29] In America long-running radio series such as *The Witch's Tale* (1931–8), *Lights Out* (1934–47), *The Hermit's Cave* (1940–3), *Inner Sanctum Mysteries* (1941–52), *Suspense* (1942–62), *The Mysterious Traveler* (1943–52), *The Black Castle* (1943–4), *Stay Tuned for Terror* (1944–5), and *Quiet Please* (1947–8) were followed by large audiences. The broadcasts were usually live, which allowed the scriptwriters considerable freedom in the choice of subject matter (as scripts were not, in the early period, routinely submitted for studio vetting, although they were mindful not to address issues that might antagonise likely sponsors).[30] Ultimately, in the late 1940s, this aural golden age of radio horror came to an end with the increasingly censorial interference of the National Association of Broadcasters and by the emergence of television. Each of these series had its own approach and style and addressed the issues of the time, from the period of economic depression to providing support for the war effort (an episode of *Lights Out* from 8 December 1942 – a year and a day after the Japanese had bombed Pearl Harbor – concludes with 'The smirking little Jap is standing at the door. He's there for you [. . .] It can happen you know. Three million dead in Europe attest to that fact').[31] In Britain the BBC ran several tales by ghost-story writers but, unlike in North America, was not so focused on producing series – the principal contribution in this respect being its *Appointment with Fear* (1943–55), whose narrator, the 'Man in Black' (Valentine Dyall), became something of a celebrity at the time.[32]

In terms of film it is significant that German expressionist films such as *The Cabinet of Dr Caligari* (dir. Robert Wiene, 1919), *The Golem* (dir. Paul Wegener, 1920), and *Nosferatu* (dir. F. W. Murnau, 1922) employ striking modernist imagery. The American horror film of the 1930s (and it is important to note that there were many silent horror films made in America in the 1920s and earlier) might seem to be far removed from such artistic concerns, and indeed the form itself might appear to have little in common with radio. However, many of the directors and technical staff on these early German expressionist films later worked in America and helped shape an emerging quasi-modernist horror aesthetic in the 1930s and beyond. Karl Freund, for example, who was the cinematographer on *The Golem* and Fritz Lang's dystopian *Metropolis* (1926), later worked in America as the cinematographer on Tod Browning's *Dracula* (1931) and Robert Florey's *Murders in the Rue Morgue* (1932).[33] Also, many of the lead actors in 1930s American horror films, such as Boris Karloff for example, also appeared in horror radio dramas.[34]

The development of non-text-based horror cannot be comprehensively covered in depth here, but this section will outline how such a form developed and discuss some, admittedly selective, landmark films. A selection of important critical texts is listed in the Guide to Further Reading.

The previous chapter concluded with an account of *Dracula*, and a good example of how the Gothic mutates from text, to play, to film, can be given in the case of adaptations of Stoker's novel. David J. Skal in *Hollywood Gothic: The Tangled Web of Dracula from Novel to Stage to Screen* explores the dramatic transformations of Stoker's novel which were first outlined in Harry Ludlam's 1962 biography of Stoker.[35] The story is a convoluted one concerning the relationship between various competing stage adaptations of the novel and

the attendant legal complexities involved in paying certain interested parties when the play was adapted for film by Universal in
1931. It is easy to get distracted by this complex tale of infighting
and belligerence revolving around some colourful characters (as
evidenced, for example, by Florence Stoker's bitter legal wrangles
with the makers and distributors of *Nosferatu* over the rights to her
husband's novel). Leaving aside such issues, it is important to
examine what these narrative transformations signified. The theatrical version developed by Hamilton Deane, which was popular
in Britain in the 1920s, was a somewhat light-hearted reprise of
Stoker's novel in which national differences were often comically
rendered. This is not to say that the Gothic possibilities of the novel
were overlooked (occasionally members of the audience fainted at
the more dramatic moments), but to acknowledge that the play did
not, and could not, represent the *fin de siècle* cultural anxieties of the
novel. Indeed, the stage production often had women playing additional, empowered roles (sometimes, for example, an actress would
play the role of a now female Dr Seward) that are not in keeping
with Stoker's reactionary attitudes towards the women's movement, but which indicate an accommodation of changing social
mores.[36] The film, however, contextually considered bears a striking resemblance to the novel. Skal in *The Monster Show: A Cultural
History of Horror* discusses 1931 as a crisis year for America because
it was the year in which the impact of the economic depression was
being profoundly felt for the first time. Whilst Stoker's novel represents a *fin de siècle* crisis, 1931–2 witnessed the production of five
seminal horror films which in different ways captured the contemporary mood of social and economic crisis in America: *Dracula*,
Frankenstein, *Dr Jekyll and Mr Hyde*, *The Mummy*, and Tod
Browning's film about circus sideshow 'freaks', *Freaks*. As Skal
notes, 'America's worst year of the century would be its best year
ever for monsters'.[37] *Dr Jekyll and Mr Hyde* and *Freaks* represent
an anxiety about economic and political instability in psychological
and physical terms. The creature in *Frankenstein* (famously played
by Boris Karloff) was dressed as a figure in shabby workmen's
clothes, which for Skal turned him into 'a poignant symbol for an
army of abject and abandoned labourers', whilst Dracula becomes
(as in Moretti's reading of the novel) 'a sanguinary capitalist [who]

relocates from Transylvania after draining the local peasants' (p. 159). This is not to say that such cultural nuances were observable to most reviewers at the time. As in the early reception of the Gothic there was some concern about the moral standing of such tales, with the *Los Angeles Times* reporter referring to *Dracula* as 'too extreme' and 'a freak picture', although other responses were more measured.[38]

Universal's domination of horror in the 1930s was later echoed in the Hammer cycle of horror films in the 1950s, 1960s, and 1970s, although there was a horror tradition (although not a specifically defined horror genre) in both American and British films in the 1920s and earlier. Hammer produced versions of the classic narratives of *Dracula*, *Frankenstein*, and *The Mummy* (which had been made in 1932 for Universal), and sequels to and variations on them, as well as adaptations of other texts – the final horror film being a version of Dennis Wheatley's *To the Devil a Daughter* in 1975.[39] These films were increasingly subject to formal censorship because of concerns that they contravened public taste. What is noteworthy is that the horror film after the Second World War was subject to a critical outrage that far exceeded that meted out to the Universal films of the 1930s. Derek Hill, for example, writing in the *Tribune* on Hammer's *The Revenge of Frankenstein* (1958), lamented that the censor had not cut a scene which seemed to echo films of the Nazi death camps which had so shocked post-war audiences: 'Now, only thirteen years after Belsen, Hammer feel they need a close-up of a charred, smouldering foot fallen from a human body pushed into a furnace'.[40] This view was elaborated by Peter Dyer, who, writing of Hammer films in *Films and Filming* in 1960, despaired that 'Not so long ago the world was terribly, profoundly shocked by the first newsreel pictures to come from Nazi prison camps . . . Now we can sit [. . .] and gloat at the same kind of thing'.[41] A new language of moral revulsion appeared in the media after the Second World War and influenced what was deemed acceptable in the 1950s and 1960s, before Hammer's introduction of soft pornography in the 1970s as public appetites changed.[42] How this film tradition subsequently developed is exemplified by some of the landmark films which followed, including *Rosemary's Baby* (dir. Roman Polanski, 1968), *The Exorcist* (dir. William Friedkin, 1973), and a more Anglo-American production, *Bram Stoker's Dracula* (dir. Francis Ford Coppola, 1992).

Before making *Rosemary's Baby*, Polanski had directed a film made in Britain, *Repulsion* (1965), which explored how the sexual hysteria of the central character, Carol (played by Catherine Deneuve), was, at least in part, generated as a response to a routinised, or day-to-day, sexual objectification. She is subject to seemingly casual sexual (and sexist) overtures from workmen in the street and the landlord of the London flat where she is staying.[43] Her anxieties escalate, leading her to commit several murders. The atmosphere of claustrophobia in *Repulsion* (where much of the action takes place in Carol's flat) is repeated in *Rosemary's Baby*, which is set in a New York tenement building and centres on a young couple (Rosemary and Guy Woodhouse, played by Mia Farrow and John Cassavetes) attempting to set up home and conceive their first child. The film is based on, and very closely follows, Ira Levin's novel, published in 1967, of the same name. The film subtly shows how Rosemary's growing anxiety is not the consequence of paranoia, as her husband and the eccentric neighbours suggest, but because her neighbours are Satanists who offer Guy the opportunity of advancing his acting career in exchange for Rosemary carrying the devil's child. Rosemary is drugged and raped by the devil, and the final scenes focus on her appalled growing awareness of this fact. However, at the end, as she nervously approaches the child's crib, she takes the baby as her own, which represents a triumph of maternal instinct over moral revulsion.[44] The film is noteworthy for many reasons. First, its incorporation of the supernatural within the apparently everyday suggests that anxiety is the only legitimate response to a world that has become demonic, a reaction which is especially relevant given anxieties at home during the war in Vietnam. This might seem to be stretching the context, but it is notable that public concerns about political mismanagement and moral legitimacy were central characteristics of debates about the war. This is not to say that the film should be read as a simple cipher for these specific concerns, but rather that it can be seen within a context in which a general mood of opposition was paralleled by feelings of disempowerment. Rosemary's optimism about the future, for example, is betrayed by those she feels closest to, as she comes to inhabit a world in which the usual moral verities are inverted – indeed one in which people have sold their souls in the interests of self-advancement. Such moral bankruptcy is suggested in how the film (like the ending of Lewis's *The Monk* some 172 years earlier) inverts Christianity in having a woman chosen to carry a child by a non-godly presence in order to make the world a worse place (also like *The Monk*, the film was subject to some specific religious criticism, when it was condemned by the National Catholic Office for Motion Pictures, which made attendance at the film a venial sin for Catholics).[45] The film's themes of disempowerment and reproduction are also to be found in Levin's novels *The Stepford Wives* (1972, filmed in 1975 and again in 2004) and *The Boys from Brazil* (1976, filmed in 1978) which, like *Frankenstein*, explore synthetic constructions of the self and forms of reproduction. In *Rosemary's Baby* the idea that the devil's son inhabits New York makes a powerful, if subtly expressed, case for the presence of corruption within the heartland of America's power base. This is a view given particular emphasis in *The Exorcist*.

The Exorcist (based on William Peter Blatty's 1971 novel) exploits a series of oppositions, between ancient and modern, Orient and Occident, and physical and spiritual, which are familiar to the Gothic, and suggests a self-conscious knowingness which has often been overlooked. Indeed the film purposively sets out to compromise notions of good and evil by raising awkward political questions concerning all kinds of colonial activities.[46]

In the beginning of the film we witness Father Merrin (played by Max Von Sydow) on an archaeological dig in northern Iraq. The film suggests that the evil he discovers there has been unleashed by his interference which effects a subtle reverse colonialism (a theme familiar from *Dracula*) as these evil forces are played out in modern-day America. The film was released in 1973 and makes reference to Vietnam and so America's own colonialist project through the film being made by the mother (Ellen Burstyn) of twelve-year-old Regan (Linda Blair). The film, called *Crash Course*, dramatises the presence of student unrest at a time when anti-Vietnam protests were widespread on American campuses. Such is the archness of *The Exorcist* that it even dismisses the possibility that Hollywood could ever make a serious film about this unrest, with Regan's mother describing it as a 'Walt Disney version of the Hoh Chi Minh story'. That this idea of colonisation (invasion, possession) and its failings is central to the film is also clear from Regan's comments to the astronaut (the film coincides with America's burgeoning space programme) who attends one of her mother's parties: 'You're going to die up there'.[47]

The revenge of the past is also apparent through the relationship of Father Karras (the younger, Italian-American exorcist, played by Jason Miller) with his mother and his faith. Karras is a boxer as well as a priest, and this bringing together of physical and spiritual worlds barely conceals an emotional disintegration occasioned by his mother's death. The apparent return of his mother through the possessed Regan unsettles even further an already troubled religious belief. The loss of Karras's mother precipitates the kind of unconscious questing which, as we have seen earlier, is familiar to the Gothic. This emphasis on the significance of motherhood (an obvious theme in *Rosemary's Baby*) is also focused through Regan's mother and is further underlined by the emblematically named Dr Klein, who initially treats Regan.[48] Indeed the idea of the absent parent is further developed in the scene where Regan's mother rows with her estranged husband (Regan's father) concerning his non-appearance on Regan's birthday.

The film develops a series of conflicts, both political and personal, which are inflicted on Regan, who in her possessed state contains within her many of the voices that in particular had so disturbed Karras's faith. Regan is thus possessed by a range of anxieties that she inherits from others. The sense of political crisis, domestic crisis (absent fathers and mothers), and spiritual crisis is all developed through Regan, who is possessed by these forces in what becomes a powerfully expressed, although displaced, comment on the failings of modern America. The ambitions of the film are thus clear as it erases the oppositions which it labours to construct in the early part of the film in order to bring together a series of apparently unrelated worlds: northern Iraq, America, Catholicism, and film production itself.

Rosemary's Baby and *The Exorcist* can both be closely related to the era which produced them. Francis Ford Coppola's version of

Dracula, entitled *Bram Stoker's Dracula*, represents a return to a 'classic' Gothic narrative which, despite its title, takes considerable liberties with Stoker's novel. The film received mixed reviews in the press because it seemed to defy narrative expectations relating to film versions of *Dracula* in general and ideas about horror in particular.[49] How to read the film is one of the interesting things about it. First, the film positions itself as a love story rather than as Gothic horror. The film's tagline of 'Love never dies' implies this, whilst simultaneously making the intriguing suggestion that love, with its pains and threatened withdrawal, functions as a curse which imbues 'love' with a Gothic ambience of thwarted longing. The lovelorn Count (played by Gary Oldman) is a tragic figure whose ambivalences (he is both melodramatic *and* decadent) position 'love' as a form of psychic disturbance. Fred Botting has noted that the film's construction of the Count as a victim represents a 'caring 1990s' reworking of vampirism which views the 'other' not as evil but as one in need of 'love, tolerance and understanding'.[50] For this reason Botting in the concluding paragraph of *Gothic* makes the claim that 'With Coppola's *Dracula* [. . .] Gothic dies, divested of its excesses, of its transgressions, horrors and diabolical laughter' (p. 180). However, the trajectory of Dracula from vampiric monster to fixated lover is similar in kind to the differences between both book and film versions of Thomas Harris's *The Silence of the Lambs* (1988, filmed 1991) and *Hannibal* (1999, filmed 2001). 'Love', its commitments, pleasures, and conflation of self with other becomes strangely reconstituted as the new Gothic presence which lurks beneath any self-conscious postmodernist intertextual play, and provides a latter-day reconfiguration of an Enlightenment scepticism of the emotions (in which 'love' and 'madness' are in danger of becoming synonymous). In this regard Botting's final claim in *Gothic* that the death of the Gothic evidenced by Coppola's film 'might just be the prelude to other spectral returns' (p. 180) can be read as an unconscious acceptance that perhaps the Gothic represented by Coppola's film indicates not the end of Gothic but rather its mutation. The monstrous Gothic body (the vampire, werewolf, mummy, zombie, and the possessed teenager) becomes replaced by a horror of emotion which, in a postmodern age, struggles to accommodate the authentic except in models of trauma which are represented by overly familiar textual props. To that degree the film is not so much about tolerating the 'other' as revealing a tacit self-loathing. Indeed, it would appear that each age gets the vampire that it deserves.

The post-war Gothic in literature provides an example of how later writers engaged with, and critically reworked, an earlier tradition, and this is the subject of the following section on post- Second World War literature from America and Britain.

CONTEMPORARY FICTION: POSTMODERN GOTHIC?

In the twentieth century the term 'Gothic' tends to become replaced with 'Horror', at least where popular literature is concerned. In part such a change in nomenclature is a recognition that the various associations that 'Gothic' has with formulaic plots involving aristocratic villains amid ruined castles, set within sublime landscapes, are not the stock-in-trade of writers such as Stephen King, James Herbert, John Saul, Dean Koontz, or Shaun Hutson, amongst many others.

The post-war boom in mass-produced pulp fiction (so called because of the poor quality of paper on which they were printed in the 1940s, 1950s, and 1960s) is not confined to horror. The post-war era was also characterised in both text- and non-text-based media by other popular modes, most notably science fiction and detective fiction.

The popularity of these novels should not detract from the fact that, in keeping with the Gothic tradition, they still address cultural anxieties. In America the Southern Gothic of the 1940s and 1950s, of writers such as Carson McCullers and Flannery O'Connor, reworks themes about region, murder, and insanity which arguably have their roots in the Gothic of Edgar Allan Poe.[51] In addition, Stephen King's novels repeatedly dwell on social problems generated within small American towns where the social limitations of such an environment become emblematic of wider issues relating to social and moral obligations. His novel *Carrie* (1974), for example, concerns the failure of family, peers, and schools to protect the vulnerable, and consequently it takes some delight in destroying much of the small town where it is set.[52] A figure of comparable standing in Britain is James Herbert, and his novel *The Rats* (1974) can, at one level, be read as a tale about inner city decay.[53] Such a popular form is not without examples of intellectual complexity. Clive Barker's work, for example, takes its place within a horror tradition but also explores a set of complex postmodern ideas about the nature of representation. His collection of tales, *Books of Blood*, includes 'Son of Celluloid' (1988), which centres on an escaped prisoner, Barberio, who is suffering from cancer. He is mortally wounded in a shoot-out with the police, and hides in a cinema behind the screen, where he dies of his wounds; however, the cancer takes on a life of its own as it searches for new victims, and does so by taking on the form of various film stars such as John Wayne, Marilyn Monroe, Peter Lorre, and Greta Garbo (thus suggesting that an apparently pristine Hollywood golden age was not as pure as it seemed).[54] Barker's novel *Weaveworld* (1988) also, as the title implies, looks at how worlds are artistically constructed through the bringing together of various forms of representation.[55]

Barker's writings mentioned here can be regarded as exercises in postmodernism. Whilst modernism focused on the fragmented nature of subjectivity (and so exploited the Gothic fascination with fractured selves), postmodernism represents a scepticism about the grand narratives (such as religion, for example) which once provided social and moral norms. In a contemporary, postmodern age one can no longer believe in coherent, universal, claims to truth which, so the argument goes, are replaced by moral relativism. Such a world is defined by the absence of absolute meaning, and in literature this becomes manifested through stylistic play in which narrative forms are run together to create synthetic worlds which foreground issues about representation above any moral or metaphysical concerns. In other words, postmodernism seems to be peculiarly suited to the Gothic because it questions the notion that one inhabits a coherent or otherwise abstractly rational world. As we shall see, some authors who have written in the Gothic mode and appear to incorporate elements of the postmodern, such as Angela Carter and Toni Morrison, are in fact sceptical about postmodernism or certain aspects of it. Carter and Morrison are not 'horror' writers in the way that King and Herbert are. Their self-conscious literary qualities distance them from such writers, even though their texts discussed here do refer back to an earlier Gothic tradition. To what extent there exists a postmodern Gothic is the issue addressed in this section. One writer whose work has been described as a forerunner to postmodernism, Shirley Jackson, helps us to see how the issues of the older Gothic are reworked within new models of 'horror' that appear to anticipate the postmodern.

Jackson's *The Haunting of Hill House* (1959) reworks Gothic tropes which are familiar from the Female Gothic. The tale is focalised by the 32-year-old Eleanor Vance, whose mother has recently died. Eleanor had nursed her mother for eleven years and her death provokes feelings of guilt over her new-found freedoms. Eleanor, as a child, had been involved in some seemingly paranormal experience when the family house was showered by stones. Dr Montague, a paranormal investigator, contacts Eleanor in an attempt to form a team of psychically sensitive individuals to take to Hill House, a renowned haunted house, in order to examine if their psychically receptive natures would help him to explore any supernatural experiences that they might encounter there. Eleanor agrees to participate in this experiment, which initially revolves around her, Dr Montague, Theodora (for whom Eleanor has implied sexual feelings), and Luke (who stands to inherit the house). This theme of the absent mother is given a twist by Jackson as she uses it to address the tensions between Eleanor's feelings of loss and her sense that such loss will enable her to forge a new identity. This becomes clear in Eleanor's initial feelings that Hill House can help her to develop an independent identity (that is, an identity that is independent of her mother's influence). She notes at one point, 'what a complete and separate thing I am, [. . .] going from my red toes to the top of my head, individually an I, possessed of attributes belonging only to me'.[56] However, this emerging sense of self is compromised by the ghostly activities within the house, which are either due to the presence of a malevolent entity or are a projection of Eleanor's highly ambivalent feelings of belonging (ones which depend on the guilty rejection of her mother).

The ghost in the house, at one level, implies the lingering presence of Eleanor's mother. Eleanor refuses to go into the library because its mustiness reminds her of her. After one terrifying visitation a chalked message is found on a wall: 'HELP ELEANOR COME HOME' (p. 146). This creates some suspicion, with Theodora accusing Eleanor of having written it herself. Later some other letters appear above Theodora's bed, 'HELP ELEANOR COME HOME ELEANOR' (p. 155), and in another scene Eleanor seems to hear her name being called. Eleanor's highly precarious sense of self is suggested in these peculiar moments of projection which imply that she has not separated herself from her mother. Haunting in that respect looks like self-haunting within a context (the house) which restages Freud's debate about the uncanny. As in the 'Uncanny', Eleanor is confronted by her fears in what appears to be a neurotically developed encounter with a double (her projected 'mother'). However, it is important to consider what is 'neurotic' about Eleanor's behaviour, because interpreted in more political (rather than psychological) terms the novel reads as a Female Gothic challenge to notions of domesticity. Eleanor's inability to escape from her mother's domestic tyranny can thus be read as a critique of the limitations imposed on women by a strict adherence to conventional, gendered, domestic roles. Darryl Hattenhauer, however, notes that the fundamental ambivalence of the novel is that 'Domestic ideology makes her believe she is free when in fact she is trapped'.[57] Eleanor thus fails to trust her initial instincts which tell her that 'Hill House is vile, it is diseased; get away from here at once' (p. 33). Eleanor is eventually forced out of the house by the others. This leaves her with nowhere to go (literally and psychologically) and she commits suicide by crashing her car in the grounds of Hill House. Her final thoughts articulate both her estrangement and her fragile grasp on her motivation: '*Why* am I doing this? Why am I doing this? Why don't they stop me?' (p. 246). Such a desperate plea for help can also be related to an earlier image of estrangement which is associated with writing.

There are repeated references to Dr Montague's leisure reading, which includes Samuel Richardson's *Pamela* (1740), a novel in which the eponymous heroine is sexually pursued by the rakish Lord B. This emphasises a theme in Jackson's novel concerning women who are placed in danger by patriarchal men, as Eleanor is in Dr Montague's experiment. The reference to texts and the dangers they refer to is further underlined in Montague's claim that the best place to try to manifest a spirit is in the library (the stale atmosphere of which Eleanor had previously associated with her mother) because 'materializations are often best produced in rooms where there are books' (p. 186). It is in the library that Eleanor, seemingly overwhelmed by the atmosphere, endangers herself by climbing a precarious staircase from which she has to be rescued. However, it is revealing that this moment of danger is staged in the library, which for Eleanor is the place in the house which she cannot enter: 'I can't go in there; I'm not allowed in there' (p. 228). Hattenhauer has noted that this foregrounding of fictionality is reflected in the many different modes of writing employed in the novel, including 'the Gothic, fantastic, fabulist, allegorical, tragic, darkly comic, and grotesque', which means that the novel anticipates 'postmodernism's writing about writing' (p. 5). In other words, the knowing use of literary references (which includes jokes about Count Dracula) foreshadows postmodernism's model of moral emptiness in which style triumphs over content. *The Haunting of Hill House* can thus be read as a complex latter-day example of the Female Gothic which stylistically cultivates a literary ambience which anticipates postmodernism's version of emptiness (which also explains Eleanor's implicit association of books with 'death'). The relationship between postmodernism and the Gothic is particularly relevant to a reading of Angela Carter's rewriting of fairy tales in *The Bloody Chamber* (1979).

Angela Carter, as well as rewriting fairy tales, also edited two collections of them for Virago Press (in 1990 and 1992), which included tales collected by Charles Perrault in the 1690s. Perrault rewrote and sanitised the older, darker, oral tales in order to use them to make moral points about the conduct of middle-class children.[58] The issue of textual ownership of such tales is a key element in their transformation (from oral tales generated within predominantly peasant cultures, to their sanitising by Perrault). In *The Bloody Chamber* Carter attempts to reclaim these tales from their seventeenth-century recompositions in order to draw out their covert gender implications. The tales also rework elements familiar from the Female Gothic concerning absent mothers and how their presence promises salvation to their daughters. 'The Bloody Chamber' is a version of the Bluebeard story in which a vulnerable young wife recounts finding the bodies of her husband's murdered former wives in a room that she has been forbidden to enter. The tale concludes with the arrival of her mother, summoned by '*maternal telepathy*' (reworking Radcliffe's heroines' unconscious pursuits of their mothers), who 'took aim and put a single, irreproachable bullet through my husband's head' leaving her, in an echo of *Jane Eyre*, to form a more equitable relationship with a blind piano teacher.[59] Carter has been criticised in feminist circles because her heroines often appear complicit in – because at some level they appear to find pleasurable – the dangers that they are ostensibly threatened by. Merja Makinen has argued that such an approach overlooks the playful nature of Carter's rewritings which mock notions of misogynistic complicity, and moves beyond it by challenging the whole idea of a binary gender divide.[60] Indeed, Carter rewrites such tales so that the typical female victims are able to gain some rapprochement with their supposed aggressors (with the obvious exception of Bluebeard). In 'The Company of Wolves' (a reworking of 'Little Red Riding Hood'), for example, the girl resists the sexual threat posed by the werewolf. When he restates the familiar refrain that his large teeth are 'All the better to eat you with', she 'burst out laughing; she knew she was nobody's meat'.[61] The tale closes on an implied post-coital moment in which 'sweet and sound she sleeps in granny's bed, between the paws of the tender wolf' (p. 159). These reworkings of older narrative forms suggest an engagement with postmodernism, but in one key respect they compromise such an association – their attempt to establish alternative models of rationality.

Aidan Day has claimed that Carter was a rationalist who deliberately worked against Enlightenment theories of reason indebted to the work of René Descartes. Descartes's famous dictum 'I think therefore I am' emphasised a binary between inner consciousness and the outer material world (or between self and other).[62] This binary opposition underpins such pairings as conscious/unconscious, rational/irrational, and masculine/feminine, the kinds of pairings which the Gothic, in its more radical guises, challenges. Carter breaks down what she regards as an artificial distinction between masculine/feminine. For Day, the roots of Carter's thinking on this are to be found in her critique of the Marquis de Sade in *The Sadeian Woman* (1979) that she was working on at the same time as *The Bloody Chamber*. There she argues that Sade reworks Descartes's objectifying dictum as 'I fuck therefore I am', which articulates a clear gender/power relationship of men over women (conceived of in Sade's penetrative terms) which she is working against.[63] For Day, Carter 'wants a model for the relationship between people that is based on the principle of reciprocity rather than self-definition by exclusion' (p. 101), a view captured in the image of the girl asleep between the paws of the wolf (an image of 'manliness') at the end of 'The Company of Wolves'. Carter's work thus challenges the view that postmodernism can be reduced to linguistic or representational play. Within her 'play' (and Carter's critique of patriarchy is fundamentally comic) there is an attempt to both rebut the claims of a postmodern relativism whilst establishing a model of identity politics which exists beyond the old Enlightenment dualisms. The issue of postmodernism has also played a role in shaping the perception of another novel that uses elements of the Gothic: Toni Morrison's *Beloved* (1987).

Beloved is based on the true story of Margaret Garner, a slave working in Ohio, who with her four children and others attempted to escape from their owner in 1855. The group was recaptured but not before Margaret Garner had killed one of her infant children and attacked the others. Garner said she had killed her child because this seemed a preferable fate than the slow death inflicted by slavery. Her actions also indicated that she claimed ownership of the children as hers, rather than acknowledging them as slaves that belonged to the slave owner. In Morrison's novel, which is set eighteen years after the killing, the role of the mother is taken by Sethe, who lives with her eighteen-year-old daughter Denver (two sons ran away when they were in their teens).[64] The house is haunted by the ghost of 'Beloved', the baby whom Sethe had killed. On the arrival of an old companion, Paul D, a former slave (the novel is set in the post-slavery era but refers back to it), he and Sethe begin an affair and he scares away the ghost. Shortly afterwards a stranger called 'Beloved' who would have been the same age as Sethe's first daughter appears and becomes like a sister to Denver and a daughter to Sethe, and drives Paul D out of the house. The ghostly presence of Beloved refers to many different histories, not only Sethe's personal history but also the history of slavery (and the novel can usefully be read in the context of the tales discussed in Chapter 3, section 3, pp. 102–9) and therefore the history of America. The novel moves backwards and forwards between the present and the past in order to examine the formative experiences in the lives of the principal characters. There is a deliberate ambivalence about Beloved, who can be read as either the return of Sethe's daughter, or as someone whose account of the past suggests that she experienced the journey on the slave ships used to transport Africans to America (the journey known as the middle passage). Morrison creates this ambivalence by indicating that Beloved can be related to personal and political pasts because personal pasts are determined by political acts (such as Sethe's claim of 'ownership' over the infant Beloved by killing her). The novel uses ghosting as a complex allegory for the reclamation of the past which requires a process of rememory. The complicated stylistics of the novel might appear to emulate the type of literary play which characterises postmodernism but, as in Carter, postmodernist ideas of absence are challenged. The novel suggests tensions between absence (as in the use of the ghost) and presence (as in what that ghost represents, what past it keeps alive). The presence of the ghost (the presence of an absence, as it were) breaks down the boundaries between the living and the dead in order to generate an allegory about African Americans' experience in which as a group they are there but not there, powerfully present but culturally and economically marginalised. Rafael Pérez-Torres notes that this constitutes a highly politicised critique of the postmodern because it challenges the notion of 'absence' by using it as a conceit for historical and cultural invisibility, so that 'while Morrison's narrative shares affinities with other postmodern texts, it also suggests a connection between its narrative strategies and the sociohistorical conditions of Africans in the Americas', which means that the apparent postmodern 'narrative pastiche' in the novel is used 'to contest history as a master narrative', because it asks questions about who produces 'history'.[65]

Jackson, Carter, and Morrison are writing within different contexts, but all of them focus on issues about representation and motherhood. They all explore the meaning of absence (mothers, children, histories) as a critique of the type of empty representation that defines one version of the postmodern. The idea that horror addresses contemporary anxieties will be developed in the following section in a close reading of Thomas Harris's *The Silence of the Lambs* (1988).

READING *THE SILENCE OF THE LAMBS*

This chapter has explored the different ways in which writers and film-makers have engaged with historical issues.[66] M. R. James's ghost stories covertly examine a perceived modernist amorality, *The Exorcist* engages with issues of American imperialism, and *Beloved* debates the relationship between past and present by exploring the connections between race, identity, and memory. Throughout this book we have explored how the Gothic needs to be understood as a mode of cultural history, one which surrenders its historical narrative once we decode its complex symbolism. How such texts engage with contemporary issues will be illustrated by a close reading of Thomas Harris's novel *The Silence of the Lambs* (1988), which was filmed in 1991. This reading reveals how a close textual historicisation can be made and indicates, as throughout this study, how the Gothic (here manifested in the guise of a superior popular thriller novel) challenges and reworks contemporary debates. A close contextualisation enables us to isolate certain themes or issues within a text, which can then be discussed in relation to the Gothic.

Harris's novel juxtaposes 'Good' and 'Evil', dwells on mutilation and murder, and explores issues concerning insanity, and moral, psychological, and physical transgression. These issues are developed as narrative tension builds in the investigation into locating a serial killer's victim and the attempt to capture or kill that serial killer. There are two, very different, serial killers in the novel. Jame Gumb murders women and flays them to use their skins to make a female 'skin' for himself. His social and sexual disturbances are a consequence of his difficult childhood and he has little sense of what motivates him. Dr Hannibal Lecter is a more intellectual figure who understands (and enjoys) the pain of others. The motivation for his behaviour is unclear in the novel (although there is some explanation for it in the sequel, *Hannibal*, 1999, filmed in

2001). However, it is around Lecter that a debate about the relationship between conceptions of 'civilisation' and what it means to be 'human' takes place. Such debates are familiar from the Gothic and are, for example, central to Brown's *Wieland*, discussed in Chapter 1. Indeed, what it means to be human and the role of education in forming that humanity is a key theme in *Frankenstein*. Such discussions are not confined to the late eighteenth- and early nineteenth-century Gothic. Postmodernism, which was referred to in the previous section to show how Carter and Morrison examine how it is possible to get at the 'truth' in an age characterised by moral relativism, is an important consideration which ghosts Harris's novel. This subtext concerning postmodernism can be decoded by contextualising the novel in relation to a book which generated considerable debate in America on its publication in 1987: Allan Bloom's *The Closing of the American Mind*.

Allan Bloom's book is a politically right-of-centre account of what he regarded as the ethically detrimental effects caused by a decline in university teaching of the classics in general and philosophy in particular. Bloom argues that the decline in the teaching of the history of political philosophy coincided with a new liberalism that emerged in the late 1960s which supported a 'cultural relativism' that refused to acknowledge the old moral and political hierarchies.[67] In such a society, Bloom claims, people become soulless because education no longer equips individuals with the life skills that enable them to grow as people. Such views are intended as a hostile rebuke to what he regards as a fashionable liberalism which is unable to commit to anything because it does not believe in anything (Bloom writes of the effects of this liberal attitude on his students: 'They can be anything they want to be, but they have no particular reason to want to be anything in particular', p. 87).[68] Bloom suggests that such liberal views now underpin the political reality of American democracy and create a culture of personal indirection and social inertia. Bloom's highly conservative reading of what he regards as a new nihilistic postmodern malaise has relevance for how we might read the figure of Hannibal Lecter.[69] First, though, it is important to note that such a contextualisation is suggested by the novel itself. There are repeated references made to an eminent psychologist that the FBI and others refer to for expert advice called Alan Bloom, who is a professor at the University of Chicago. Allan Bloom was a professor of political philosophy at the University of Chicago and his idea that culture civilises people by nurturing their soul is addressed in the relationship between Lecter and Clarice Starling.

The novel makes a number of references to education. Starling first met Jack Crawford (her FBI boss) when he spoke at a class she took whilst studying psychology and criminology at the University of Virginia. When taunted by Frederick Chilton (the psychologist in charge of the institute where Lecter is held) about the possibility that she may find Lecter intimidating, she retorts, 'I graduated from the University of Virginia with honors, Doctor. It's not a charm school'.[70] The emphasis on Starling's educational background, which is reiterated throughout the book, is meant to chart her social progress as she came from a poor family background and spent some time raised in an orphanage. This sets the scene for the meeting with Lecter, who initially refers to her as 'student Starling' because she is an FBI trainee. He mocks the social background that is only thinly hidden by her professional ambitions, 'Do you know what you look like to me, with your good bag and your cheap shoes? You look like a rube. You're a well-scrubbed, hustling rube with a little taste' (p. 22). Lecter by this point has underlined his claim on high culture by drawing from memory scenes from Florence to decorate his windowless cell. The encounter between them takes on a teacher–student dynamic as Lecter attempts to educate Starling generally about psychopathology, and later about the specific profile of the serial killer for whom they are searching. The role of Lecter is ambivalent in this because although he possesses the kind of education that Bloom regarded as essential to develop the soul, he is nevertheless a barbarian who has murdered nine people in extremely violent ways (often eating parts of his victims), and therefore appears to be 'evil'. Bloom, as part of his rebuttal of liberal ideas, claims that students were unable to understand 'evil' as a malaise of the soul, because they preferred to 'believe that evil deeds are performed by persons who, if they got the proper therapy, would not do them again – that there are evil deeds, not evil people' (p. 67). In this first meeting Lecter also mocks the behaviourist trend in psychology which explains complex human behaviour in terms of quantifiable patterns (Allan Bloom also critiqued behaviourism). When Starling asks him about his past he replies, 'Nothing happened to me, Officer Starling. *I* happened. You can't reduce me to a set of influences. You've given up good and evil for behaviourism' (p. 21). Lecter proceeds to critique, in true Bloomian fashion, the consequences of this new moral relativism: 'You've got everybody in moral dignity pants – nothing is ever anybody's fault. Look at me [. . .] Can you stand to say I'm evil? Am I evil, Officer Starling?' (p. 21). Starling's reply, 'I think you've been destructive. For me it's the same thing', is challenged by Lecter's response: 'Evil's just destructive? Then *storms* are evil, if it's that simple. And we have *fire*, and then there's *hail*' (p. 22).

Lecter's role is not just to provide clues about Jame Gumb's identity (and he knows from the start who the killer is and strategically releases information in order to barter for better conditions for himself): it is to provide Starling with a series of tutorials designed to illustrate her inability to grasp the nature of 'evil'. Their second meeting, which takes place after the abduction of Catherine Martin, is also associated with references to high culture (although they are not specific to Lecter), including Starling's impromptu misquotation of a line from T. S. Eliot's 'Ash Wednesday' (1930) and her discovery that Barney, one of Lecter's warders at the institute, is reading Jane Austen's *Sense and Sensibility* (1811). The tutorial continues with Lecter's examination of Starling's past as he invites her to confront the unconscious reasons as to why it is so personally, rather than professionally, important for her to catch the killer. There is a third and final meeting which concludes these tutorials. It takes place after Lecter has been moved to a new seemingly secure location by trading information about the killer (Catherine Martin's mother is a senator, which gives the investigation an added importance and a sense of urgency).

Lecter is held in a former courthouse which has been converted into municipal offices. The building is 'a massive Gothic-style structure' (p. 221), and Lecter's prefabricated cell is situated on a floor in the building which is normally associated with the holdings of the Shelby County Historical Society, and Starling notices how the place smells of 'library paste' (p. 223). These incidental links to history and books provide the context in which Lecter gives Starling some defining clues about the psychology of the killer. Lecter begins, however, by mocking a speech which Crawford had made the previous year to the National Police Academy (a report of which Lecter has read). For him the speech illustrates Crawford's inferior intellectual skills because he quoted the Roman emperor Marcus Aurelius (whose *Meditations* were written around AD 170) from a secondary source. For Lecter, 'If he understood Marcus Aurelius, he might solve his case' (p. 226). Starling asks him to explain and he replies, 'When you show the odd flash of contextual intelligence, I forget your generation can't read' (pp. 226–7). This is a view suggested in *The Closing of the American Mind*, where Bloom comments that students 'have not learned how to read, nor do they have the expectation of delight or improvement from reading' (p. 62). Lecter then leads Starling through a train of thought prompted by Marcus Aurelius: 'Of each particular thing, ask: What is it in itself, in its own constitution? What is its causal nature?' (p. 227). This line of reasoning leads to the conclusion that the killer covets his victims' skin and therefore had prior proximity to those victims (a subsequent clue given by Lecter leads Starling back to the first victim, and ultimately to the discovery of Gumb's whereabouts). The novel therefore appears to support the view that it is through an understanding of philosophy and history that the 'soul' of others can be explained, and that Lecter possesses some now nearly lost cultural knowledge that civilisation needs. In this instance the Gothic monster that is Lecter helps catch the other 'monster', Gumb, and does so through his supposedly superior reading.

Bloom's book can be read as a latter-day version of Nordau's *Degeneration* in its lament over a perceived cultural decline. However, it is important to question the extent to which Harris's novel mocks Bloom's pessimism (because Starling is the heroine) or endorses Bloom's views (because, despite everything, Lecter is 'right'). A hint to how we might solve this conundrum is suggested in the name of Hannibal Lecter. Eric Griffiths, reviewing the novel in 1991, claimed that the origin for the name was Baudelaire's poem 'Au Lecteur' ('To the Reader'), published in *Les Fleurs du mal* in 1855.[71] The poem concludes with reference to 'Hypocrite lecteur' who is both the twin of the poet and by implication that of the reader. The poems in the collection have a Gothic ambience, and

'Au Lecteur' addresses the supposedly human fascination with 'evil', despite our claims on civilisation and decency. Reference is made to how 'His Majesty, / Satan Thrice-Great, lulls our charmed soul' (ll. 9/10) and how:

> He holds the strings that move us, limb by limb!
> We yield, enthralled, to things repugnant, base;
> Each day towards Hell, with slow, unhurried pace,
> We sink, uncowed, through shadows, stinking, grim.
> (ll. 13–16)[72]

The poem thus suggests that our impulse to do good is compromised by our fascination with evil (which makes hypocrites of us all). This explains Lecter's cruelty, and it is a poem which Allan Bloom also mentions in his analysis of a contemporary world that he sees as soulless because of its failure to grasp moral and intellectual absolutes. For Bloom, 'Baudelaire presented sinning man as in the Christian vision, but without hope of God's salvation, piercing pious fraudulence, *hypocrite lecteur*' (p. 205, emphasis in original), which, for Bloom, foreshadows the disappearance of religious ethics in modern life. Hannibal Lecter is thus, in Bloom's terms, part of the problem (because he suggests that we live in a godless world) and the solution (reading the classics). He is thus twinned (both Good and Evil) in a clear echo of Baudelaire's jaded metaphysics.

The novel's engagement with Bloom's ideas can also be illustrated by how the psychologist 'Alan Bloom' is represented. First, his expert advice does not help catch the killer. The advice is generalised, built around notions of certain psychological types and therefore does not provide an insight into the emotionally complex life of a character such as Gumb. After one television interview, Starling's roommate, Ardelia Mapp, comments that his opinion was little more than 'Slick obfuscation and facile bullshit' (p. 120). Later Lecter asks Starling if she had looked him up in Bloom's book: 'How did he describe me?' 'A pure sociopath.' 'Would you say Dr. Bloom is always right?' (p. 146).

Reading *The Silence of the Lambs* for this type of detail reveals how it reworks ideas about the 'truth' (it is, after all, at one level a detective novel), notions of 'humanity', and conceptions of 'Good' and 'Evil', and thus reconfigures the tangled relationship that the Gothic had with the Enlightenment in the eighteenth century. The limitations of reason (here represented in the figure of 'Alan Bloom') do not capture the complex importance of irrationality and feeling which were central to the Romantics (and become represented in the novel by the Baudelairean twinning of 'Good' and 'Evil'). This ambivalence is maintained at the end when, although Gumb is killed, Lecter escapes, so that neither rationality nor the irrational ultimately triumphs in a novel which avoids any easy sense of closure.[73]

Approaching *The Silence of the Lambs* in this way generates a particular interpretation. This is not the only way in which the novel can be examined but it illustrates how Gothic symbolism can be understood within the context of certain contemporary debates which, ostensibly (because they are about a perceived malaise in American higher education), bear little relationship to a tale about contrasting psychopaths. Reading closely for detail and cultural context thus helps to generate highly specific interpretations of texts, which also addresses how familiar Gothic themes are reworked in the process.

SUMMARY OF KEY POINTS

- A modernist Gothic emerges in the early twentieth century.
- The Gothic is taken up by new non-text-based media.
- 'Pulp' horror becomes a popular mode of the Gothic.
- The Gothic critically engages with postmodernism after the 1970s.

QUESTIONS AND POINTS FOR DISCUSSION

- What are the key characteristics of the modernist Gothic?
- How does the literary Gothic compare and contrast with non-text-based Gothic?
- How does the Female Gothic develop and/or move beyond the Radcliffean Gothic?

- How does the Gothic respond to postmodern ideas of representational play?

NOTES

1. David Punter, *The Literature of Terror: The Modern Gothic* (London and New York: Longman, 1996), vol. 2, p. 67. All subsequent references given in the text are to this edition.

2. Williams Hughes, *The Handbook to Gothic Literature*, ed. Marie Mulvey-Roberts (Basingstoke: Macmillan, 1998), p. 143.

3. Julia Briggs, *The Rise and Fall of the English Ghost Story* (London: Faber & Faber, 1977), p. 135, cited at p. 85 in Punter, *Literature of Terror*. I am conscious that this implies that the Gothic is an inherently radical form, whereas it can often be used to conservative ends. However, the critical material on James suggests that the Gothic simply fails to appear as Gothic at any politically discernible level (whether radical or reactionary).

4. Clive Bloom, 'M. R. James and his Fiction', in *Creepers: British Horror & Fantasy in the Twentieth Century*, ed. Clive Bloom (London: Pluto, 1993), pp. 64–71, p. 69.

5. M. R. James, 'The Mezzotint', in *The Collected Stories of M. R. James* (London: Edward Arnold, [1931] 1970), pp. 36–53, p. 40. All subsequent references in the text are to this edition. I develop these arguments in 'M. R. James's Gothic Revival' in a special issue of *Diegesis* on 'Horror', ed. Gina Wisker, 7 (Summer 2004), 16–22.

6. M. R. James, 'The Haunted Dolls' House', in *The Collected Stories of M. R. James* (London: Edward Arnold, [1931] 1970), pp. 472–89.

7. This is a point made by E. F. Bleiler in his Introduction to *Best Ghost Stories of Algernon Blackwood* (New York: Dover, 1973), p. viii.

8. Algernon Blackwood, 'The Willows', in *Best Ghost Stories of Algernon Blackwood* (New York: Dover, 1973), pp. 1–52, pp. 2–3.

9. Algernon Blackwood, 'The Wendigo', in *Best Ghost Stories of Algernon Blackwood* (New York: Dover, 1973), pp. 158–207.

10. Algernon Blackwood, 'The Empty House', in *Best Ghost Stories of Algernon Blackwood* (New York: Dover, 1973), pp. 276–92, p. 288. All subsequent references in the text are to this edition.

11. E. F. Benson, 'Mr. Tilly's Séance', in *The Tale of an Empty House and Other Ghost stories* (Guernsey: Black Swan, 1986), pp. 156–72, p. 157. All subsequent references in the text are to this edition.

12. E. F. Benson, 'How Fear Departed from the Long Gallery', in *The Tale of an Empty House and Other Ghost Stories* (Guernsey: Black Swan, 1986), pp. 80–96, p. 80.

13. E. F. Benson, 'Caterpillars', in *The Tale of an Empty House and Other Ghost Stories* (Guernsey: Black Swan, 1986), pp. 27–36, p. 27.

14. E. F. Benson, 'The Face', in *The Tale of an Empty House and Other Ghost Stories* (Guernsey: Black Swan, 1986), pp. 11–26.

15. E. F. Benson, 'The Room in the Tower', in *The Tale of an Empty House and Other Ghost Stories* (Guernsey: Black Swan, 1986), pp. 109–23.

16. E. F. Benson, 'Expiation', in *The Tale of an Empty House and Other Ghost Stories* (Guernsey: Black Swan, 1986), pp. 37–55, p. 53.

17. T. S. Eliot, *The Waste Land*, in *Selected Poems* (Harmondsworth: Penguin, [1948] 1952), part V, 11. 377–84.

18. For an extended examination of this influence, see Andrew Smith and Jeff Wallace (eds), *Gothic Modernisms* (Basingstoke: Palgrave, 2001). The relationship between the Gothic and modernism is an interesting one and can be found not just in literature but also in German expressionist films such as Murnau's *Nosferatu*, Wiene's *The Cabinet of Dr Caligari*, and Wegener's *The Golem*. In music we also find Schoenberg's 'A Theme Tune for an Imaginary Horror Film'. The German title is 'Begleitungsmusik zu einer Lichtspielszene', Op. 34 (1930).

19. James Joyce, *Ulysses* (Oxford: Oxford University Press, [1922] 1993), p. 47.

20. David Seed, '"Psychical" Cases: Transformations of the Supernatural in Virginia Woolf and May Sinclair', in *Gothic Modernisms*, ed. Smith and Wallace, pp. 44–61, p. 54.

21. May Sinclair, *Uncanny Stories* (New York: Macmillan, 1923).

22. See Seed, '"Psychical" Cases', and David Glover, 'The "Spectrality Effect" in Early Modernism' in *Gothic Modernisms*, ed. Smith and Wallace, pp. 29–43.

23. May Sinclair, 'Finding the Absolute' in *Uncanny Stories* (New York: Macmillan, 1923), pp. 329–62.

24. May Sinclair, 'The Nature of the Evidence', in *Uncanny Stories* (New York: Macmillan, 1923), pp. 209–34, p. 229. All subsequent references in the text are to this edition.

25. Diana Wallace, 'Uncanny Stories: the Ghost Story as Female Gothic', in *Gothic Studies*, 6:1 (May 2004), 57–68, 62.

26. May Sinclair, 'The Villa Désirée', in *The Penguin Book of Erotic Stories by Women*, ed. Richard Glyn Jones and A. Susan Williams (Harmondsworth: Penguin, 1996), p. 84.

27. See Wallace, 'Uncanny stories', p. 63.

28. Wallace, 'Uncanny stories', p. 61.

29. Richard J. Hand, *Terror on the Air! Horror Radio in America, 1931–1952* (New York: McFarland, 2006), pp. 5–11.

30. See Hand, *Terror on the Air!*, p. 19.

31. 'Scoop', quoted in Hand, *Terror on the Air!*, p. 19.

32. See Kim Newman (ed.), *The BFI Companion to Horror* (London: Cassell, 1996), p. 265. The series was suggested by the thriller writer John Dickson Carr as part of the war effort.

33. See entry on Freund in Newman, *BFI Companion*, p. 128.

34. Hand, *Terror on the Air!*, p. 10.

35. David J. Skal, *Hollywood Gothic: The Tangled Web of Dracula from Novel to Stage to Screen* (New York: Faber and Faber, [1990] 2004). All subsequent references in the text are to this edition. Harry Ludlam, *A Biography of Dracula: The Life Story of Bram Stoker* (London: Foulsham, 1962): see pp. 152–78.

36. See Skal, *Hollywood Gothic*, pp. 103–37, for an account of the theatrical versions of *Dracula*.

37. David J. Skal, *The Monster Show: A Cultural History of Horror* (New York: Faber and Faber, [1993] 2001), p. 115. All subsequent references in the text are to this edition.

38. Skal, *Hollywood Gothic*, p. 199.
39. For an account of Hammer see David Pirie, *A Heritage of Horror: The English Gothic Cinema* (London: Gordon Fraser, 1973), and Jonathan Rigby, *English Gothic: A Century of Horror Cinema* (London: Reynolds & Hearn, [2000] 2004).
40. David Hill, 'Five Parts Boredom to One of Nausea', *Tribune*, 12 September 1958, quoted in Rigby, *English Gothic*, p. 68.
41. Quoted in Rigby, *English Gothic*, p. 81.
42. Note an early example of this transformation, *The Vampire Lovers* (dir. Roy Ward Baker, 1970), a loosely adapted version of Le Fanu's *Carmilla*.
43. See Rigby, *English Gothic*, pp. 142–3, for an outline analysis of the film.
44. See Skal, *Monster Show*, pp. 292–4, for a reading of the film.
45. Skal, *Monster Show*, p. 293.
46. This reading closely follows my review of the film in *Gothic Studies*, 2: 3 (December 2000), 368–9.
47. The film was made in 1973 which, paradoxically, was within a year of the end of Vietnam and the last moon landing (both 1974). I am grateful to my colleague Richard J. Hand for pointing this out, and for his many very helpful comments on this section.
48. Melanie Klein was a noted psychoanalyst of childhood (and motherhood), whose writings include *The Psychoanalysis of Children* (1932), *Contributions to Psychoanalysis, 1921–1945* (1948), *Narrative of a Child Analysis* (1961), and *Our Adult World and Other Essays* (1963).
49. See Skal, *Hollywood Gothic*, p. 278.
50. Fred Botting, *Gothic* (London and New York: Routledge, 1996), p. 179. All subsequent references in the text are to this edition.
51. See A. Robert Lee on 'Southern Gothic' in *The Handbook to Gothic Literature*, ed. Marie Mulvey-Roberts (Basingstoke: Macmillan, 1998), pp. 217-20, where he makes this link with Poe.
52. Stephen King, *Carrie* (London: New English Library, 1974).
53. James Herbert, *The Rats* (London: New English Library, 1974).

54. Clive Barker, 'Son of Celluloid', in *Clive Barker's Books of Blood*, vol. 3 (London: Sphere, 1988), pp. 1–35.

55. Clive Barker, *Weaveworld* (Glasgow: Collins, 1988). See Andrew Smith, 'Worlds That Creep Up on You: Postmodern Illusions in the Work of Clive Barker', in *Creepers: British Horror and Fantasy in the Twentieth Century*, ed. Clive Bloom (London: Pluto, 1993), pp. 176–86.

56. Shirley Jackson, *The Haunting of Hill House* (London: Constable, [1959] 1999), p. 83. All subsequent references in the text are to this edition.

57. Darryl Hattenhauer, *Shirley Jackson's American Gothic* (New York: State University of New York, 1999), pp. 160–1. All subsequent references in the text are to this edition.

58. For an extended analysis of Perrault's 'Little Red Riding Hood' see Jack Zipes, *The Trials and Tribulations of Little Red Riding Hood* (London: Routledge, 1993).

59. Angela Carter, 'The Bloody Chamber', in *The Bloody Chamber* (Harmondsworth: Penguin, 1979), pp. 7–52, p. 51.

60. Merja Makinen, 'Angela Carter's *The Bloody Chamber* and the decolonisation of feminine sexuality', in *Angela Carter: New Casebooks*, ed. Alison Easton (Basingstoke: Macmillan, 2000), pp. 20–36.

61. Angela Carter, 'The Company of Wolves', in *The Bloody Chamber* (Harmondsworth: Penguin, 1979), pp. 148-59, p. 158. All subsequent references in the text are to this edition.

62. Aidan Day, *Angela Carter: The Rational Glass* (Edinburgh: Edinburgh University Press, 1998), see pp. 91–106. All subsequent references in the text are to this edition.

63. Angela Carter, *The Sadeian Woman* (London: Virago, 1979), p. 26, cited in Day, *Angela Carter*, p. 97.

64. See Toni Morrison, *Beloved* (London: Vintage, 1987).

65. Rafael Pérez-Torres, 'Between Presence and Absence: *Beloved*, Postmodernism and Blackness', in *Beloved: A Casebook*, ed. William L. Andrews and Nellie Y. McKay (Oxford: Oxford University Press, 1999), pp. 179–201, p. 184, p. 194.

66. Arguably films are not the product of just the director's input, as writers and producers are also involved.

67. Allan Bloom, *The Closing of the American Mind* (New York:

Simon & Schuster, 1987), p. 30. All subsequent references in the text are to this edition.

68. Bloom's book is highly contentious in many of its claims, not least its attack on feminist readings of philosophical texts, and the book should be understood as a part of a backlash against critical theory.

69. It should, however, be noted that Bloom never uses the term 'postmodernism'.

70. Thomas Harris, *The Silence of the Lambs* (New York: St Martin's Press, 1988), p. 11. All subsequent references in the text are to this edition.

71. Eric Griffiths, book review in *The Modern Review*, 0: 0 (summer 1991), p. 7.

72. Charles Baudelaire, 'Au Lecteur', in *Three Poems from Selected Poems from Les Fleurs du mal: A Bilingual Edition*, trans. Norman R. Shapiro (Chicago: University of Chicago Press, 1998). Accessed at: http://www.press.uchicago.edu/Misc/Chicago/039250.html

73. Lecter returns in the sequel, *Hannibal* (1999). That novel explains more about his past and plays out the relationship between Lecter and Starling as a romance. It is a novel in a different narrative key to *The Silence of the Lambs*, one more in keeping with Coppola's attempt to turn *Dracula* into a love story.

Conclusion

This book has examined a range of different Gothic texts (and non-textual media such as radio and film) from the eighteenth century onwards. The aim has been to provide an overview of the Gothic combined with some close analysis of particular texts. Such an introduction to the Gothic is, by definition, merely the starting point for further discussion, rather than the last word.

This study has examined texts which are often included on the Gothic curriculum (as well as looking at some texts which are usually not), although it is important to note that what typically constitutes a Gothic canon is subject to change. The growing availability of texts which had been difficult to obtain, the production of new contributions to Gothic scholarship, and the addition of what became new landmark Gothic texts and films help to develop the curriculum. The teaching of Ann Radcliffe and Matthew Lewis, for example, can now be supplemented because of the republication of texts by other authors in the period. Since 2005 Zittaw Press have published some hitherto difficult to obtain copies of eighteenth-century novels. They have also reprinted (since 2003) an extensive series of Blue Books which were popular shortened versions of Gothic narratives first published in the early nineteenth century.[1] In addition, source material from the Sadleir-Black collection of early Gothic fiction, housed at the University of Virginia, is now available on microfilm from Adam Matthews Publications.[2] These new means of easy access to sources which were once almost the preserve of academic researchers help to deepen and enrich the pedagogic possibilities for exploring the Gothic.

However, in considering likely developments within the Gothic it is helpful to return, if only briefly, to the notion of a self-reflexive postmodernist impulse which in, different ways, Angela Carter and Toni Morrison respond to. There has been a strand in recent popular cinema, most notably in the *Scream* series of films (1996, 1997, 2000), which incorporates jocular self-reflections on the generic expectations of, in particular, the so-called slasher films of the late 1970s and 1980s. The discussions about the nature of such films might seem to indicate the emergence of a new form of anti-Gothic which deconstructs the Gothic even as it works through some of its more or less familiar props, issues, and characterisations. However, although such films are wittily self-reflexive, they still function as horror films in their own right, even though any potential 'transgression' is inevitably circumscribed by a self-awareness that implies that they do not take themselves too seriously. The *Nightmare on Elm Street* series (released between 1984 and 1994; the first and last films were written and directed by Wes Craven, who directed the *Scream* series) also increasingly used ironic humour, but nevertheless focused on recognisably Gothic themes of insanity, the unconscious, and sexuality. Such films might suggest the emergence of a strangely blended hybrid form which develops shocks even whilst it parodies itself. However, films like those in the *Scream* series can also be read as lampoons of consumerism because they mock the concept of standardised mass production. The films make the viewer acutely aware that they are not buying a standardised, predictable, cheaply made product, but rather a film which ironically comments on such buying (or viewing) habits. Gothic ambivalence haunts these films by suggesting that their potential radicalism has to be seen within the context of the film industry itself (especially of the late 1970s and 1980s, when this 'type' of films, many of them going straight to video release, were made). However, this only represents one strand within the horror film, and it is important to acknowledge just how diverse the culture of the horror film is. Films such as *The Others* (2001), *My Little Eye* (2002), and *28 Days Later* (2002), to name just three recent, unusual horror films, take themselves rather more seriously and address a range of contemporary concerns, including voyeurism, science, and insanity. There has been a considerable amount of academic interest shown in the horror film genre, and this represents a growing area of scholarship which is likely to continue. Television series such as *Buffy the Vampire Slayer* (1997–2003) are also increasingly the subject of academic analysis, and the history of television Gothic is an area of developing critical inquiry.

One of the key issues explored in this volume has been sexuality. In part this is because of a critical perception that the Gothic often trades in tabooed representations of desire. Indeed, because the Gothic so often focuses on issues of gender and identity it means that sexuality and politics are frequently foregrounded. There has also been recent interest in exploring the Gothic through queer theory, which not only examines work by gay writers but also explores what Eve Kosofsky Sedgwick has termed 'homosexual panic' as one of the underlying dynamics in representations between men in the Gothic (the title of her study is *Between Men*, 1985).[3] Paulina Palmer's critical study *Lesbian Gothic* (1999) has also proved to be groundbreaking,[4] and there has been a special issue of the journal *Gothic Studies* on 'Queering Gothic Films' (2005, edited by Michael Eberle-Sinatra).[5] In terms of recent literature, Sarah Waters's *Affinity* (1999) can be read as a lesbian reprise of the Female Gothic in its evocation of a Victorian world of taboo, insanity, and incarceration.[6] In addition Michael Rowe has edited two anthologies of gay Gothic horror tales, *Queer Fear* (2000) and *Queer Fear II* (2002), which Clive Barker has acknowledged as an important outlet for gay writers of the Gothic such as himself.[7] The relationship between queer theory, which examines the construction and deconstruction of gendered identities, provides an important approach to a form such as the Gothic which is also characterised by its ambivalent approach to identity and gender. This is likely to be a highly productive area for further critical enquiry.

This book has examined some of the major texts and debates associated with the Gothic in the British and American traditions. However, it is also important to note that there is emerging scholarship which has considered in depth the debt which the British and American Gothic owes to a European Gothic tradition.

Avril Horner's edited collection *European Gothic: A Spirited Exchange* (2002) readdresses this Anglo-American imbalance and explores how Gothic writing in French, Spanish, Russian, and German enables us to re-evaluate matters of national provenance.[8] Nationally inflected Gothic, such as, for example, Irish Gothic, has also received considerable critical attention, and nationality and the Gothic is an area which will see a growth in scholarship in years to come.[9]

The academic journal *Gothic Studies* and the conference activities of the International Gothic Association to which it is linked also provide clues as to how scholarship may advance. The May 2002 issue of *Gothic Studies* carried an article by Sara Martin entitled 'Gothic Scholars Don't Wear Black: Gothic Studies and Gothic Subcultures'. Martin notes that the Goth subculture emerged in the UK in the 1980s around a music scene associated with bands including The Cure and Siouxsie and the Banshees.[10] She also notes that this coincided with the emergence of Gothic studies as an area of respectable academic enquiry. However, the Goth subculture, which will be the focus of the remainder of this chapter, has rarely been subject to the same form of critical analysis as the literary culture. In part Martin acknowledges that this is a matter of methodology because the cultural studies approach to reading subcultures is different in kind to the analytical reading practices of most Gothic scholars. She also acknowledges that academics do not, in the main, inhabit such subcultures (that is, they 'don't wear black') and so are likely to neglect them. Martin, however, makes a convincing case that in order to understand the Gothic of any era it is important that we take into account the wider cultural picture. She notes that, when examining the eighteenth-century Gothic, scholars tend to address the integration between 'Gothic literature, drama, architecture, painting, decoration and other Gothic cultural phenomena', which leads her to claim that:

> Likewise, twentieth century Gothic Studies demands that the scholar's attention be directed not only towards the literature of the past and towards the twentieth century academic methods but also towards the manifestations of the Gothic that are happening right now in most of the Western world.[11]

Martin sees the emergence of such scholarship as initially appearing around the analysis of the Goth music scene. This is a subject which has also recently increasingly found its way into academic conferences on the Gothic. Music provides a cultural reference point in which songs can be read as part of an evolving Gothic tradition (one which the critic James Hannahan claims begins with Screamin' Jay Hawkins's 'I Put a Spell on You', 1957) and subject to the same type of textual scrutiny as any Gothic text.[12] However, in order to understand the dynamics of the Goth subculture it becomes necessary, according to Martin, that we move beyond music to embrace the wider semiotic transformation of the Gothic implied within the Goth subculture. She claims that in the present day 'many consumers of Gothic texts have chosen to *incorporate Gothic into their everyday life* as a way of living in today's contradictory complex world' (p. 33). The wider question concerns the ways in which such contradictions are negotiated and whether a Goth subculture represents a radical alternative or produces paradoxes of its own which reflect the fundamental ambivalences of much Gothic fiction. A clue about this is suggested in David Punter's claim that 'The central contradiction [...] from which all the others follow, is this: that Gothic can at one and the same time be categorized as a middle-class and as an anti-middle-class literature', a view which is implicit in analysis of the nonconformist outlooks of those in the Goth subculture.[13]

Paul Hodkinson's *Goth: Identity, Style and Subculture* (2002) is a sophisticated and important analysis of the subculture. Studies of subcultures as musically orientated youth cultures have been an important, and popular, area of sociological investigation since Dick Hebdiges's *Subculture: The Meaning of Style* (1979). Such analyses typically explore the aspirations and class, gender, and racial compositions of such subcultures. Hodkinson, an academic and a member of the Goth scene, sociologically examines the kinds of identity politics involved in becoming part of the subculture. What is notable in the analysis and the testimonies of members of the scene is an openness to versions of 'otherness'. Indeed, one could perhaps expect that such a subculture would embrace 'otherness' with some enthusiasm. However, much of this appears to be largely a matter of individual outlook rather than a key aspect of group membership. Hodkinson's analysis of the class, racial, and sexual identifications of an admittedly statistically small group of Goths who completed a questionnaire at the biannual Whitby Gothic Weekend suggests a predominately white, heterosexual, young, middle-class subculture. Such a subculture typifies outsiders as 'trendies' who slavishly follow trends rather than buck them. In particular, argues Hodkinson, the subculture perceives itself as anti-commercialist and asserts economic attachments that are Goth-specific (buying certain types of clothes, music, and so on) that set them aside from 'individualized postmodern consumers'.[14] This suggests a 'closed' subculture (perhaps a definition of a subculture) which paradoxically appears to be both 'middle class' in composition and 'anti-middle class' in attitude. It would be too crude to dismiss the Goth scene as little more than a white middle-class youth subculture. Rather, it seems to provide an interesting latter-day example of how a Gothic ambience is being renegotiated in class-inflected terms, especially through a resistance to conventional notions of middle-class 'respectability'. Hodkinson's study reveals that despite some variations within the subculture there is a consensus that the scene is opposed to a largely abstract notion of the mainstream (identifiable as the 'norm'). However, what actually constitutes the mainstream is much more problematic to define, especially given that many of the members of the subculture would appear to have class backgrounds that imply association with it. Such paradoxes relocate Punter's identification of class paradox as the defining aspect of the Gothic. However, there is also a sense of parody in much of this. The faux decadence of the scene appears to mock models of middle-class 'civilised' behaviour, and the extensive use of white make-up could be read as a lampoon of the largely mono-racial aspects of the subculture (and of a certain kind of conventionally understood middle-class identity).

Agnes Jasper in an article on the Dutch Goth scene has examined how members of the subculture express a wariness about seeming too Goth.[15] The paradox that Jasper identifies (who, like Hodkinson, is a Goth and an academic) is that strict conformity to the Goth scene is not regarded as non-conformist (and therefore is not properly 'Goth'). The problem is how to find a space for individuality within what appears to be a heavily stylised scene. The subculture is able to treat this issue with some humour, and Jasper refers to a cartoon by a contemporary artist, 'Voltaire' (the name is an ironic Enlightenment reference), which whilst acknowledging an inevitable discrepancy between fantasy and reality in a young Goth's life nevertheless contains a reference which problematically reworks one of the more troubling aspects of the Gothic literary tradition. The cartoon jokingly refers to a figure who fantasises that he is a vampiric version of Vlad the Impaler, but in reality is a teenager named Bernie Weinstein. Such a link between Jewishness and vampirism reasserts images of anti-Semitism that Carol Margaret Davison has identified as a key dynamic within the British Gothic tradition.[16] Indeed, there are many readings of *Dracula*, for example, which interpret the Count as representing a popular *fin de siècle* anti-Semitism.[17] This is not to say that the Goth scene is anti-Semitic, but that this casual evocation of elements of the Gothic tradition unwittingly, but nevertheless worryingly, repeats some of the political dramas of an earlier age.

The Goth scene is one contemporary manifestation of the Gothic which reworks some of its tensions and raises questions about class which are also relevant to an understanding of the literary tradition. It is also a subculture which has its own texts, including magazines and fanzines. Mick Mercer's *Hex Files: The Goth Bible* (1996) is a reference guide, broken down as an A–Z of nations, to Goth-related activities worldwide, including information on fanzines, music, and the local fetish scene.[18] Gavin Baddeley's *Gothic Chic: A Connoisseur's Guide to Dark Culture* (2002) discusses the Goth scene within a wider analysis of the cultural traditions of the Gothic (including literature, film, television, radio, and music), whilst Nancy Kilpatrick's *The Goth Bible: A Compendium for the Darkly Inclined* (2005) is a wide-ranging and somewhat light-hearted account of the Goth experience which refers to itself as 'a lifestyle handbook for today's creatures of the night'.[19] Further investigation into the scene, its practices, and its texts can helpfully shed light on the continuing presence and inevitable mutation of the Gothic tradition in the twenty-first century. In addition, the continuing presence of scholarship on the literary Gothic and on the related emerging research areas sketched here ensure that our understanding of the Gothic is as continually evolving as the form itself.

NOTES

1. A full list of their publications can be found at: http://www. zittaw.com/.

2. *Gothic Fiction: Rare Printed Works from the Sadleir-Black Collection of Gothic Fiction at the Alderman Library, University of Virginia*, on microfilm, ed. Marie Mulvey-Roberts, Alison Milbank and Peter Otto (Marlborough, Wiltshire: Adam Matthew, 2003).

3. Eve Kosofsky Sedgwick, *Between Men: English Literature and Male Homosocial Desire* (New York: Columbia University Press, 1985).

4. Paulina Palmer, *Lesbian Gothic: Transgressive Fictions* (London: Cassell, 1999).

5. Michael Eberle-Sinatra (ed.), 'Queering Gothic Films', special issue, *Gothic Studies*, 7 : 2 (November 2005).

6. Sarah Waters, *Affinity* (London:Virago, 1999).

7. Michael Rowe (ed.), *Queer Fear* (Vancouver: Arsenal Pulp, 2000), and *Queer Fear II* (Vancouver: Arsenal Pulp, 2002).

8. Avril Horner (ed.), *European Gothic: A Spirited Exchange* (Manchester: Manchester University Press, 2002).

9. See Jarlath Killeen, *Gothic Ireland: Horror and the Anglican Imagination in the Eighteenth Century* (Dublin: Four Courts, 2005). See also Joseph Valente, *Dracula's Crypt: Bram Stoker, Irishness and the Question of Blood* (Urbana: University of Illinois Press, 2002).

10. A more recent manifestation of a Goth scene in North America has associations with musicians such as Marilyn Manson.

11. Sara Martin, 'Gothic Scholars Don't Wear Black: Gothic Studies and Gothic Subcultures', in *Gothic Studies*, 4: 1 (May 2002), 28–43, 33.

12. See James Hannahan, 'Bela Lugosi's Dead and I Don't Feel So Good Either: Goth and the Glorification of Suffering in Rock Music', in Karen Kelly and Evelyn McDonnell (eds), *Stars Don't Stand Still in the Sky: Music and Myth* (London: Routledge, 1999). See Martin, 'Gothic Scholars Don't Wear Black', 36. As well as Goth music there has also been the emer-

gence of Gothic-influenced graphic novels. Unfortunately space precludes analysis of the form.

13. David Punter, *The Literature of Terror*, 2 vols (London: Longman, [1980] 1996), vol. 2, p. 203.

14. Paul Hodkinson, *Goth: Identity, Style and Subculture* (Oxford: Berg, 2002), p. 96.

15. Agnes Jasper, ' "I am not a Goth!" The Unspoken Morale of Authenticity Within the Dutch Gothic Subculture', in *Etnofoor*, 17 (1–2), 90–115. Jasper views the subculture (and perhaps this is more relevant to the Dutch context) as not as class-specific as Hodkinson claims for the UK experience.

16. Carol Margaret Davison, *Anti-Semitism and British Gothic Literature* (Basingstoke: Palgrave, 2004).

17. See Daniel Pick, *Faces of Degeneration: A European Disorder, c.1848–c.1918* (Cambridge: Cambridge University Press, 1989), p. 173. See also Jules Zanger, 'A Sympathetic Vibration: Dracula and the Jews', *English Literature in Transition, 1880–1920*, 34 (1991), 33–44.

18. Mick Mercer, *Hex Files: The Goth Bible* (New York: Overlook, 1996).

19. Gavin Baddeley, *Gothic Chic: A Connoisseur's Guide to Dark Culture* (London: Plexus, 2002), and Nancy Kilpatrick, *The Goth Bible: A Compendium for the Darkly Inclined* (London: Plexus, 2005), quotation from book jacket.

Student Resources

This essay was written by a student taking a final year module entitled 'Gothic Literature 1790s–1900' taught by me at the University of Glamorgan. The module looks at a number of texts which are referred to in this book, and seminar discussion of them also shaped some of the ideas in the submitted essays (such as here, for example, in a brief discussion of social and psychological incompletion in *Christabel* and some references to rationality in *Lamia*). However, this is a model essay for a number of reasons and it achieved a passing grade of first class (although not at the top of that range, for reasons which will be explained in the Commentary). Paragraphs are numbered for ease of reference.

Discuss images of vampirism in Romantic poetry

[§ 1] Images of vampirism can be found in 'Vampire legends [that] appear nearly everywhere' (Punter and Byron, 2004, p. 268), dating as far back as the vampiric *lamia* of Greek Mythology. However, the vampire initially makes its appearance in English Literature during the eighteenth century, where early images of vampirism can be found in poetry, such as Goethe's 'The Bride of Corinth' (1797). Polidori's *The Vampyre* (1819) signifies the entry of the vampire into prose fiction shortly afterward, early in the nineteenth century, and images of vampirism can also be found in the early nineteenth-century Romantic poetry of John Keats and Samuel Taylor Coleridge. Throughout this essay Keats's *Lamia* (1819) and Coleridge's *Christabel* (1816) will be examined in order to explore the extent to which the vampiric figures of Lamia and Geraldine share the characteristics of the Gothic vampires, including 'the vampire[s'] associat[ion] with sexuality' (Punter and Byron, 2004, p. 268), while illustrating how they also conform to many of the conventions of Romantic poetry. It will be shown how the Romantic representations of vampirism are intrinsically linked to the inner life of the imagination and emotions, and how this complicates the Gothic portrayal of vampires as 'monsters [and as a source of] evil' (Punter and Byron, 2004, p. 270).

[§ 2] Lamia initially inhabits a secular pre-Christian world of 'fairy broods', 'nymph[s]' and 'satyr[s]' (Keats, 1:ll. 1–2). This is a place that is so full of the Romantic sense of 'originality [and] wonder' (Drabble ed., 2000, p. 872) that it is even beyond the limits of the imagination of the poet; it is 'strewn [with] rich gifts, unknown to any muse' (Keats, 1:l. 19). There is a sense that poetry itself is inadequate to describe the vampiric Lamia's world. Lamia, herself, is also a truly Romantic figure, as a *lamia* or a vampire she is an 'outcast' (Drabble ed., 2000, p. 874), who leaves her world of wonder in an attempt to satiate the imaginative longings and humanising emotions of her inner life. While Lamia is imprisoned in a snake's body 'she will[s], her spirit' (Keats, 1:l. 205) to roam humanity, allowing her imagination to 'feast and riot' (Keats, 1:l. 214) on all she sees. 'And once, while among mortals dreaming thus, / She saw the young Corinthian Lycius . . . And fell into a swooning love of him' (Keats, 1:ll. 215–219). Lamia is, in true Romantic style, a force of 'imaginative spontaneity, visionary originality, wonder and . . . self-expression' (Drabble ed., 2000, p. 872). After her transformation into female form and gaining Lycius's love, she prepares her 'place unknown' (Keats, 1:l. 388) for their wedding feast. Once again, Lamia's 'imaginative spontaneity' comes to the fore as she creates a tropical wonderland of 'splendour' (Keats, 2:l. 137), where she ensures that 'her viewless servants . . . enrich / The fretted splendour of each nook and niche' (Keats, 2: ll. 136–137). With the help of her supernatural abilities Lamia is creating a kind of paradise on earth, a version of Eden, through a process of creativity that demonstrates 'the autonomy of the all-important creative imagination' (Drabble ed., 2000, p. 872), of the Romantic writer.

[§ 3] Since the vampiric Lamia is portrayed as a force of creativity and not of destruction, it is difficult to deny that she is a vampiric figure who complicates the typical nineteenth-century portrayal of the vampire as a source of evil and destruction. Throughout the course of Keats's poem, Lamia becomes a Romantic symbol of 'poetry, idealism and dreaming' (Strachan ed., 2003, p. 159), despite initially being portrayed as a deceptive manipulator who uses her preternatural faculty to mesmerise her victim, Lycius. As a result Lamia, unlike most vampiric figures, fails to materialize into a convincing source of evil. Lamia does not want to wreak death and destruction but instead longs for love and sensual pleasure. She wants to 'move in a sweet body fit for life / And love and pleasure, and the ruddy strife / Of hearts and lips' (Keats, 1:ll. 39–41). She is a sensual vampiric figure who, like Le Fanu's Countess Carmilla, is a seductress. Lamia leaves her sexualized world of the 'wanton . . . and licentious' (Cotterell, 1996, p. 59) 'hoofed satyrs' (Keats, 1:ll. 15) of Greek Mythology, in order to snare Lycius 'in her mesh' (Keats, 1:l. 295) of unearthly pleasure, where 'bliss / . . . [and not] distrust and hate' (Keats, 2:ll. 9–10) can flourish. Lamia creates 'a place unknown' (Keats, 1:l 388) in the middle of Corinth that is a representation of her inner life of sensations and pleasurable emotions.

[§ 4] Coleridge's *Christabel* also contains many Romantic elements. The poem begins in the style of a medieval romance, using the stock props of a 'castle' (Coleridge, l. 1) complete with a 'moat' (Coleridge, l. 118), and Christabel, the 'high-born damsel, . . . [who is] laying herself down . . . to dream' (Lamb in Matthews ed., 1971, p. 157) about another stock prop of medieval romance, her 'betrothed knight' (Coleridge, l. 28). Also in true Romantic style, *Christabel*, like *Lamia*, places an emphasis on the inner life, as it dwells on the importance of dreams and dreaming. The poem tells how Christabel 'had dreams all yesternight' about her absent knight, and how this leads her out into the 'midnight wood' (Coleridge, l. 31), where she first encounters the vampiric Geraldine. Later, 'Bracy the bard' (Coleridge, l. 472) recounts, what the reader knows to be, a prophetic dream that he has had to Sir Leoline,

Christabel and Geraldine. He tells how, in his dream, on hearing Christabel 'uttering fearful moan' (Coleridge, l. 523), he finds a 'dove' with 'a bright green snake / Coiled around its wings and neck' (Coleridge, ll. 536–537). The importance that Romantic writing places upon the inner life becomes clear through this dream, because within the context of the poem it serves as a prophetic allegory of the relationship between Christabel and the vampiric Geraldine.

[§ 5] In addition to conforming to many Romantic conventions, Romantic images of vampirism also contain clear links to the vampires of Gothic fiction. Lamia makes her appearance as 'a palpitating snake' (Keats, 1:l. 9); however, as she is bargaining with Hermes she reveals 'I was a woman once' (Keats, 1:l.117). Like many of the Gothic vampires, Lamia 'is a 'shape-shifter' (Motion, 1998, p. 433), however, unlike most Gothic vampires, for example Bram Stoker's Count Dracula, she cannot execute her transformation at will. In order to regain her 'woman's shape' (Keats, 1:l.118), Lamia has to bargain with Hermes and then undergo a painful transformation that leaves her with 'Nothing but pain and ugliness' (Keats, 1:l.164), before allowing her to emerge as a 'full-born beauty new and exquisite' (Keats, 1:l.172). When Lamia beseechingly asks " 'When from this wreathed tomb shall I wake?' " (Keats, 1:l.38), she is openly acknowledging her vampiric nature as she compares her life as a snake to a living death. Like Lamia, Coleridge's Geraldine has the ability to shape-shift, though not in the same explosive way. Geraldine's transformation is terrifyingly subtle in comparison to Lamia's. Geraldine looks at Christabel, and just as 'A snake's small eye blinks dull and shy, / . . .the lady's eyes they shrunk in her head, / Each shrunk up to a serpent's eye' (Coleridge, ll. 571–3). This subtle transformation in Geraldine echoes the image of the snake from Bracy the bard's dream, which was discussed earlier. In traditional vampire style, Coleridge also has the victim, Christabel, begin to assume some of Geraldine's vampiric characteristics as the poem employs a language of disease and corruption; she 'Shuddered aloud with a hissing sound' (Coleridge, l. 579), and 'did imitate / . . . [Geraldine's] look of dull and treacherous hate . . . With forced unconscious sympathy' (Coleridge, ll. 593–597). Christabel is changing against her will and she is powerless to prevent her emergent likeness to the serpentine and vampiric Geraldine, and also to Keats's Lamia. In addition, when Geraldine says 'In the touch of this bosom there worketh a spell' (Coleridge, l. 255), it becomes clear that, like Keats's Lamia and Le Fanu's Carmilla, Geraldine also possesses preternatural powers. Although, Geraldine's powers do not appear to cause the same sense of rapture in Christabel as those feelings that Lamia and Carmilla create in Lycius and Laura, Geraldine uses her preternatural powers to help her to ensure Christabel cannot tell her father about 'her bosom and half her side' (Coleridge, l. 246), which is 'A sight to dream of not to tell' (Coleridge, l. 247). She ensures Christabel's silence by becoming 'lord of . . . [her] utterance' (Coleridge, l. 256).

[§ 6] The vampiric Geraldine, like Keats's Lamia, also complicates nineteenth-century ideas that regard vampires as being a source of evil. The poem provides a sense that Geraldine has been created, or 'Raised up' (Coleridge, l. 361), by the internal lives of her victims. At the opening of the poem Sir Leoline is mourning his long dead wife, in whose memory the 'sacristan / . . . duly pulls the heavy bell / Five and forty beads' (Coleridge, ll. 327–329) at dawn everyday. The heroine, Christabel, is also missing absent loved ones. Unable to sleep, she leaves her father's castle to go into the wood to 'pray / For the weal of her lover that's far away' (ll. 29–30). It is while Christabel is praying beneath an oak tree, that she hears the moans of 'a damsel bright, / Drest in a silken robe of white' (ll. 58–9), providing a sense that Geraldine is conjured up by, and in response to, Christabel's inner turmoil. This feeling that the 'damsel' has been conjured up by the sense of absence and the need for solace felt by her victims continues throughout the poem as Geraldine later attempts to supplant the position of authority that Christabel's dead mother held. She orders the dead mother's ghost, Christabel's 'guardian spirit' (Coleridge, l. 327), to be " 'Off, woman, off!' " (Coleridge, l. 205), and 'holds the maiden in her arms . . . . As a mother with her child' (Coleridge, ll. 287–9). This not only reinforces the sense that Geraldine is created by the emotions that reside in the internal life, but is also in accord with the Gothic realm where there are many absent mothers, such as the world of Radcliffe's Ellena Rosalba.

[§ 7] It has already been argued that the vampiric Geraldine appears as a result of the sense of absence and sorrow felt by her victims, and that her initial appearance coincides with Christabel lamenting the absence of her lover. However, there are ambiguities in the language that Coleridge utilises, that also allow the poem to suggest that Geraldine appears in order to supplant the lover's position in Christabel's affections. This places Geraldine, like Lamia, squarely in the position of a seductress, who appears in order to fulfil a need in Christabel that only a lover can satisfy. Despite initially being seen as 'The maid devoid of guile and sin' (Coleridge, l. 587), ambiguities within its language allow the poem to suggest that Christabel's dreams about her absent lover, which make 'her moan and leap / As on her bed she lay in sleep' (Coleridge, ll. 29–30), may not be as innocent as they appear. This sense is compounded by the fact that Christabel tells Geraldine that " 'to my room we'll creep in stealth / And you tonight must sleep with me' " (Coleridge, ll. 116–117); she deliberately sneaks Geraldine into the castle without her father knowing. The poem is allowing the possibility that Christabel's world may not be as pristine as it at first appears, it can also be seen as a sexualised world where Christabel is free to indulge her sexual fantasies about the absent knight, and also possibly about the hypnotic Geraldine. In the light of this reading of the poem, Christabel's innocent virtuous world of medieval romance slides into the sexualised world of the nineteenth century Gothic vampire, a world such as that inhabited by Le Fanu's Countess Carmilla.

[§ 8] However, it is the sense that Geraldine is created by the inner life of emotions and desire that complicates the nineteenth-century portrayal of vampires as sources of evil. Since it has been argued that Geraldine is conjured up by need and absence, despite coming from the natural world outside the castle, she is an internal, and not an external, threat. Through Christabel and the vampiric Geraldine, the poem is exploring what happens when you look within. It is ultimately suggesting that evil and danger are not external threats; it is proposing instead that they are troubles that come from within. In this sense evil and danger can be seen as expressions of the inner life of the imagination and emotions. However, the fact that Geraldine appears to materialize in an attempt to fill the positions of absent loved ones as a response to her victims' need for comfort and solace also suggests that the vampiric Geraldine somehow completes both them, and their world.

[§ 9] As discussed earlier, the vampiric Lamia is not the main source of evil in Keats's representation of vampirism. The main source of evil in the Romantic world of *Lamia* comes instead from the secular world of philosophy and science, in the guise of Apollonius. Lamia's first encounter with Apollonius ensures that the reader's sympathies are firmly on the side of Lamia. 'With curled gray beard, sharp eyes, and smooth bald crown, / Slow-stepped, and robed in philosophic gown' (Keats, 1:ll.364–365), Apollonius is a cold and unsettling figure who causes Lamia to 'tremble' and 'shudder' (Keats, 1:ll.368–369). Keats's poem is portraying the vampiric Lamia as exhibiting the human emotions of love and fear, whilst conversely, the human Apollonius is depicted as cold and emotionless. Lamia's fear increases to a terror when Apollonius arrives as an 'uninvited guest / To force himself upon . . . [them], and infest / With an unbidden presence the bright throng of younger friends' (Keats, 2:ll. 165–167). Lamia recognizes that Apollonius is a symbol of 'the analytical rationalism . . . [and] the coldly calculating mentality of . . . philosophy' (Drabble, 2000, p. 872), against which the Romantic spirit seems compelled to revolt. She knows, that as a source of magic, the philosophical Apollonius cannot understand her because she is 'not a mathematical truth' (Hunt in Matthews ed., 1971, p. 169). The poem states how 'all charms fly / At the mere touch of cold philosophy' (Keats, 2:ll. 229–230), and then reveals how 'Philosophy will clip an angel's wings, / Conquer all mysteries by rule and line, / Empty the haunted air, and gnomed mine, / [and] Unweave a rainbow' (Keats, 2:ll. 234–238). It becomes clear that the poem 'makes the power of the philosopher an ill-natured and disturbing thing' (Hunt in Matthews ed., 1971, p. 169), a 'thing' that deliberately sets out to destroy the wonder that can be found in the natural world. As such, 'Keats's portrayal of Apollonius [can be interpreted] as an attack upon a sour rationalism at the touch of which poetry and the imagination is destroyed' (Strachan ed., 2003, p. 159). It is sadly ironic that when Apollonius destroys Lamia, in order to save Lycius from the 'foul dream' (Keats, 2:l. 271) that he views her as being, 'He becomes a form of [the] evil that he banishes' (Motion, 1998, p. 436).

[§ 10] In conclusion, it has been shown how the images of vampirism that can be found in the Romantic poetry of Keats and Coleridge conform to both Romantic and Gothic conventions. It has been illustrated how the Romantic vampires, Geraldine and Lamia, are both seducers who are associated with the sexualised world of much Gothic fiction. In the tradition of many nineteenth-century vampires, it has also been shown how Geraldine and Lamia are shape-shifters who exercise the use of their preternatural powers to help ensnare and entrap their victims. However, it has also been illustrated that whilst utilising, and adhering to, many Gothic conventions and props, *Lamia* and *Christabel* are quite clearly products of Romantic imaginations. In true Romantic style, Lamia and Geraldine are outcasts who revolt against the nineteenth-century portrayal of vampires as a source of evil. Lamia, it has been shown, possesses characteristics that are traditionally categorised as evil, characteristics such as duplicity and the ability to manipulate. Despite this, she is clearly a figure who holds the reader's sympathy because the poem allows her to be a force of creativity, someone who has the humanising emotions that are linked to 'love' and 'bliss', and not to grief or destruction. Similarly, Coleridge's Geraldine also complicates the idea of a vampire as being a source of evil. Whilst it can be argued that she is an evil figure, it can also be argued that she is created by the inner life where emotions and desire exist. In view of this, Coleridge's Geraldine, it has been shown, can be seen as completing her victims, making them emotionally whole again. The figures of Lamia and Geraldine 'endorse the Romantics' view of the human mind as organically created' (Drabble, 2000, p. 872). Finally, it has been revealed that in the world of Romantic poetry, the source of evil is a representation of a cold and calculating view of philosophy. Through Apollonius, the poetry portrays philosophy as being an evil and destructive force, a force that has the power to 'intrude upon the sanctities of the human heart' (Drabble, 2000, p. 872).

Bibliography

Coleridge, Samuel Taylor. *Christabel* in Wu, Duncan ed. *Romanticism: An Anthology*. Oxford. Blackwell, (first published 1994).

Cotterell, Arthur. *The Encyclopaedia of Mythology*. London. Anness Publishing Ltd., 1999 (first published 1996).

Drabble, Margaret ed. *The Oxford Companion to English Literature*. Oxford. Oxford University Press, 2000.

Hunt, Leigh in G. M. Matthews, ed. *Keats: The Critical Heritage*. London. Routledge, 1971.

Keats, John. *Lamia* in Wu, Duncan ed. *Romanticism: An Anthology*. Oxford. Blackwell, (first published 1994).

Lamb, Charles in G. M. Matthews, ed. *Keats: The Critical Heritage*. London. Routledge, 1971.

Motion, Andrew. *Keats*. London. Faber and Faber, 1998 (first published 1997).

Punter, David and Glennis Byron. *The Gothic*. Oxford. Blackwell Publishing, 2004.

Strachan, John ed. *The Poems of John Keats*. London. Routledge, 2003.

COMMENTARY

First, to the strengths of the essay. Note how the opening paragraph contextualises the literary representations of vampirism in a succinct but informed way. The paragraph also provides a clear statement of the student's aims and ambitions. Paragraph 2 indicates how the student is routing their analysis of the poem through a close reading of it. This is an important approach when looking at any text, but poetry (and especially Gothic poetry) demands this type of close exploration because it is vital, as we have seen in the discussion of poetry in this volume, to examine how language is used. The opening of the third paragraph acknowledges that the complexities of the poem should be understood within the context of certain generic expectations concerning literary representations of vampirism. This helps both to locate the poem in historical and literary terms and to indicate how, and why, the poem challenges such expectations. In paragraph 4 the student introduces *Christabel* by attempting to place it in the context of Romanticism. Paragraph 5 begins to develop links between Romanticism and the Gothic, and establishes a context relating to other literary representations of vampires. It also makes effective comparison between the two poems in order to complicate and advance the argument. Again, the reading of *Christabel* is routed through a close analysis of the text in paragraphs 5, 6, and 7. Paragraphs 8 and 9 are a clear recap of the key issues in the poems and the final paragraph is, in the main, a lucid summary of the principal arguments. Also, the essay is a very well-written, eloquent answer. It is well paced, with no sense of either rushing the argument or indirection at any point. The student has made excellent use of a limited range of secondary sources and throughout is aware of the necessity of balancing the demands of close reading against the needs of contextualising the argument. However, there are a number of ways in which the essay could have been improved.

First, the essay discusses the poems without due respect for their chronology. Because Coleridge is a first-generation Romanticist this places him in a slightly different context from that of Keats. Coleridge was working on *Christabel* in the late 1790s, even though its formal publication was shortly before *Lamia*, and by discussing the poems non-chronologically it becomes difficult to explore matters of likely influence of one poet upon another. Paragraph 3 makes reference to Le Fanu's *Carmilla*, but this was published in 1872, so the most that can be claimed is that *Lamia* foreshadows what would appear in the Gothic, but this weakens any rigorous engagement with specific matters of influence because *Carmilla* is not a text that is discussed in any depth (a problem which resurfaces at the end of paragraph 7). Paragraph 4, although referring to the Romantic context, does not properly define what the principal concerns of the Romantics were. This would have been the space in which to outline the relationship between Romanticism, the Gothic, and the Enlightenment. The end of paragraph 6 refers to the theme of absent mothers in *Christabel* but makes only the briefest reference to Radcliffe, whereas a more complete discussion of how the poem might be situated in terms of the Female Gothic would have been helpful. Throughout the student has been diligent in establishing the correct contexts, but in these instances they have not been as thoroughly developed as they might. The concluding paragraph is an intelligent synopsis but there is always the danger of oversimplification, and this is apparent in the claim that 'it has been revealed that in the world of Romantic poetry, the source of evil is a representation of a cold and calculating view of philosophy'. This one generalisation aside, the essay is on the whole a model of how to read poetry and the Gothic for its detail.

When writing essays it is important that due care is taken with establishing the correct context. This means spending some time outlining the critical view of the topic, or author, and then using this as the context in which to develop your arguments. It is not necessary to always agree with critics, but it is important to engage with them to help critically position your own arguments. It is also helpful to have some sense of the historical period, although this might not necessarily apply if you develop a purely psychoanalytical reading, for example. A more materialist reading would need to provide information about the cultural and historical contexts. Here, the student makes brief reference to *Carmilla*, and it would be possible to examine images of lesbianism as one way of creating a context in which to discuss, for example, *Christabel* and Le Fanu's tale. However, it would also be important to acknowledge that the Romantic context is quite different from the one in which Le Fanu is writing and that this plays a role in shaping his work. Reading for context also enables us, as this essay makes clear, to account for the detail of a text as it enables us to understand why it is dealing in specific forms of representation, themes, and issues. It is also important, as this essay demonstrates, to properly balance close reading of the text with a wider understanding of the context which produced it.

The Guide to Further Reading provides information on the type of secondary material that you need to engage with in order to develop the necessary contextual work. Some of these texts are general and others relate to more specific periods and forms: a combination of such scholarship is often helpful in establishing the required critical framework.

GLOSSARY

Ambiguity

A key concept that explains many of the hesitations and contradictions which are so often found in Gothic texts. David Punter in *The Literature of Terror* (1980, revised 1996) sees the term as central to understanding the middle-class provenance of the Gothic and its peculiar anti-middle-class tendencies. The Gothic also delights in images of sexual taboo but because they are tabooed it is unclear, or ambiguous, as to where the coherent moral or political vision of the text is to be found.

Enlightenment

An eighteenth-century movement associated with the triumph of reason (as well as religious tolerance). For the Romantics this privileging of reason ignored 'human' qualities such as feeling and the imagination. The Gothic's exploration of the irrational and focus on heightened emotional states provides a counterpoint to an Enlightenment confidence in scientific method.

Female Gothic

A term coined by Ellen Moers in 1976 and used by her to describe Gothic literature written by women in the late eighteenth and early nineteenth centuries. The Female Gothic influenced many of the aspects of sensation fiction in general and the writing of Wilkie Collins in particular. Central themes and issues include female incarceration within coded domestic spaces (castles, aristocratic milieux, and so on), and the restoration of female identity usually through the discovery of a 'lost' mother, or by that mother's intervention. Typically the form is characterised by a subtle feminism and an optimism concerning the possibility of social advancement for women.

Fin de siècle

The end of the nineteenth century, for conservative commentators in Britain, characterised by decadence and degeneration. Oscar Wilde, for example, was represented as a degenerate figure in Max Nordau's *Degeneration* (1892), which is a pseudo-scientific analysis of decadent decline. Theories of degeneracy were explored by writers as diverse as Bram Stoker and H. G. Wells, and played an important role in shaping Gothic narratives concerned with nationality, empire, and conventional gender scripts.

Horror

A concept which in the eighteenth century is contrasted with Terror. In Radcliffe, Terror is represented through gesture and implication, and so stimulates the imagination and feelings. In contrast Horror has an explicitness that overwhelms, or negates, the imagination. Terror is linked to the subtleties of the Female Gothic, whilst the explicitness of Horror is linked to images of violence found in the male Gothic of Matthew Lewis. Horror retains this association with visually explicit violence as a characteristic of horror novels and horror films of the twentieth and twenty-first centuries.

Modernism

A literary and cultural movement of the early twentieth century which was influenced by the Gothic. This can be seen in German expressionist films such as *The Cabinet of Dr Caligari* (1919), *The Golem* (1920), and *Nosferatu* (1922), as well as in the work of T. S. Eliot, James Joyce, and Virginia Woolf. The Gothic's reliance on images of physically and emotionally damaged selves appears to have had a particular resonance with modernist writers, artists, and film-makers working in the period.

Postmodernism

Art and literature from the 1970s onwards of a self-referential kind regarded as illustrating the end of the grand narratives which once gave coherence to culture, society, and everyday experience. The decline in shared values, so the argument goes, is replaced by moral relativism. Not a movement as such, more of a concept and one taken issue with by some of the writers discussed in this book (notably by Angela Carter and Toni Morrison).

Romanticism

A literary, artistic, and philosophical movement which began in different countries (Britain, mainland Europe, and America) in the late eighteenth and early nineteenth centuries. In Britain it is characterised by anti-Enlightenment tendencies and championed the importance of the imagination over the dictates of natural science. Romanticism provides an important context for the Gothic because it shares with it an interest in sublimity and emotion. Many Romantics such as Byron, Coleridge, Keats, and Percy Shelley were influenced by the Gothic.

Sensation fiction

Emerging in the 1860s, the popular literary form of its day. Novels typically explored issues about insanity and lost identities, set within plots involving manipulative aristocrats which reworked elements of the earlier Gothic tradition. Critics have noted how its use of either threatened or actual female imprisonment (often in asylums) reworks aspects of the Female Gothic. The use of amateur detectives tends to provide an image of triumphant rationality. The form can be read as a secular, non-supernatural, continuation of an earlier Gothic tradition.

The Sublime

A conceptualisation of nature and the role of the imagination. Although discussions of sublimity go back to classical times they took on an especial significance for the Romantics in the late eighteenth and early nineteenth centuries. Typically, in the sublime moment the subject feels overwhelmed by their experience of nature, the majesty of which suggests the presence of a divine creator. However, Burke argued that Terror is the most powerful, and therefore the most sublime, emotion. He developed this theory in his treatise *A Philosophical Enquiry* (1757), which proved to be influential on a generation of Gothic writers working in the eighteenth century. His treatise suggested a model of trauma which underpins the later 'Uncanny'.

Terror

A model of anxiety and fear which in the eighteenth century is often contrasted with Horror. Conceptions of Terror in the eighteenth century are underpinned by Burke's idea of sublime Terror. Burke's idea that a fear of death was the most sublime emotion was used and modified by Gothic writers at the time. Ann Radcliffe, for example, in her essay 'On the Supernatural in Poetry' (1826) contrasts Terror with Horror, arguing that Terror expands the soul and so produces a pleasurable fear, whereas Horror overwhelms the imagination.

Transgression

A term that has associations with ambiguity. On a formal level the Gothic typically transgresses models of realism by dwelling on fantastical experiences. On a more sophisticated level it also transgresses notions of conventional values, whether social, cultural, or sexual. However, often the transgressor ('monster', vampire, ghost, and so on) is associated with 'evil', which renders the moment ambivalent because of a hesitation between the pleasures of transgression and a demonising language of 'evil'.

Uncanny

A post-Romantic conceptualisation of unease which has played a significant role in the critical analysis of the Gothic. Sigmund Freud's essay 'The Uncanny' (1919) examined feelings of unease as they appear within seemingly commonplace experience. Feelings of uncanniness (the *unheimlich*) are initially contrasted with ideas of the home (the *heimlich*) and the domestic security that it represents. However, the Oedipus complex suggests that the home is where sexual secrets are propagated, so that the home becomes traumatic, or uncanny, as a result. This trauma is manifested as a repetition compulsion, and Freud explores how a culture repeats the past in tales of the dead in which the past comes back to life (or is repeated). This conclusion has relevance for a consideration of the ghost story and the images of the double (the living and the dead) in the Gothic.

GUIDE TO FURTHER READING

General

Aguirre, Manuel, *The Closed Space: Horror Literature and Western Symbolism* (Manchester: Manchester University Press, 1990).

Armitt, Lucie, *Theorising the Fantastic* (London: Arnold, 1996).

Botting, Fred, *Gothic* (London: Routledge, 1996).

Botting, Fred (ed.), *The Gothic* (Cambridge: D. S. Brewer, 2001).

Bronfen, Elisabeth, *Over Her Dead Body: Death, Femininity and the Aesthetic* (Manchester: Manchester University Press, 1992).

Byron, Glennis and David Punter (eds), *Spectral Readings: Towards a Gothic Geography* (Basingstoke: Macmillan, 1999).

Castricano, Jodey, *Cryptomimesis: The Gothic and Jacques Derrida's Ghost Writing* (Montreal: McGill-Queen's University Press, 2001).

Cavallaro, Dani, *The Gothic Vision: Three Centuries of Horror, Terror and Fear* (New York: Continuum, 2002).

Clemens, Valdine, *The Return of the Repressed: Gothic Horror from the Castle of Otranto to Alien* (Albany, NY: Albany State University Press, 1999).

Davison, Carol Margaret, *Anti-Semitism and British Gothic Literature* (Basingstoke: Palgrave, 2004).

Ellis, Markham, *The History of Gothic Fiction* (Edinburgh: Edinburgh University Press, 2000).

Fisher, Benjamin F., *The Gothic's Gothic: Study Aids to the Tradition of the Tale of Terror* (New York: Garland, 1988).

Frank, Frederick S. (ed.), *The Guide to the Gothic, III: An Annotated Bibliography of Criticism, 1994–2003* (Lanham: Scarecrow, 2005).

Grixti, Joseph, *Terrors of Uncertainty: The Cultural Contexts of Horror Fiction* (London: Routledge, 1989).

Hoeveler, Diane Long and Tamar Heller (eds), *Approaches to Teaching Gothic Fiction: The British and American Traditions* (New York: The Modern Language Association of America, 2003).

Hogle, Jerrold E., *The Cambridge Companion to Gothic Fiction* (Cambridge: Cambridge University Press, 2002).

Horner, Avril (ed.), *European Gothic: A Spirited Exchange, 1760–1960* (Manchester: Manchester University Press, 2002).

Howells, Coral Ann, *Love, Mystery and Misery: Feeling in Gothic Fiction* (London: Athlone, 1978).

Jackson, Rosemary, *Fantasy: The Literature of Subversion* (London: Methuen, 1981).

Kilgour, Maggie, *The Rise of the Gothic Novel* (London: Methuen, 1995).

MacAndrew, Elizabeth, *The Gothic Tradition in Fiction* (New York: Columbia University Press, 1979).

Moretti, Franco, *Signs Taken for Wonders* (London: Verso, 1983).

Mulvey-Roberts, Marie (ed.), *The Handbook to Gothic Literature* (Basingstoke: Macmillan, 1998).

Punter, David, *The Literature of Terror: A History of Gothic Fictions from 1765 to the Present Day* (London: Longman, [1980] 1996).

Punter, David, *Gothic Pathologies: The Text, the Body and the Law* (Basingstoke: Macmillan, 1998).

Punter, David (ed.), *A Companion to the Gothic* (Oxford: Blackwell, 2000).

Punter, David and Glennis Byron, *The Gothic* (Oxford: Blackwell, 2004).

Sage, Victor, *Horror Fiction in the Protestant Tradition* (Basingstoke: Macmillan, 1988).

Sage, Victor (ed.), *The Gothick Novel: A Casebook* (Basingstoke: Macmillan, 1990).

Sedgwick, Eve Kosofsky, *The Coherence of Gothic Conventions* (London: Methuen, 1986).

Smith, Andrew and William Hughes (eds), *Empire and the Gothic: The Politics of Genre* (Basingstoke: Palgrave, 2003).

Smith, Andrew, William Hughes and Diane Mason (eds), *Fictions of Unease: The Gothic from Otranto to the X-Files* (Bath: Sulis, 2002).

Todorov, Tzvetan, *The Fantastic: A Structural Approach to a Literary Genre*, trans. Richard Howards, 2nd edn, ed. Louis A Wagner (London: Case Western University, 2002).

Romantic

Baldick, Chris, *In Frankenstein's Shadow: Myth, Monstrosity and Nineteenth-Century Writing* (Oxford: Clarendon, 1987).

Behrendt, Stephen C. (ed.), *Approaches to Teaching Shelley's Frankenstein* (New York: The Modern Language Association of America, 1990).

Botting, Fred (ed.), *Frankenstein: A Casebook* (Basingstoke: Macmillan, 1995).

Brown, Marshall, *The Gothic Text* (Stanford: Stanford University Press, 2004).

Bruhm, Steven, *Gothic Bodies: The Politics of Pain in Romantic Fiction* (Philadelphia: University of Philadelphia Press, 1994).

Clery, E. J., *The Rise of Supernatural Fiction, 1762–1800* (Cambridge: Cambridge University Press, 1995).

Clery, E. J. and Robert Miles (eds), *Gothic Documents: A Sourcebook, 1700–1820* (Manchester: Manchester University Press, 2000).

Cottam, Daniel, *The Civilised Imagination: A Study of Ann Radcliffe, Jane Austen, and Sir Walter Scott* (Cambridge: Cambridge University Press, 1985).

Gamer, Michael, *Romanticism and the Gothic: Genre, Reception, and Canon Formation* (Cambridge: Cambridge University Press, 2000).

Ketterer, David, *Frankenstein's Creation: The Book, the Monster, and the Human Reality* (Victoria, BC: University of Victoria Press, 1979).

Kiely, Robert, *The Romantic Novel in England* (Cambridge, MA: Harvard University Press, 1972).

Levine, George and U. C. Knoepflmacher (eds), *The Endurance of Frankenstein: Essays on Mary Shelley's Novel* (Berkeley: University of California Press, 1979).

Mellor, Anne K., *Mary Shelley: Her Life, Her Fiction, Her Monsters* (New York: Methuen, 1988).

Miles, Robert, *Gothic Writing, 1750–1820: A Genealogy* (London: Routledge, 1993).

Miles, Robert, *Ann Radcliffe: The Great Enchantress* (Manchester: Manchester University Press, 1996).

Mishra, Vijay, *The Gothic Sublime* (New York: State University of New York Press, 1987).

Napier, Elizabeth R., *The Failure of Gothic: Problems of Disjunction in an Eighteenth-Century Form* (Oxford: Clarendon, 1987).

Norton, Rictor (ed.), *Gothic Readings: The First Wave, 1764–1840* (New York: Continuum, 2000).

Praz, Mario, *The Romantic Agony* (Oxford: Oxford University Press, 1933).

Railo, Eino, *The Haunted Castle: A Study of the Elements of English Romanticism* (New York: Humanities, 1964).

Smith, Andrew, *Gothic Radicalism: Literature, Philosophy, and Psychoanalysis in the Nineteenth Century* (Basingstoke: Macmillan, 2000).

Thomkins, J. M. S, *The Popular Novel in England, 1770–1800* (Lincoln: University of Nebraska Press, 1961).

Thompson, G. R. (ed.), *The Gothic Imagination: Essays in Dark Romanticism* (Pullman: Washington State University Press, 1974).

Voller, Jack G., *The Supernatural Sublime: The Metaphysics of Terror in Anglo-American Romanticism* (DeKalb: Northern Illinois University Press, 1994).

Watt, James, *Contesting the Gothic: Fiction, Genre, and Cultural Conflict* (Cambridge: Cambridge University Press, 1999).

Victorian

Bloom, Clive (ed.), *Nineteenth Century Suspense* (Basingstoke: Macmillan, 1990).

Brantlinger, Patrick, *Rule of Darkness: British Literature and Imperialism, 1830–1914* (Ithaca: Cornell University Press, 1988).

Brennan, Matthew C., *The Gothic Psyche: Disintegration and Growth in Nineteenth-Century English Literature* (Columbia, SC: Camden House, 1997).

Briggs, Julia, *Night Visitors: The Rise and Fall of the English Ghost Story* (London: Faber, 1977).

Carter, Margaret L., *The Vampire and the Critics* (London: UMI Research, 1988).

Cvetcovich, Ann, *Mixed Feelings: Feminism, Mass Culture, and Victorian Sensationalism* (New Brunswick, NJ: Rutgers University Press, 1992).

Dalby, Richard and William Hughes, *Bram Stoker: A Bibliography* (Westcliff-on-Sea: Desert Island, 2004).

Day, William Patrick, *In the Circles of Fear and Desire: A Study of Gothic Fantasy* (Chicago: University of Chicago Press, 1985).

DeLamotte, Eugenia C., *Perils of the Night: A Feminist Study of Nineteenth-Century Gothic* (Oxford: Oxford University Press, 1990).

Dickerson, Vanessa R., *Victorian Ghosts in the Noontide: Women Writers and the Supernatural* (Columbia: University of Missouri Press, 1996).

Dijkstra, Bram, *Idols of Perversity: Fantasies of Feminine Evil in Fin-de-Siècle Culture* (Oxford: Oxford University Press, 1986).

Dryden, Linda, *The Modern Gothic and Literary Doubles: Stevenson, Wilde and Wells* (Basingstoke: Palgrave, 2003).

Garrett, Peter K., *Gothic Reflections: Narrative Force in Nineteenth-Century Fiction* (Ithaca, NY: Cornell University Press, 2003).

Glover, David, *Vampires, Mummies, and Liberals: Bram Stoker and the Politics of Popular Fiction* (Durham: Duke University Press, 1996).

Hughes, William, *Beyond Dracula: Bram Stoker's Fiction and its Cultural Context* (Basingstoke: Macmillan, 2000).

Hughes, William and Andrew Smith (eds), *Bram Stoker: History, Psychoanalysis and the Gothic* (Basingstoke: Macmillan, 1998).

Hughes, Winifred, *The Maniac in the Cellar: Sensation Novels of the 1860s* (Princeton: Princeton University Press, 1980).

Malchow, Howard, *Gothic Images of Race in Nineteenth-Century Britain* (Stanford: Stanford University Press, 1996).

Melada, Ivan, *Sheridan Le Fanu* (Boston: Twayne, 1987).

Mighall, Robert, *A Geography of Victorian Gothic Fiction: Mapping History's Nightmares* (Oxford: Oxford University Press, 1999).

Miyoshi, Masao, *The Divided Self: A Perspective on the Literature of the Victorians* (New York: New York University Press, 1969).

Pick, Daniel, *Faces of Degeneration: A European Disorder, c.1848–c.1918* (Cambridge: Cambridge University Press, 1989).

Pykett, Lyn, *The 'Improper' Feminine: The Woman's Sensation Novel and the New Woman Writing* (London: Routledge, 1992).

Robbins, Ruth and Julian Wolfreys (eds), *Victorian Gothic: Literary and Cultural Manifestations in the Nineteenth Century* (Basingstoke: Palgrave, 2000).

Sage, Victor, *Le Fanu's Gothic: The Rhetoric of Darkness* (Basingstoke: Palgrave, 2004).

Schmitt, Cannon, *Alien Nation: Nineteenth-Century Gothic Fictions and English Nationality* (Philadelphia: University of Pennsylvania Press, 1997).

Senf, Carol A., *The Vampire in Nineteenth-Century English Literature* (Bowling Green, OH: Bowling Green State University Popular Press, 1988).

Showalter, Elaine, *Sexual Anarchy: Gender and Culture at the Fin de Siècle* (New York: Viking, 1990).

Smith, Andrew, *Victorian Demons: Medicine, Masculinity and the Gothic at the Fin de Siècle* (Manchester: Manchester University Press, 2004).

Smith, Elton E. and Robert Haas (eds), *The Haunted Mind: The Supernatural in Victorian Literature* (Lanham: Scarecrow, 1989).

Wolfreys, Julian, *Victorian Hauntings: Spectrality, Gothic, the Uncanny and Literature* (Basingstoke: Macmillan, 2002).

Twentieth Century

Armitt, Lucie, *Contemporary Women's Fiction and the Fantastic* (Basingstoke: Macmillan, 2000).

Cornwell, Neil, *The Literary Fantastic: From Gothic to Postmodernism* (Brighton: Harvester, 1990).

Daly, Nicholas, *Modernism, Romance and the Fin de Siècle: Popular Fiction and British Culture, 1880–1914* (Cambridge: Cambridge University Press, 1999).

Day, Aidan, *Angela Carter: The Rational Glass* (Edinburgh: Edinburgh University Press, 1998).

Sage, Victor and Allan Lloyd Smith (eds), *Modern Gothic: A Reader* (Manchester: Manchester University Press, 1996).

Smith, Andrew and Jeff Wallace (eds), *Gothic Modernisms* (Basingstoke: Palgrave, 2001).

Thurschwell, Pamela, *Literature: Technology and Magical Thinking* (Cambridge: Cambridge University Press, 2001).

Wilt, Judith, *Ghosts of the Gothic: Austen, Eliot, and Lawrence* (Princeton: Princeton University Press, 1980).

American

Bailey, Dale, *American Nightmares: The Haunted House Formula in American Popular Culture* (Bowling Green, OH: Bowling Green State University Popular Press, 1999).

Bloom, Clive (ed.), *Gothic Horror: A Reader's Guide from Poe to King and Beyond* (Basingstoke: Macmillan, 1998).

Bloom, Harold (ed.), *Stephen King: Modern Critical Views* (Philadelphia: Chelsea, 1998).

Brogan, Kathleen, *Cultural Haunting: Ghosts and Ethnicity in Recent American Literature* (Charlottesville: University Press of Virginia, 1998).

Carpenter, Lynette and Wendy Kolmar (eds), *Haunting the House of Fiction: Feminist Perspectives on Ghost Stories by American Women* (Knoxville: University of Tennessee Press, 1994).

Christophersen, Bill, *The Apparition in the Glass: Charles Brockden Brown's American Gothic* (Athens: University of Georgia Press, 1993).

Crow, Charles (ed.), *American Gothic: An Anthology, 1787–1916* (Oxford: Blackwell, 1999).

Davis, Jonathan P., *Stephen King's America* (Bowling Green, OH: Bowling Green State University Popular Press, 1994).

Docherty, Brian (ed.), *American Horror Fiction: From Brockden Brown to Stephen King* (Basingstoke: Macmillan, 1990).

Edwards, Justin D., *Gothic Passages: Racial Ambiguity and the American Gothic* (Iowa City: University of Iowa Press, 2003).

Fiedler, Leslie, *Love and Death in the American Novel* (Cleveland, OH: Meridian, 1964).

Goddu, Teresa A., *Gothic America: Narrative, History, and Nation* (New York: Columbia University Press, 1999).

Gross, Lewis S., *Redefining the American Gothic: From Wieland to Day of the Dead* (Ann Arbor: UMI Research, 1989).

Halttunen, Karen, *Murder Most Foul: The Killer and the American Gothic* (Cambridge, MA: Harvard University Press, 1998).

Hattenhauer, Darryl, *Shirley Jackson's American Gothic* (Albany: State University of New York, 2003).

Kerr, Howard and John William Crowley (eds), *The Haunted Dusk: American Supernatural Fiction, 1820–1920* (Athens: University of Georgia Press, 1983).

Lloyd-Smith, Allan, *American Gothic Fiction: An Introduction* (London: Continuum, 2004).

Magistrale, Tony, *Landscape of Fear: Stephen King's American Gothic* (Bowling Green, OH: Bowling Green State University Popular Press, 1988).

Magistrale, Tony and Michael Morrison (eds), *A Dark Night's Dreaming: Contemporary American Horror Fiction* (Columbia: University of South Carolina Press, 1996).

Malin, Irving, *New American Gothic* (Carbondale: Southern Illinois University Press, 1962).

Martin, Robert K. and Eric Savoy (eds), *The American Gothic: New Interventions in a National Narrative* (Iowa City: University of Iowa Press, 1998).

Meindl, Dieter, *American Fiction and the Metaphysics of the Grotesque* (Columbia: University of Missouri Press, 1996).

Mogen, David, Patrick Scott and Joanne B. Karpinski (eds), *Frontier Gothic: Terror and Wonder at the Frontier in American Literature* (Rutherford: Fairleigh Dickinson University Press, 1993).

Ringe, Donald A., *American Gothic: Imagination and Reason in Nineteenth-Century Fiction* (Lexington: University Press of Kentucky, 1982).

Sonser, Anna, *A Passion for Consumption: The Gothic Novel in America* (Bowling Green, OH: Bowling Green State University Popular Press, 2001).

Wardrop, Daneen, *Emily Dickinson's Gothic: Goblin with a Gauge*

(Iowa City: University of Iowa Press, 1996).

Weinstock, Jeffrey Andrew (ed.), *Spectral America: Phantoms and the National Imagination* (Madison: University of Wisconsin Press, 2004).

Wilczynski, Marek, *The Phantom and the Abyss: The Gothic Fiction in America and Aesthetics of the Sublime, 1798–1856* (Frankfurt: Peter Lang, 1999).

Winter, Kari J., *Subjects of Slavery, Agents of Change: Women and Power in Gothic Novels and Slave Narratives, 1790–1865* (Athens: University of Georgia Press, 1992).

Female Gothic

Becker, Susanne, *Gothic Forms of Feminine Fictions* (Manchester: Manchester University Press, 1999).

Clery, E. J., *Women's Gothic: From Clara Reeve to Mary Shelley* (Tavistock: Northcote House, 2000).

Ellis, Kate Ferguson, *The Contested Castle: Gothic Novels and the Subversion of Domestic Ideology* (Urbana: University of Illinois Press, 1989).

Fleenor, Juliann E. (ed.), *The Female Gothic* (Montreal: Eden, 1983).

Gilbert, Sandra M. and Susan Gubar, *The Madwoman in the Attic: The Woman Writer and the Nineteenth-Century Literary Imagination* (New Haven: Yale University Press, 1979).

Heiland, Donna, *Gothic and Gender: An Introduction* (Oxford: Blackwell, 2004).

Heller, Tamar, *Dead Secrets: Wilkie Collins and the Female Gothic* (New Haven: Yale University Press, 1992).

Hoeveler, Diane Long, *Gothic Feminism: The Professionalisation of Gender from Charlotte Smith to the Brontës* (Liverpool: Liverpool University Press, 1998).

Kelly, Gary (ed.), *Varieties of Female Gothic*, 6 vols (London: Chatto, 2001).

Massé, Michelle A., *In the Name of Love: Women, Masochism and the Gothic* (Ithaca: Cornell University Press, 1992).

Meyers, Helene, *Femicidal Fears: Narratives of the Female Gothic Experience* (New York: SUNY, 2001).

Milbank, Alison, *Daughters of the House: Modes of the Gothic in Victorian Fiction* (Basingstoke: Macmillan, 1992).

Miles, Robert (ed.), *Women's Writing: The Elizabethan to Victorian Period*, 1: 2 (1994) [special issue: Female Gothic Writing].

Moers, Ellen, *Literary Women* (London: Women's Press, 1978).

Smith, Andrew and Diana Wallace (eds), *Gothic Studies*, 6: 1 (May 2004) [special issue: Female Gothic].

Williams, Anne, *Art of Darkness: A Poetics of Gothic* (Chicago: University of Chicago Press, 1995).

Gender/Sexuality/Queer Theory

Andiano, Joseph, *Our Ladies of Darkness: Feminine Daemonology in Male Gothic Fiction* (University Park: Penn State University Press, 1993).

Castle, Terry, *The Female Thermometer: Eighteenth-Century Culture and the Invention of the Uncanny* (Oxford: Oxford University Press, 1995).

Eberle-Sinatre, Michael (ed.), *Gothic Studies*, 7: 2 (2005) [special issue: Queering Gothic Films].

Halberstam, Judith, *Skin Shows: Gothic Horror and the Technology of Monsters* (Durham, NC: Duke University Press, 1995).

Hendershot, Cyndy, *The Animal Within: Masculinity and the Gothic* (Ann Arbor: University of Michigan Press, 1998).

Hurley, Kelly, *The Gothic Body: Sexuality, Materialism and Degeneration at the Fin de Siècle* (Cambridge: Cambridge University Press, 1996).

Palmer, Paulina, *Lesbian Gothic: Transgressive Fictions* (London: Cassell, 1999).

Schoene-Harwood, Berthold, *Writing Men: Literary Masculinities from Frankenstein to the New Man* (Edinburgh: Edinburgh University Press, 2000).

Sedgwick, Eve Kosofsky, *Between Men: English Literature and Male Homosocial Desire* (New York: Columbia University Press, 1985).

Sedgwick, Eve Kosofsky, *Epistemology of the Closet* (London: Harvester Wheatsheaf, 1991).

Film

Berenstein, Rhona J., *Attack of the Leading Ladies: Gender, Sexuality, and Spectatorship in Classic Horror Cinema* (New York: Columbia University Press, 1996).

Chibnail, Steve and Julian Petley (eds), *British Horror Cinema* (Routledge: London, 2002).

Clover, Carol J., *Men, Women, and Chain Saws: Gender in the Modern Horror Film* (London: British Film Institute, 1993).

Crane, Jonathan Lake, *Terror and Everyday Life: Singular Moments in the History of the Horror Film* (Thousand Oaks: Sage, 1994).

Creed, Barbara, *The Monstrous Feminine: Film, Feminism, Psychoanalysis* (London: Routledge, 1993).

Eisener, Lotte, *The Haunted Screen* (London: Secker and Warburg, 1973).

Grant, Barry K. (ed.), *Planks of Reason: Essays on the Horror Film* (London: Scarecrow, 1984).

Grant, Barry K. (ed.), *The Dread of Difference: Gender and the Horror Film* (Austin: University of Texas Press, 1996).

Hopkins, Lisa, *Screening the Gothic* (Austin: University of Texas Press, 2005).

Hutchings, Peter, *Hammer and Beyond: The British Horror Film* (Manchester: Manchester University Press, 1993).

Hutchings, Peter, *The Horror Film* (Longman: London, 2004).

Jancovich, Mark (ed.), *Horror: The Film Reader* (London: Routledge, 2002).

Kracauer, Siegfried, *From Caligari to Hitler: A Psychological History of German Film* (Princeton: Princeton University Press, 1947).

Krzywinska, Tanya, *A Skin for Dancing in: Possession, Witchcraft and Voodoo in Film* (Westport, CT: Greenwood, 2005).

Newman, Kim (ed.), *The BFI Companion to Horror* (London: British Film Institute, 1996).

Pirie, David, *A Heritage of Horror: The English Gothic Cinema, 1946–1972* (New York: Equinox, 1974).

Powell, Anna, *Deleuze and Horror Film* (Edinburgh: Edinburgh University Press, 2005).

Prawer, S. S., *Caligari's Children: The Film as Tale of Terror* (New York: Da Capo, 1980).

Rigby, Jonathan, *English Gothic: A Century of Horror Cinema* (London: Reynolds & Hearn, 2004).

Silver, Alain, *More Things than Are Dreamt Of: Masterpieces of Supernatural Horror from Mary Shelley to Stephen King in Literature and Film* (New York: Limelight, 1994).

Skal, David J., *The Monster Show: A Cultural History of Horror* (Harmondsworth: Penguin, 1994).

Skal, David J., *Hollywood Gothic: The Tangled Web of Dracula from Novel to Stage to Screen* (London: Faber & Faber, 2004).

Tudor, Andrew, *Monsters and Mad Scientists: A Cultural History of the Horror Movie* (Cambridge, MA: Basil Blackwell, 1989).

Twitchell, James B., *Dreadful Pleasures: An Anatomy of Modern Horror* (Oxford: Oxford University Press, 1985).

Waller, Gregory A. (ed.), *American Horrors: Essays on the Modern American Horror Film* (Urbana: University of Illinois Press, 1987).

Wright, Bruce Lanier, *Nightwalkers: Gothic Horror Movies: The Modern Era* (Dallas: Taylor, 1995).

Wood, Robin, *Hollywood from Vietnam to Regan* (New York: Columbia University Press, 1986).

Radio

Hand, Richard J., *Terror on the Air! Horror Radio in America, 1931–1952* (Jefferson: McFarland, 2005).

Goth subculture

Hodkinson, Paul, *Goth: Identity, Style and Subculture* (Oxford: Berg, 2002).

Index